SACRAMENTAL
THEURGY
FOR
WITCHES

About the Author

Frater Barrabbas Tiresius is a practicing ritual magician who has studied magic and the occult for over forty years. He believes that ritual magic is a discipline whose mystery is unlocked by continual practice and by occult experiences and revelations. Frater Barrabbas believes that traditional approaches should be balanced with creativity and experimentation, and that no occult or magical tradition is exempt from changes and revisions.

Over the years, he found that his practical magical discipline was the real source for all his creative efforts. That creative process helped him build and craft a unique and different kind of magical system, one that is quite unlike any other yet based on common Wiccan practices. So, despite its uniqueness, this magical system is capable of being easily adapted and used by others.

Frater Barrabbas is also the founder of a magical order called the Order of the Gnostic Star and he is an elder and lineage holder in the Alexandrian tradition of Witchcraft.

SACRAMENTAL THEURGY FOR WITCHES

ADVANCED LITURGY REVEALED

FRATER BARRABBAS

Chicago, IL

First Edition. 2024.

Paperback ISBN: 978-1-959883-26-5
Library of Congress Control Number on file.

Cover design by Wycke Malliway.
Edited by Becca Fleming.

Published by:
Crossed Crow Books, LLC
6934 N Glenwood Ave, Suite C
Chicago, IL 60626
www.crossedcrowbooks.com

Printed in the United States of America.

Other Books by Frater Barrabbas

Spirit Conjuring for Witches, Llewellyn
Elemental Magic for Witches, Llewellyn
Talismanic Magic for Witches, Llewellyn

Forthcoming Titles

Transformative Initiation for Witches, Crossed Crow Books
Mastering the Art of Witchcraft, Crossed Crow Books
Disciple's Guide to Ritual Magick, Crossed Crow Books
Mastering the Art of Ritual Magick, Crossed Crow Books
Liber Nephilim, Crossed Crow Books

DEDICATION

This book is dedicated to my friend and great sage Steven Posch; to Kerwidyn, forever maid of the woods; to Jonathan Nightshade, Witch extraordinaire; and the Avalon Baphomet Bunch, who taught me to venerate the Horned God, the Stang, and revitalize my Witchcraft faith; to my wife Joni, who taught me how to write books; and to Lynxa, my feline muse.

ACKNOWLEDGMENTS

Many thanks to Keith Ward for his artistic assistance and visions, and to the Great Goddess, who I shall not name, who has taught me all I know about sacramental theurgy.

TABLE OF CONTENTS

NOTE BY THE AUTHOR

This is my fourth book in the *For Witches* series, and it represents all of the lore that I have developed, shared, and learned from others and now pass on to you, my readers. In my previous books, I had covered all the magical technology that I had developed and mastered many years ago on my path as a Witch and ritual magician. However, there was an important body of lore that I had not covered in those previous books. I felt that this lore was of vital interest to those who seek to deepen their practice of modern Witchcraft. Therefore, I have written this book, *Sacramental Theurgy*, to include those very special kinds of magical rites that are also a form of advanced liturgy and sacramental magic. Since Witchcraft, from my perspective, is a religion that freely mixes both magic and religious practices, I wanted to promote a kind of practice that would help Witches to engage and act through the Goddesses and Gods to make dramatic and profound changes in the material world.

I have performed these kinds of practices since the early days of my Witchcraft tradition, but I have developed and evolved them into a very powerful methodology of magic. It has an ancient provenance going back to antiquity and the practices of Neoplatonic philosophers as well as Pagan magicians even before them, and it was also brought into the Catholic church as a form of magical liturgy. Of course, in the last century, the Catholic church has done everything it could to remove the magical elements and perspectives from the mass and the use of sacraments.

However, this kind of magic is so natural and built into the Pagan mindset that it was simple to even unknowingly borrow it for use in forms of Witchcraft magic. Later on, my appropriation of Catholic rituals and practices became more deliberate as I found the original Pagan perspectives to be a perfect fit for modern Witchcraft. The Catholic church had discarded the Tridentine Mass and its associated rites as being too magical back during Vatican II. I have resurrected and transformed them to the service of Witchcraft liturgy and magic. I have appropriated what is no longer sanctioned or used by the Catholic church, so my borrowing of ritual patterns is allowable but likely seen as illicit and controversial.

Sacramental Theurgy is a unique work that reveals all of these methods and techniques that I have used over the decades to direct and project the magical powers of my Deities into the material world to make changes, to aid, heal, and protect others. It is doing the work of the Gods and Goddesses in this world, acting as an agent for distributing their blessings, sacraments, and magical transformations. This book, although it is a part of the *For Witches* series, represents a methodology that does not completely rely on any of the other books in that series for it to be mastered. They can be merged together to fashion an even greater potent magical capability. What this book does require is a deepening relationship with the Deities and Notaries of Witchcraft that is more intimate, active, engaged, and empowered. May you find in this work the means to bring peace and abundance to yourself, your clan and coven, and the world at large.

Frater Barrabbas

PART ONE

INTRODUCTION TO SACRAMENTAL THEURGY

CHAPTER ONE

Theurgy and
Modern Witchcraft

"The excellence of the soul is understanding;
for the man who understands is conscious,
devoted, and already godlike."
—Hermes Trigmagistos

Witchcraft today has two basic dimensions; it is a religion and it is a form of magic. Typically, the magic that Witches perform often has little to do with the Deities that are worshiped simply because the magical objective is mundane and material based. Witches are more inclined to work objective forms of ritual magic instead of performing votive rites and begging their Deities to fulfill their objectives. This is likely because, before the modern age, Witchcraft was exclusively a form of magic employed mostly by women, but also some men, and was only peripherally involved with any kind of religious devotion or praxis.

Christian authorities who persecuted Witches believed that Witchcraft was a diabolic religion that worshipped the Devil, and it was demonic powers that gave Witches their supernatural abilities. This belief was invented from whole-clothe by a small group of theologians in Switzerland in the fifteenth century and grew to become a kind of pervasive Christian propaganda.[1] The reality was

---

1 Michael D. Bailey, *Origins of the Witches' Sabbath*, pp. 1–2.

that Witchcraft, at that time, was mostly a system of magic that may have given a tacit acknowledgment to the fairies, earth-spirits, demons, or diabolic intermediaries who gave them their powers; but it was mostly a magical methodology divorced from any kind of religious beliefs or practices.

It was only much later, in the twentieth century, that a notion of a Witchcraft religion began to be developed. It is probably because the religious practices of modern Witchcraft are still being developed today that the idea of engaging with the Pagan-based Witchcraft Deities to intercede and to make changes in the material world through the artifice of votive offerings, prayer, meditation, communion, sacrifice, and godhead assumption has not become a common practice. To mix Witchcraft magic with Witchcraft religious practices is to formulate a kind of Witchcraft-based theurgy.

Theurgy is defined as a magical operation that induces the Deity to perform a paranormal operation to benefit an individual or a group or to refrain or block an occurrence that would cause harm. The Greek word *theurgy* is interpreted to mean "God Work," so it is a form of high magic that directs the supernatural powers of the Deity to either make something materialize or to block something from happening. A theurgist is someone who has the ability to directly converse with the Gods and Goddesses and to either urge them to act or to abrogate their powers and assume their identity and then perform the desired work. Pagan philosophy, particularly among the late Neoplatonists, stated that the highest achievement was to become a magus who wielded the powers and wisdom of the Deities, performing the art of theurgy for the benefit and blessing of humankind.

While this kind of religious magic was considered the ultimate mastery possessed by Neoplatonic philosophers of late antiquity, such a practice and its associated perspectives are very relevant today for modern Pagans and Witches. It is, in fact, the natural evolution of our practices of liturgy and magic that the two approaches should become united into an advanced formulation of magic, a kind of Witchcraft Theurgy. This evolution is already occurring today, and in fact, it represents the cutting-edge of Witchcraft practices that certain select senior members or innovators within our community are developing and practicing in private gatherings, covens, and groves.

So, what kind of magic is Witchcraft Theurgy? How is it different than what modern Witches have been doing for the last several decades? This kind of magic is a natural progression from the basic religious practices that consist of votive offerings, godhead assumption, sacramentation, and communion. When the salt and water are charged, blessed, and mixed, then a sacrament is produced which is lustral water. Anointing oils used in initiation and the Great Rite are typically blessed before being used, as are the magical tools of wand and athame. Some Witches offer food and drink to their Deities and burn candles and incense as offerings to them.

There is typically a regimen of meditation, summoning, and calling to the Deities of the coven, and Mystery observances for the four seasons and the lunation cycle. The Great Rite itself is defined as a system of sacramentation where two individuals assume complimentary godheads to perform the sacred act of consecrated sexual union. There are the kisses bestowed by the leaders to the members of the coven as blessings, and there are the lashes of the scourge that represent the pain and sacrifice associated with learning and mastering life. There are also the cords that bind and release, and in some cases, blood from shallow wounds is used to bind and mark the elect. All of these typical practices can become fully magical and used to greatly enhance the power of magical operations if they are used with the intention to engage the Deities in the magical work.

Witchcraft Theurgy can be divided into two basic categories: sacramental magic and the mysteries of transformation. In both of these categories, the Deities are engaged and their impact enlarged so that the magic performed is done explicitly through them. This would require not only defining the Deities in greater intimate detail than what is typical in a coven or group, but it would also require expanding the scope of Deities so that the world surrounding these Witches would be filled with Deities representing the cosmic, regional, and local geographic domain of the covenstead.

If the world becomes a place of sacramentation then it must also logically be filled with Deities so that everything within it becomes holy and imbued with spirit. This requires a shift in perspective for modern Witches, but it is one that is more compelling and logical within the context of a Pagan and polytheistic perspective. It begins with the Deity within one (the Familiar Spirit) and expands to include all of the natural world, including the underworld. Recognizing these many Deities and properly worshiping at least some of them will give the Witch an endless number of spiritual allies to call upon to help them with their theurgical and magical workings.

Sacramentation is defined as making sacraments and altering or modifying material substances to be imbued with the essence of the Deities. This magical concept is closely related to the idea of transubstantiation, which was central to the idea of the Catholic Mass. Yet, this idea was not originally Christian, but was taken as a symbolic act of a more ancient practice, that of animal sacrifice. Since the Catholic Church has gone to great lengths to remove the magic and its association with the bloody sacrifice from the act, we can acknowledge the true source of this practice and appropriate it in turn, so that it becomes once again a Pagan Mystery and a magic action.

We can consecrate bread and wine, or beer, as the body and blood of the sacrificial Deity of nature itself, or we could even perform an animal sacrifice in the same manner as the Pagans of antiquity. However, performing an actual animal sacrifice requires a knowledge and expertise that is lacking in most Pagan and Wiccan communities so that the animal doesn't suffer, and its body and blood are carefully used to further the offering to the Deities and participants. The victim animal would also be one that is typically part of the human food chain, such as a chicken, goat, lamb, or calf. If a practiced and knowledgeable farmer and butcher is not available for such a practice, then I would recommend using food and drink instead of a live animal for a sacrifice. Wisely, sacrifice as depicted in Witchcraft ceremonies is largely symbolic or staged.

Still, the subject of sacrifice, whether it be a living animal or food and drink, is changed to be a suitable representation of the specific Deity that represents the gift of life and death that joins humans and Deities together in communion. That is the magic of transubstantiation, and what is sacralized through this artifice can also be used to charge, empower, and sacralize magical operations. To harness this power of sacramentation, I will present two rituals: a magical mass and a magical benediction, aligned to a specific set of Deities and used to produce magical sacraments that can be used to empower and enhance magical operations. These will use consecrated food and drink, as well as lustral water and charged oils, to act as magical tools.

Sacramentation would also include more advanced techniques of godhead assumption where the Deity that is worshipped by a group or gathering would be fully personified by an individual who has not just assumed this godhead but has made it a focus of a much deeper liturgical and psychological connection. The assumptive Operator has become temporarily, for an event, the living and breathing personification of that Deity, for the benefit and blessings of the gathered community. The focus for such a working is the transformative operation of the consecrated mask, garb, jewelry, and face and body makeup that aids in transforming the body and appearance into that of the Deity, the donning of such cultic apparel and the intense and powerful godhead assumption that goes with it.

Other forms of sacramentation would include the creation of amulets, the consecration and realization of outdoor groves, and the building and erecting of place-markers for the Deity such as a Stang, besom, a sacred well, a cairn, henge, or a gateway. It would also include the talismanic animation of a statue or bust. All of these artifacts and constructions can be used in a magical operation to fulfill a magical objective. However, all of these artifacts would require a greater and intimate connection to a specific Deity in order to facilitate the operation of imbuing them with the spiritual essence of that Deity.

The Operator would need to perform many liturgical rites, godhead assumptions, and votive offerings before they could summon and project the spiritual essence of their chosen Deity into that artifact. They would, in fact, need to briefly assume and personify that Deity in order to project its powers and intelligence. The target artifact would have to be consecrated and given as an offering to that Deity, requiring that the Operator possesses the votive *key* to unlock it for a given magical rite.

The mysteries revolve around the cycle of light and darkness, life and death, the lunation cycle, the four seasons, the Mystery of Transformative Initiation, and the Mystery of the nature and ubiquity of Spirit, the Deities, and the One that binds them together. While the typical modern Witch will already know and practice liturgical rites for the full moon as the esbats and the eight seasonal rites for the sabbats, there is much more beyond and behind these operations that will lend powers and secret knowledge to the Witch who can realize and utilize them. We should, therefore, examine these Mysteries in greater depth to define and present rituals that embody the lunation cycle and the solar cycle so that these events can be harnessed to cause internal psychic transformations in the participants and also to unleash the powers of the Earth, Sun, and Moon to make material changes in the world.

Traditional modern Witchcraft has two initiation ordeals and a sacramental communion of the Great Rite that confers the full attainment of the religious magic of the Craft. However, since these Mysteries are based loosely on the three degrees of Blue Lodge Masonry, then it should follow that there is a third ordeal that is missing. A Witch should, in my opinion, undergo three ordeals if they are to be considered fully initiated, having passed through the three gateways of the Mysteries in order to be properly prepared for the rite of sexual consecration. I have previously developed such a rite, but it has never been given serious consideration, and we will not examine it in this work. Of course, such a rite would only be useful for those Witches who believe that the traditional three degrees are necessary and important.

For those who don't particularly believe in or abide by this traditional concept, where one initiation is more than sufficient, we could discuss the nature of transformative initiation. This kind of initiation is based on the natural literary cycle of the Hero's Journey, which has a powerful psychological function within the psyche of all spiritual seekers. This cycle has a mythic and, therefore, a magical and liturgical component that is available for those who see its value and can harness its symbols, using them as triggers and controlling symbols for the achievement of powerful psychic transformations. I have examined and written about this mythic and cyclic structure and how to magically apply it in my book *Mastering the Art of Ritual Magick*, but I will not be re-examining it in this work.[2]

The location for the Mysteries, the place where these operations are performed, is typically an indoor room in the house designated as the covenstead. However, a completely different approach, and one that is in many ways more profound and sacred, is the outdoor grove. There is not a lot of information about a grove and its use in the books on Witchcraft and Paganism, but it is—or should be—a foundational practice for any group whose focus is the magic and sacredness of nature. Unlike an indoor room that functions as a temple, the grove never needs to be consecrated to be made ready for use. It is naturally consecrated, and all one has to do is change their awareness and perception to realize that fact. The powers and Mysteries that one finds in a grove are intrinsic to nature itself, but often, these features are missed due to the necessary assumption of a different way of seeing and experiencing a sacred grove. While a permanent place for such a grove is a desired objective, any private natural setting can function as a grove, including a public campground (so long as it is secluded for the rites).

If Witches have changed their perspectives regarding the ubiquity of many Deities, then the grove becomes a veritable domain filled to bursting with magical spirits, nature beings, and Gods and Goddesses. Any of these can be called upon and assumed to enhance a religious magical working. What is required is to erect and establish place markers for them to emerge from out of the fabric of the natural grove and become accessible. Of course, such a place marker would require a period of familiarization, votive offerings, and the development of an image and name for this Deity, as well as establishing a connection and link to it. This can be done within the span of one or two days for a practiced Operator, or such a working could call and summon one of the greater Deities of the covenstead, such as the Goddess of the Trees or the Horned God of feral nature. The possibilities for liturgical magic (theurgy) are nearly endless in a living and breathing sacred grove.

---

2 Frater Barrabbas, *Mastering the Art of Ritual Magick – Omnibus Edition*, pp. 127–139.

As you can see through these examples stated above, Witchcraft Theurgy is a natural process of extending and deepening the liturgical practices that modern Witches have been performing for decades. These are not the same practices espoused by the Neoplatonic philosophers for antiquity, nor are they overly philosophized practices of the Ceremonial Magician or modern Neoplatonist. Neoplatonism has little to say about these practices since they are antique Pagan magical practices that have their origin in the far and mysterious past. These rites, although based on simple concepts, can become complex and highly developed, however, they can also be simple and easily accessible to the experienced and seasoned Witch.

Since Witchcraft Theurgy is so integral to the practice of Witchcraft magic and liturgy, the question posed about why someone *would* want to perform this kind of magic becomes, instead, why *wouldn't* someone want to practice this magic once they have mastered the basic rituals and worked magic for a while. I don't have to make arguments about these techniques and methods for Witchcraft Theurgy when their use would provide a deeper and more potent form of Witchcraft for them to engage in and practice. The question becomes something in the order of whether the Witch in question wants to remain practicing their Craft as they always have or to embark upon a journey that will deepen and intensify their religious and magical experiences. That is the choice confronting the Witch who is reading this book, and I believe that by itself, such a guaranteed outcome will be sufficient to attract Witches to engage with the contents of this book and to immerse themselves into a new and more empowered praxis.

My targeted readers for this book are those who have mastered the basic religious practices and rites of modern Witchcraft. They would also have knowledge and experience and find it comfortable to practice magic through a Witchcraft foundation. This is, unfortunately, not a book for beginners or those who have not learned to assume a godhead, consecrate food and drink, summon and call their Deities, give votive offerings, engage with their Deities in a direct manner, or develop an intimate connection with a targeted Deity. Those techniques must already be a part of the repertoire of the practicing Witch in order for the rites in this book to be accessible.

There are many beginning books on Witchcraft, not to mention an internet chock full of beginning concepts, rites, and practices, that I don't feel the need to write about those subjects. Instead, I want to reach out to those who have already mastered these practices and who now seek to advance their practices by taking the next natural and logical step forward.

There are Witches in our various communities who are already practicing forms of Witchcraft Theurgy, although they might not call it by that label and would have naturally followed the progression that their knowledge and experience had brought them. However, what I am presenting in this book is the whole package that expands the basic practices of Witchcraft at each and every point. If the seasoned Witch has also taken upon themselves the additional teachings of spirit conjuration, advanced energy workings, and talismanic magic in addition to theurgy, then I believe that such a one will have fully mastered the spectrum of Witchcraft religion and magic. They will have become a Pagan Magus and be able to re-engineer their lives and the lives of their loved ones to better fulfill their religious and magical obligations. These four different pathways will come together to forge a life and a way of being that is a doorway to godhead in our Pagan and natural world. It is a doorway that all are invited to enter, and it is one that can enlarge, enrich, empower, and charm the lives of all who pass through it.

Let us, therefore, progress through this lore and share these sacred rites of magic so that the final piece of the Witchcraft puzzle might be revealed and activated. We will follow this pathway in a sequential manner so that each action in the liturgical practices in Witchcraft religious rites will become a powerful and expanded magical capability. I have already said that Witchcraft Theurgy consists of two distinct categories, and these are sacramental magic and magical Mystery rites. So, this book will be divided into two parts to accommodate these two types of practices. Here is a list of those topics that we will cover within the two parts.

Sacramental Magic

1. **Expanding and deepening the connection with Deities:** The methodology of formulating a state of union with a chosen Deity through advanced devotion.
2. **Art of Sacramentation:** Making sacramental medicines, food and drink, unguents, and artifacts.
3. **Art of Transubstantiation:** The rituals of the magical mass and benediction rite.
4. **Godhead Personification:** The rite of the mask, adornment, and beautification of the living Deity.
5. **Art of amulets and charms:** The crafting of godhead links within consecrated artifacts.
6. **Constructing sacred and magical placeholders for the godhead residence.**
7. **Statue Animation:** The talismanic charging of a godhead link focused on a statue or bust.
8. **The Greater Great Rite:** Enhancing the Great Rite through full godhead assumption and emulating the Deity Marriage or *Hieros Gamos* rite.

Magical Mystery Rites

1. **Defining and incorporating the Mysteries of the natural world into a ritual praxis.**
2. **Lunar Mystery rites of the Eightfold Lunation Cycle.**
3. **Solar Mystery rites of the Eightfold Seasonal Cycle.**
4. **Sacred Grove and the magical Mysteries of Nature as Deity.**
5. **Rite of the Grand Sabbat:** Where the sacred grove meets the godhead personification.

These are the topics that I will be covering in this work. I will include ritual examples and patterns along with the necessary information that you need to work this kind of magic. Some of the rites may be a bit more complex than what you are used to using, and one in particular (statue animation) requires a knowledge of talismanic magic in order to be grasped.

All of these practices and rites are grouped under the definition of theurgy that we discussed in the first part of this chapter. Yet, they are not beyond the provenance of traditional modern Witch-craft, and, in fact, act as an advanced extension to what is likely already being practiced by you.

What I am presenting in this work, the various rites and techniques, are a part of my Witchcraft practice. I would not be writing a book and including rituals that I have not had extensive experience performing myself. They are a part of my praxis and what I would teach students if I had to function as an instructor of Witchcraft magic. They represent the body of lore that I would share and discuss in detail after the student had learned to perform more advanced forms of Witchcraft magic. I would present the techniques and methods for spirit conjuring, advanced energy magic, and talismanic magic before embarking on the studies of Witchcraft Theurgy simply because I could then be certain that the student had enough experience and knowledge to make the most of these kinds of studies and practices.

Now, let us begin our journey into the specialized knowledge and practices that will help you master the advanced arts of Witchcraft Theurgy. I think that you will find this a fascinating journey that will add a number of strategic skills to your repertoire of religious rites and magic.

CHAPTER TWO

POLYTHEISM FOR WITCHES— A PRACTICAL SPIRITUAL APPROACH

"A religion without a goddess is
halfway to atheism."
—DION FORTUNE

When I was just a Witchling and first starting my journey on the path of Witchcraft, I learned that there was a Goddess and a God and that these two Deities gave birth to all that naturally exists in the world. The Goddess was a combination of a deification of nature and the cosmos, symbolized by the Moon. The God was a Horned Deity who was the stern guardian of the underworld and its Mysteries, and the shepherd of the dead, helping them on the road to rebirth. He was a bit like Hades, Pan, or Janus, mixed with a bit of the Sabbath Goat and a pinch of the Christian Devil to give him some street cred. Then there were the Dread Lords protecting the four quarters of the sacred circle of the covenstead, and a singular Deity representing the union of the Goddess and the God, called the Dreighton.

The Goddess and God were given names as part of the Mystery and confidentiality of the coven, and these names were often taken from the adopted cultural mythology of the tradition and the coven. If the tradition and adopted culture were Welsh, then the associated Goddesses and Gods of that tradition were incorporated into the rites. If it were Celtic, Greek, or even Roman, then

14

the Deities of those cultural traditions were used. The traditional Gardnerian or Alexandrian *Book of Shadows* may or may not name these Deities, and it often occurred that they were written as blank lines to be filled in by the knowledgeable initiate. Needless to say, the theological representation for modern Witchcraft was a kind of duotheology, and although it was neither Christian nor monotheistic, it wasn't particularly Pagan, either. It functioned as a kind of modern Western approach to the ancient Chinese Taoist concepts of Yin and Yang, although precedence was given to the Goddess over that of the God.

In addition, there were other Deities to be found in Modern Witchcraft, such as the Sun God, earlier named Lucifer (in the 1950s and 1960s) and then given the name of Lugh, Helios, Sol, or Apollo. The Sun God functioned in contradistinction with the Moon Goddess, and they were considered brother and sister. This likely was borrowed from the book *Il Vangello delle streghe*, or the *Witches' Gospel (of Aradia)*.[3] Of course, the daughter of the Goddess named Aradia was often featured in the mythology of modern Witchcraft and is particularly important in the Gardnerian tradition.

There was also the Green Man who appears during the beginning of Summer (Beltane) and lives until autumn, and the Oak King and the Holy King, who act as representations of the changing seasons and the eternal conflict of light and darkness. Some groups proposed that the Goddess had a mortal lover or son who dies and is reborn, only to die again every autumn. Sometimes, it was the daughter who was taken into the underworld, similar to the tale of Persephone. So, what you have in this situation is a loosely defined deified family consisting of a mother, father, daughter, and son, representing a more traditional approach to polytheism than a simple duotheology.

What is occurring here, while I am enumerating the many faces of Deity that one can find in modern Witchcraft, is the natural human proclivity that when allowing for more than one Deity, ultimately, a multitude begins to appear. The Greater Mystery is that polytheism allows for the occurrence of a multitude of Deities because the occurrence of spirit in nature is multifold and shaped

---

3   Charles Leland, *Aradia, or the Gospel of the Witches*, 1899.

by the geography of place and the constant cyclic change of light and darkness, life and death, summer and winter, and the mystery that surrounds them all. It is naturally pluralistic and based on a pantheistic approach to spirituality.

We are surrounded by spirits everywhere, and some of them are Deities. Some of these Deities reside in the places where we live, whether in the city or the country, taking residence in lakes, streams, rivers, underground aquifers, hills, canyons, mountains, woods, forests, cultivated fields, swamps, upon the land as living things, underneath the ground, and above us in the sky. One can even find a myriad of spirits and Deities residing in city parks, tunnels, sewers, or in tall buildings as corporate egregores. The grass growing in the cracks of pavement and asphalt roads show the emergence of the spirits of life. With such a massive variety of spiritual entities all around us, and with some of them aggregated or elevated to formulate Deities, it seems quite limiting to subscribe to worshipping and engaging with just two.

A duotheology, as practiced in classical Witchcraft, is really an illusion, and such a perspective denies the true polytheistic nature of Witchcraft. It is, in my opinion, just as unfounded to subscribe to just a Goddess and a God (whether named or even unnamed and generalized with the appellation of the word "The" to determine their overall mutability and inclusion of all such Deities) in the guise of a religion that lionizes sexual polarity and natural fertility. There is that factor operating in Witchcraft, but it isn't the only viable perspective. Just like in human society, a cisgender-based masculine Deity mated with a cisgender feminine Deity, as father and mother, only represents a small percentage of everything that is living in the natural world. It must also be true of Deities based on this fact of nature as well, and if we comb through polytheism as it was and is practiced in the world, we will find a plurality of manifestations and representations that would include transgender and even agender Deities. It would include amalgamations of human and animal, fabulous mythic beasts, and iconized animals and human beings.

Therefore, it is important to expand the list of possible Deities to include the cosmic, sky, earth-based, and underworld beings as well as the Deities of place representing one's home and geographic location. Wherever we are in the world, there may be a Deity representing the Moon and the Sun, the storms, winds, and the stars in the sky, but also the Deity residing in an old, gnarled oak in your backyard, the nearby lake or river, the woods and fields, hills and depressions, and the underground streams and wells. All of these Deities are valid, and if they are unnamed, they are only waiting for the opportunity to present themselves to you, the active Witchcraft practitioner. A veritable and vast pantheon awaits your active research and examination of the very place and location of your home, where your family members live, and where relatives and friends reside; a comprehensive diaspora of Deities and spiritual beings are waiting to be named and engaged.

It is also important to have specific Deities to represent strategic themes that are found in the Mysteries of Light and Darkness. All forms of life are born, grow to maturity, and then die. If a Deity is to impart that Mystery to us and direct us through it, then it must share in that process of death and transition. What we have then is a Deity that dies and is reborn. Additionally, the underworld and overworld represent the places where life thrives or resides in stasis at certain times of the cycle of light and darkness, so a Deity representing earthly fertility would need to occupy the overworld and underworld to represent the seasons of growth and dormancy. The place between the light and darkness, where the transition occurs, is occupied by a lintel Deity who represents the powers of time, change, and transformation, but also of stillness and the unchanging state of the source of all things.

The sun's passage across the sky and its transformation and rebirth during the night to reemerge with the dawning light is also another cycle of the never-ending Mystery of Light and Darkness. This particular cycle represents the cosmogonic cycle of the cosmos, the birth, life, death, and rebirth of the sun through the event of a single day, symbolizing the occurrence of the archetypal day and night at the beginning of time and the ending.

Correspondingly, the dance of the Sun, Moon, and Earth represents the phases and shifting of the moon as it passes through the lunation cycle. Here, three Deities are engaged in this dance, the Sun, Moon, and the Earth, and when given archetypal genders, it could be two Goddesses and a God performing the dance, or it could be two Gods and a Goddess, where the subscribing of a Deity to a cosmic body has no rules or requirements. Egypt had both a Moon Goddess and Solar God in one cult, and a Moon God and a Solar Goddess in another. A creative approach will yield a richer formulation than if such a determination is approached in a narrow and dogmatic manner.

This fourfold pattern is also represented in the life cycle of plants, animals, and human beings. The phases of birth and childhood, puberty, maturity, and old age are reflected in the four seasons, with the promise or expectation of renewal and rebirth after death. One could also see this fourfold cycle represented by the four sacramental philosophies of Eros (procreation), Agape (friendship or sodality), Thelema (will to power), and Thanatos (diminishment and death). It is the cosmogonic cycle of creation, a golden age, an age of mankind (death), and the end-times of dissolution. Certainly, there are also aspects of Deity that would represent the child, the lover, the parent, and the wise old one, since Deity must share in the cycles of life and death that it has created from within and is a part of itself. In Paganism, the Deity is never considered to be outside or separate from the world and the life that it has created.

Pagan Deities have an intimate and immanent relationship with the material universe. It is only in the evolution of monotheism that creator Deities are seen to be separate and distinct from their creations, and also when pantheons are reduced to a single great Deity (a process called *macranthropy*), such as what occurred to Amen-Ra, Jupiter-Sol, Zeus, or Marduk.

These various thematic Mysteries are populated with Deities, and these Deities must become defined, developed, worshipped, and consciously assumed in order for the magical powers and wisdom inherent in their Mysteries to be harnessed. Therefore, the practice of Witchcraft should follow the natural path of extending the list of Deities to include those in one's locality but also to characterize the Mysteries themselves, making them accessible to the members of the covenstead. This step of extending the covenstead pantheon (or the pantheon of an individual's practice) is the first step required by anyone who seeks to engage the Deities within a framework of magical operations to impact the material world. That framework is named *God-Work*, or more aptly, *theurgy*. This is also the topic of this book, Witchcraft Theurgy.

Dying God and the Mysteries

The principal Mystery, from the standpoint of polytheism, is both birth and death. While science has explained the process of birth and death from a material perspective, what it has failed to explain is that quality which uniquely animates living beings and what is lost when a living being dies. Life and death are the greatest Mysteries for humanity, since despite the brilliance of science, we know no more about what happens after death and what happens prior to birth than we did in antiquity.

What is the nature of Spirit that gives some kind of continuity to these Mysteries, and how do the Deities share in that Mystery of life and death, light and darkness? Do people ever return from death, and is there any substance to the belief in reincarnation? If reincarnation does act upon living things, then how does that happen? What lives past the termination of life, and what is reborn when one life passes on to another? This is the great, and likely unsolvable, Mystery that has preoccupied human beings since the beginning of conscious self-awareness.

Our religious faiths and doctrines have attempted to answer these questions since science is unable and incapable of answering them—at least for the time being. How a religious doctrine perceives this Mystery says a great deal about the human perspective of that faith. For Christians, death is more important than life, and like most systems of monotheism, it is the final occurrence that ends with either an eternal reward or punishment for what remains of the self, which is the soul. Eastern traditions see a continual cycle of rebirths that occurs forever, or at least until one is released through a form of enlightenment or extreme piety. In all cases, there is some kind of indestructible attribute of the self that survives death, but religions tend to be nebulous about their definitions when it comes to delineating the nature of that indestructible aspect of the self. It is called variously the soul, spirit, atman, higher self, or one's fame or legacy.

We can only define this indestructible attribute of self by comparing it to what it cannot be—anything that is perishable. People are born with a specific set of genetic traits inherited from their parents and live their lives in a specific time, place, and within a specific social-economic strata. They are determined and loosely ruled by a unique set of physical and social circumstances, and all of this is perishable since it is based on the mind and body, location, and time. Anything that would be separate and distinct from this unique human being with all their qualities and history would not be based on the physical body and its brain-based conscious mind. It is something that is practically indefinable and inexplicable, and whatever it is must partake in the life of a person but also be completely separate from it—a profound paradox!

Thus, a person's spirit or soul would have to be both immanent and transcendent in order to function after the death of the individual's physical body. We are only rarely aware of this spirit or soul, and then only through the filter of our conscious minds, which tends to distort what we are experiencing.

A being that is based on super-ordinary consciousness that is both immanent and transcendent to individual existence is probably the best definition of a Deity that one could consider, so the spirit that animates all living people is, therefore, a God. Our God or Goddess Within is what survives our death, and that inner Deity does not function separately or distinctly from the Well of Spirit that is the One and the eternal source of everything. Separation and distinctness, from a spiritual standpoint, are very likely an illusion; but it is an illusion that consciousness supports, both from the perspective of individual beings and individual Deities. While perceiving this unity is a foundation of ultimate human wisdom, we cannot function long within its grasp without having to re-assume the mundane requirements of life.

If that indestructible spirit merges into the wholeness of the One, then it can also reemerge from that One to participate in individual human life once again. This is how I define reincarnation. There is no teleology or destiny involved, and no cyclic evolution. Just the continuous cycle of life and death, rebirth, and death again. The egoic self does not participate in this endless cycle since it is extinguished at death. There is no need to escape or stop what is a natural process of Spirit participating in the life cycle of individual beings. We can assume that something in the One is growing or evolving through this experience, but the nature of the One is that it contains all potential, so anything that might occur to an individual life has already occurred in some fashion, and is, therefore, not unique.

I believe that the Mystery of life and death is really the mystery of Deity in its myriad formulations and its unity. What this means is that our dead ancestors are really Gods and Goddesses, that the multiform of Deity engages intimately in the creation of life to partake and project their spiritual essence into physical beings at their birth, and that we live as godheads completely unaware of our unique divinity until we die. The world around us is filled with Deities representing all living things, and our minds and unconscious beings are surrounded and infused by them.

This is evident even through the tragedy and misery as well as the moments of bliss and glory in life that befall us. All that is required of us living in the world today is to realize on a conscious level our own divinity and our connection to all things divine, both living, dead, and inanimate. We seek meaning in our lives, and we determine our destinies through our choices or indecisiveness; but our lives are nothing more or less than the dance and gyrations of millions of Deities, obscured and hidden by their outer forms but still, in some manner and at times, sensible to us.

Life, in whatever form it occurs, is a gift of the Deities, and death is nothing more than our gift back to those same beings. It is in the giving and receiving of gifts that the relationship between humanity and Deity is based, and these holy gifts are called *sacrifices*. We surrender something as a gift or offering to the Deity, and we receive something in return for our offering. That surrender does not always entail something being killed, as in the bloody sacrifice of ancient practice, but it does represent the gift of life and love, whether as food or drink, votive lights, incense, oils and perfumes, or precious objects. What is received in return contains the essence of that Deity, it is therefore called a *sacrament*.

Since human beings have within themselves a God or Goddess, when they die, they surrender that God or Goddess Within to the greater God or Goddess Without. We are, therefore, a totem of the Dying God, which is both within us and also without. The Mystery of the Dying God plays out in our lives as it plays out in the changing of the seasons of growth and harvest, the diurnal cycle of light and darkness, the phases of the moon, and the periodic liturgies of sacrifice and sacrament. We are both an Officiant and a sacred offering in this never-ending holy ritual of life and death. Therefore, it is important that we realize, and also make a place for, this most important Deity in our liturgical and magical work since it represents both the sacramental and theurgical components of our essential practice of Witchcraft. It is also the central Mystery of life and death in which we all participate and celebrate.

Characterizing the Dying God in modern Witchcraft might be complicated due to the fact that Christianity has preempted any claim on a Deity that dies and is resurrected through the mythic artifice of Jesus Christ. However, the concept of a Dying God is very ancient and is likely to be found at the very dawn of human consciousness and the beginnings of religious practices. Frazier and his associates promoted the idea of the dying and resurrecting Deity as a preeminent mythic factor in all religions, whether ancient, primitive, or even modern. Later anthropologists debunked this iconology of a single myth and instead have shown that many of the Dying Gods didn't resurrect in their former forms, and other resurrecting Gods only took on a likeness of death before resuming their former form.[4]

What this phenomenon reveals to us is that, as opposed to a single myth, there are, in fact, many different myths found in various cultures and times throughout the world. The formulation of this Deity is the power of transition and transformation, the change in state from matter to spirit and from spirit to matter. There is the ever-changing and ephemeral nature of the phenomenon of material existence, and there is the still-point that represents the unchanging nexus or gateway through which all spirit and matter proceed.

Many non-Christian examples of the Dying God exist in the timeline of various Western cultures, not even counting the Eastern and New World cultures. There is Dionysus Zagreus, Osiris, Tammuz, Dumuzi, Ba'al, Adonis, Attis, and Baldr, to name a few. Goddesses have also shared this feature, with Deities such as Persephone, Proserpine, Blodeuwedd, and Modren. The Sumerian Goddess Inanna entered the underworld and experienced death for

---

4 Jonathan Z. Smith, *Dying and Rising Gods*, in *The Encyclopedia of Religion* Vol. IV, edited by Mircea Eliade, Macmillan, pp. 521–527.

three days until rescued by her father, Ea. Later, she was known as Ishtar by the Akkadians but still was associated with that underworld transit. The Egyptian God Ra undergoes a daily cyclic death and rebirth, traversing the underworld and regaining his life through the power and intercession of Osiris. Often, the Dying God is brought back in another form altogether, such as Osiris manifesting in the abundance of the crops from the Nile's annual inundation, Dionysus Zagreus, whose divine body parts were mixed with matter (of the Titan Gods) to become the base material for the dual nature of humanity or even the transformation of John Barleycorn into whiskey.

The Dying God is the Deity sharing in our own mortality, representing the holy communion between itself and humanity. Yet, to present this Mystery and to direct the power and authority of the Dying God requires an agent, a priest or priestess who can act momentarily in the guise of the Deity. Whether that godhead assumption is only used temporarily to consecrate sacraments with the touch, word, and breath of the blessing of the godhead, or if it is a fully materialized personification using the consecrated mask and hallowed adornment (jewelry, garb, and makeup) for a Grand Sabbat cultic visitation, an agent to act as the Deity is required.

Like any priestess or priest, the agent of the Deity must be experienced and deeply aligned with the Deity that they are to represent. There are degrees of engagement and intensity, depending on what level of godhead materialization is required. The highest level of materialized assumption used for the Grand Sabbat does, of course, require the deepest and fullest level of assumption possible for a human being. There is a methodology that can be used by the priestess or priest to make this possible, and we should cover those techniques as a necessary part of this book.

The theological premise of Witchcraft needs to be expanded to include the Dying God, the Deities of place and locale, one's ancestor spirits (who are also Gods), and the most important godhead of one's familiar spirit or inner godhead. All of these Deities should have a place in the liturgical and magical work of the accomplished Witch. The Witch's temple shrine should include representations of all of these Deities, and they should be participants in their daily, weekly, monthly, and seasonal liturgy. Only such active and activated Deities can be engaged in magical workings, so it is important that they receive offerings and religious attention. Feeding the Goddesses, Gods, ancestors, and one's personal Deity should be a part of the Witch's praxis, since obtaining and maintaining such an alignment is important for receiving blessings and materialized sacraments—the sacralized food and drink for humanity.

Still, these Deities do not exist in a vacuum since they are part of a pageantry of cyclic Mysteries through which they manifest their power and maintain their relevance. The Mysteries represent the cycle of light and darkness, life and death, and are the core of the observances and practices of modern Witchcraft. While Deities represent the personalities that populate the spiritual and material worlds combined, the cyclic Mysteries represent the passage of time and symbolize the ephemeral nature of all things in the material world. These events are the signposts for meaning and magic that occur and then disappear, only to reappear again at the appointed time.

Five Mysteries and Cycles of Change

Theurgical magic is governed by what I call the Five Mysteries associated with time. I had previously written about what I discovered as the Five Natural Mysteries, but that was before I began to deeply examine the theurgy present in Witchcraft magic.[5] I have found that these Five Mysteries fit perfectly into the expressions and manifestation of sacramental magic, and that is the ever-changing and ongoing cycle of time. If life is a holy sacrament to Witches, then the changing seasons and the lunar cycle symbolize the periodic manifestation of the Deities into the material world.

The Five Mysteries, as I had defined them, consist of the constant cycles that are both amazing and banal occurrences that we typically take for granted. The core of these Mysteries is time itself, particularly the attribute of that which changes everything but remains unchanged, which is a definition of the monistic Mystery of the One.

---

5 Frater Barrabbas, *Mastering the Art of Ritual Magic – Omnibus Edition*, pp. 150–161.

Here are the Five Mysteries, as I defined them some years ago.

1. The Cycle of Day and Night (Light and Darkness)
2. Lunar Cycle—28 days within four phases and eight lunation stages
3. Solar Cycle—365 days broken into four seasons and eight astrological points (called *sabbats* by Witches and Pagans)
4. The Cycle of Birth, Life, Death, and Individual Transcendence
5. Paradoxical Nature of Spirit, Deity, and the One

The cycle of Individual Transcendence consists of two coexisting processes: the five-stage cosmogonic cycle and the seventeen-stage Hero's Journey. These two processes join at the point where the hero receives the boon that transforms them into the apotheosis or living Deity. The boon is, of course, the vision of the cosmogonic cycle and the hero's role and place within it.

With this knowledge, the hero becomes like a God and is filled with a profound purpose and unitary function in the evolution of the conscious universe. Of course, this state of affairs lasts only briefly and is lost when this insight and wisdom is translated into the waking world and solidified by necessity and the context of life. The message is still important and significant, but it rarely meets with the god-like sensation when it was first delivered within the mythic and psychic world. The twenty-two stages of the combined cycle can be readily equated with the twenty-two Trumps of the Greater Arcana of the Tarot.

Day and night are normal occurrences that are easily taken for granted, as are the phases of the moon and the seasons of the sun. We live our lives and pay no attention to the Mystery cycles constantly shifting and moving around us. Yet, at night, in the dark of the moon, or at the nadir of the winter solstice, we pause to dream and sleep in our singular ways.

During the night, between waking and sleep, the mysterious rebirth of the sun is happening in the mythic world of our souls. The Sun rises in the morning, circles the sky, and sets in the west, having lived an entire life in half a day. Still, the battle between light and darkness happens while most people sleep and dream. The Sun dies and is rekindled so that it might arise and ascend in the morning sky. This mythic pattern of life, death, and rebirth happens in the four seasons and the monthly cycle of the moon, so if we are not attentive, it will all happen behind the scenes of our daily lives, and we will be less alive because of our inattention.

All of these Mysteries are interrelated with the cycles of the sun and the moon, and these are emulated in the life cycle of all living beings on this planet. This constant and relentless change consists of both regular and predictable changes, as well as stochastic changes when things abruptly begin or end with a flourish of chaos and social perturbations.

In the center of this constant change is the mysterious double-headed lintel godhead who is the beginning and the ending, and yet beyond—the Deity of Time who resides within the timeless center. As Witches and Pagans, we must focus on these Mysteries and make them more than just a joyous part of our liturgy; for the Earth and its constant change is our companion in life and death. Yet, when we endeavor to practice forms of theurgy, we must focus on these Mysteries because they are the foundation of the magical power and wisdom that we seek to wield in order to change ourselves, our family and friends, and the material world at large.

CHAPTER THREE

ANATOMY OF
GODHEAD ASSUMPTION

"I will give you a new heart and put a new spirit within you;
I will remove your heart of stone
and give you a heart of flesh."
—EZEKIEL 36:26

One of the most beautiful and amazing experiences that a
modern Witch or Pagan can have is experiencing the core
liturgical rite of Drawing Down the Moon, the Sun, or the Horned
God. It is, in fact, a godhead assumption that is often a central part
of the religious liturgy of modern Pagan-based religions. All things
flow out from it that vitalize, sacralize, and substantiate the tenets
of these modern religions. It is also a kind of lighter version of a full
Deity personification since it doesn't require the necessary greater
preparations and testing that a full personification would require.
A full personification is used for a community gathering, such as
a Grand Sabbat, and it requires a committed and highly trained
Operator. What I am discussing here is the kind of rite performed
for a small group, such as a coven. Still, this enactment, in whatever
format, can be a deeply moving mystical experience for the novice
and the seasoned practitioner alike, but in some cases, it can also be
a tool of coercion and control.

I have long maintained that the basic hierarchical structure of
Witchcraft covens and Pagan groves promotes a static leadership

that doesn't have any checks or balances. This is not true for all traditions (such as Reclaiming Witchcraft), of course. It is, however, an issue in the British Traditional Witchcraft (BTW) lineages. As one senior BTW priestess has put it, the members of a coven vote their dissatisfaction with the coven High Priestess or High Priest with their feet, meaning that poor leaders often lose their members if they show a consistent behavior of unmitigated incompetence or authoritarianism.

Conversely, I believe that any group or gathering of individuals should function as equals in that group regardless of prior experience, community status, or assumed authority. Being a High Priestess or High Priest in a coven is a role, and in fact, I think that using the term "High" is very much misleading and vests the individual with an unquestionable authority, training, and pedigree that they might actually lack. Thus, I prefer the term *priestess* or *priest*, which denotes that the role is temporary, and the authority only extends to acting within the consensus and mandate of the whole group.

In badly run groups, the godhead assumption becomes a tool for lending the authority, wisdom, and magic of the covenstead Deity to bolster the weak ego and lack of experience of the priestess or priest. Who would question the actions or the motivations of someone who is invested with the power and authority of the very Deity that is worshipped in this group? Such a person would be quickly branded as an apostate and unbeliever, and in a short time, ejected from the group.

Ego inflation is a risk to anyone who leads a group and also assumes the godhead for the members of that group without having certain controls and a method for objectively judging that assumption. If an individual assumes a godhead to work magic outside of an organization, then there is little risk of this kind of phenomenon. This occurrence of godhead-inspired ego inflation is jokingly referred to in various traditional Craft communities as the High Priestess or High Priest syndrome, where the individual becomes intoxicated with a state of self-infatuation and imagined powers and insights that makes a sad mockery of the central tenet of modern Witchcraft. The consequences for this kind of behavior, over time, are very tragic and it has an overall negative impact on the religious experiences of those who are forced to withstand it. Such an experience could even make someone leave that tradition altogether.

What I want to discuss in this chapter is not the occurrences of bad or wrong-headed godhead assumptions within a group, but instead, how this central tenant can be controlled and properly judged by the members of that group. I also believe that it is important within such groups that the person who is going to assume the godhead of the covenstead pantheon should not be the person who is assuming the role of priestess or priest for liturgical and magical workings for the group. They should be separate roles so that authority and potential godhead intoxication are not in any way linked. This also allows the individual who is to assume a godhead to be free of all responsibilities so that they can prepare and concentrate on the operation and not have to engage in any other activity.

I would also recommend that the members of the group take turns performing this operation and that it be a part of the training regimen for the group. If there is a greater emphasis on preparation, training, and controls established by the group to be able to objectively judge their experience, then I think that the religious experience of this central practice will be greatly enhanced and become, most importantly, one that is shared within that group. It will also help the members realize the Deities of their group so that they might become more intimately manifest and tangible to them.

One of the most important considerations that I feel should be a part of this wondrous Mystery of the Drawing Down godhead assumption is that the target Deity should not be vague or open-ended. What I mean by vague and open-ended is that the target Deity is either completely unnamed or only tentatively defined. The Deities of the covenstead need to be defined in a thorough manner, including a full definition of their characteristics and the mythic supporting documentation in which they appear.

Where excesses can and do occur is when the target Goddess or God is a nebulous, unnamed, and unqualified entity. That allows the manifestation of the Deity to readily assume the qualities of the ego and personality of the person undergoing the Drawing Down rite. Without definitions, there can be no limitations imposed by the known characteristics and traits of a well-defined Deity. A well-developed definition of the Deity and an exposition of its various mythic stories act as a control, a limitation, and a focus for the person who will be assuming that godhead. Any unjustifiable actions, spoken words, or characterizations can be judged as representing a poor or defective Drawing Down rite.

Another important consideration is that not every Drawing Down rite will produce a high-level godhead assumption. Sometimes it will be weak, or even distorted, and other times it will be awesome and accompanied by paranormal phenomena. A high-level godhead assumption should be considered a rare event, and a typical one would be at the middle point between a failure and a mind-blowing experience. Also, as in magic and the Mysteries, sometimes a rite is successful and sometimes it isn't. That should be considered okay, and it invites the kind of scrutiny that becomes an important learning situation.

Being truthful, transparent, and fully aware of the quality of the godhead assumption, for both the performer and the group, will help individuals to learn, grow, and become more accomplished. A new practitioner might produce an exemplary Drawing Down the first time they attempt it, just as a seasoned initiate might have a poor showing due to various circumstances. There should never be any shame in a weak Drawing Down rite, just as there should never be any great pride or ego inflation in a very successful one. The point in any individual performing a godhead assumption is the tangible presence of the Deity occurring through them. They are only an instrument of the Deity, and not to be mistaken for any kind of avatar of that Deity.

To ensure that the central rite of the Drawing Down is done in a proper and fully acceptable manner, the individual who performs this rite and the participants must follow some very specific directions. I am not trying to dictate liturgical preferences or act as some kind of authority to state these conditions. What I am trying to do is to make certain that the Drawing Down rite adheres to commonsense conditions and controls so that the immanent manifestation of Deity is maintained as an optimal part of modern Witchcraft and Pagan religions.

Witches and Pagans don't *believe*—they experience! That is to say, we don't base our faith on rites and practices alone, but on the immanent experience of the Deities that we worship. If that central tenet is shown to be distorted, fake, illusory, or based on the personality disorders of the performer, then the whole edifice must fall. Keeping the experience of the Goddesses and Gods in modern Witchcraft and Paganism as integral and true when someone is performing a Drawing Down rite should be the first and highest priority of the traditions where such a religious occurrence is central.

So, what will help to maintain the integrity and the authenticity of the Drawing Down rite are some simple guidelines that will not impinge on how this ritual is performed. We should then discuss the all-important preparations that should be performed before this rite is enacted, the controls and limitations determined by the coven, and a method or scale for judging the quality of the manifestation of the Deity. I will also endeavor to examine the ritual actions for the godhead assumption and distinguish them from those actions that are done for a personal godhead assumption prior to a solitaire working. This body of instruction and associated considerations will be part of my anatomy of godhead assumption that will ensure a more consistent and successful outcome.

Finally, you might be wondering why I am proposing these guidelines and controls on the Drawing Down rite performed in a coven or grove. Since this kind of godhead assumption is being enacted for a group of fellow worshipers, and that from this rite follows the obligatory sacramental rites of communion, empowerment, group magical workings, and Deity oracles and blessings, one would assume that a more successful godhead assumption would make the sacramental rites more potent and tangible.

Because this book is about sacramental theurgy as practiced in modern Witchcraft and Paganism, the foundation is that of a proper and enhanced Drawing Down rite. Our religious beliefs allow for the impersonation of our Deities under certain conditions, and that doing so makes them fully realized, immanent, and materialized. If the Drawing Down rite is more rigorously defined, prepared, and practiced, then there is a greater opportunity for the art of theurgy to be employed.

Preparations for Godhead Assumption

The elected person who will be assuming the godhead for the Drawing Down (whom I will call *the Medium*) should have no other responsibilities other than this operation. What this does is allow them to focus exclusively on this task and not have any other responsibilities that might distract or lessen the degree of godhead assumption that they are able to achieve. In fact, it would be a good idea if they were placed in seclusion up until the time that the Drawing Down rite is planned to occur. That means that the group meet-and-greet, working preparations, group meditation, and the consecration and empowering of the magic circle and the temple would be done without them being present.

I will assume that the working where this Drawing Down rite is enacted to this degree of intensity and focus would be for a full moon esbat or a special seasonal sabbat, such as one of the equinoxes or solstices for the Sun God, or one of the cross-quarter gatherings for the Horned God. Of course, the chosen Deity might not be any of these entities (think polytheism), so the coven would choose their Deity for this working. It should possibly occur during one of the esbats or sabbats to make it more momentous. My assumption also includes that there would be some other accompanied magical workings, such as blessings, healings, petitions for material achievements, or seeking oracular guidance and advice from the Deity. All of these preparations for the actual workings are planned and decided without the knowledge of the Medium. They are, for this operation, excluded from all coven deliberations and group decisions.

How I define a powerful and successful godhead assumption for the Drawing Down rite is the self-control and mastery that the Medium demonstrates as they enter into the conscious being of the Deity. This can only occur if the Medium is intimately familiar and comfortable with the Deity that they have chosen to assume. Until there is a high degree of confidence and comfort in performing this rite with the targeted Deity, a Medium should not undertake a Drawing Down rite that is singly focused, intense, and possibly even preternatural. A beginner could perform this kind of rite, but only one that has abilities and talents that would mark them as particularly gifted and blessed by the target Deity.

Therefore, the Medium should have already established an intense engagement with the targeted Deity that might have been in process for weeks or even months before the working. This would entail a process of spiritual alignment that would allow them to gain an exclusive connection to the godhead. They would be performing regular and periodic devotions to it consisting of votive offerings, prayers, and meditations. They would be aware of the ebb and flow of the lunar cycle and also the varying of light and darkness associated with the changing seasons as they engage with this discipline. These actions would also include any kind of volunteering or service to the community at large, all done discreetly in the name of the Deity. All of these activities would make the candidate Medium properly prepared to perform the godhead assumption, and in fact, they may periodically perform that rite silently alone as additional preparation.

The key to a successful godhead assumption, in my opinion, is that the Medium must temporarily surrender themself, their conscious being, to that of the Deity. Not everyone is equipped to handle this kind of requirement since it takes a level of trust that might be daunting for some. Also, some individuals may not be able to achieve this degree of openness. Certainly, the Medium is most vulnerable in this type of working, but trust and love will hopefully suffice to make this requirement acceptable and achievable.

During this period of group activity where they are preparing for the working, the Medium is sequestered in a part of the temple domicile that is quiet, settled, and far from the temple and rooms where the coven will meet and perform the initial rites to set the temple for the working. This period of sequestration should be filled with a long period of meditation, prayer, and making votive offerings to the target Deity. The room can be temporarily set up to be a mini shrine to the target Deity, with votive candles lit, flowers, incense burning, and perhaps even some low-volume meditative music. There should also be a statue or picture depicting the image of the Deity. The Medium should focus on the image and charac-teristics of the Deity and seek to identify themself within the full range of the persona of that being. This means that they should be garbed, adorned, and made up to look as much like that Deity as possible. This period is also characterized by a calling, summoning, and a passionate connection to the target Deity, like a lover searching for their lost beloved.

I would recommend a couple of hours or slightly more for this activity, and it can commence before the coven members even arrive for the working. It might start with a purification bath, anointing with consecrated oils, and a ritualized adornment activity using the help of a maid to assist the Medium in achieving their dressing and appearance. At the end of this period of focused and intense activity, the Medium should achieve the first stage of a deep trance, where they are only partially aware of their surroundings.

While the Medium is undergoing their preparations, the coven will assemble to decide the objective of the working, reducing it to a single word or phrase. That word or phrase will act as one of the controls for the Drawing Down rite. The members will know and share this word or phrase, but the Medium, who isn't present, will not know it. This word or phrase will be the focus of the group's meditation so that it is well planted into the minds of coven members.

Once the preliminary work of the meditations, circle consecration, and temple empowerment are completed, then the priestess will open a gateway to the northwest angle, and while they hold it open, the maid and helpers will go and retrieve the Medium from their sequestration and bring them to the edge of the circle. The priestess will welcome the Medium and bring them into the circle in the traditional way. They should then be seated on a temporary throne (a comfortable chair draped with a fancy cloth) and then given time to assume a deeper trance state, completing the preparation process. I recommend that the Medium be allowed to sit instead of standing so that they will be able to assume a deep trance without worrying about falling over. Also, being seated is better than lying down since reclining would induce the Medium to fall asleep instead of assuming a trance state.

As you can see, using these steps and sequestering the Medium would allow for the maximum achievement of the godhead assumption, since it would be the only activity that they would have to engage in for that specific working. I believe, based on actual experience over many years, that sequestering the Medium produces the optimal godhead assumption.

Drawing Down Rite Analyzed

I have discussed this rite of godhead assumption in my book *Spirit Conjuring for Witches*, but that version of the ritual was written for an individual assuming their personal godhead as part of their regular magical workings, particularly the work of spirit conjuration.[6] However, in this specific instance of godhead assumption, we are discussing the methodologies of performing a Drawing Down rite for the benefit of a group or coven.[7] What is required here is much more rigorous, although similar in many respects. The main difference is that the Medium would not perform the ritual actions and they would be seated on their temporary throne. The ritual actions will have to be adjusted for this kind of working.

While the Medium is seated and seeking to develop a deep trance state, the coven members sit around them and engage in a period of meditation, focusing on the Medium and perceiving them as the proper vessel of the Deity. There could be some adoration involved in that focused meditation, but it is, of course, for the Deity and not the individual posing as the Deity.

Then, the priest or priestess would stand before the seated Medium and perform the basic ritual structures for the Drawing Down rite. My preference is that a priestess should perform the ritual actions if the Medium is representing a male Deity, and a priest would perform these actions if the Deity is female. However, gender preferences such as these are to be determined by the coven and do not need to follow my preferences. Since I am an elder, I tend to see things from that perspective, although times are radically changing, and the tendencies of a cisgender male could very well be irrelevant. The Officiant performing the ritual actions might not even be the coven priestess or priest, since it might be prudent to have the Officiant be someone who has a link with the Deity and the Medium.

---

6 Frater Barrabbas, *Spirit Conjuring for Witches*, pp. 91–94.

7 Stewart and Janet Farrar, *A Witches' Bible: The Complete Witches' Handbook*, pp. 39–43. See the traditional Witches' Drawing Down ritual and associated communion.

Whoever is going to function as the Officiant and perform the actions of the Drawing Down rite should use a consecrated wand (or an anointed hand) to touch the bodily power points that are charged during the ritual. Thus, there won't be the traditional five-fold kiss. While the designated Officiant is performing the ritual actions, the Medium should visualize what they are doing and the effects on their body so that there is reciprocity and alignment between the priest and Medium.

Whether the coven members are garbed or skyclad, the Medium is fully garbed in some fashion, even if it is mostly body paint as in the case of the Horned God or any other nature Deity. The reason for less intimate contact is that it is less distracting to the Medium. Once again, this is my suggestion, and the coven may decide differently.

The following represents the basic steps as found in many traditions of Witchcraft, with the suggested differences associated with this fully realized godhead assumption instead of the typical variety used in the more frequent gatherings. The coven members are gathered around the seated Medium and standing before them is the Officiant, armed with a wand, with arms crossed over their chest. The preliminary period of meditation has already been completed and the members are ready to perform the rite.

1. **Introit:** A coven member rings a bell three times. The Officiant begins the rite with a short prayer and exhortation to the Deity, said with great passion and focused intent. This prayer should be fully memorized and is the preliminary introduction to the working, establishing the name of the Deity to be summoned.

2. **Ascending Wave:** The Officiant, using the wand, points and gently touches the feet, knees, groin, breasts, lips, and the area above the forehead while visualizing an energized light traveling up the Medium's body. The Officiant draws an invoking spiral above the Medium's head and sees the energy go through the ceiling of the temple and beyond.

3. **Primary Invocation:** The Officiant, holding the wand perpendicular to the floor in the right hand, intones the invocation of the Deity, perhaps even using barbarous

words of evocation, and entreats the Deity to descend to its worshipers and bless them with its presence. This invocation should also be memorized.

4. **Descending Wave:** The Officiant, using the wand, draws an invoking spiral above the head of the Medium and then touches the lips, breasts, groin, knees, and feet, visualizing an energized light descending from above the Medium slowly down to their feet.

5. **Mantle of Glory:** The Officiant, using the wand, draws an equal-arm cross on the torso of the Medium, starting from the right shoulder to the left, and from the head to the groin, visualizing an energized light forming a pulsating equal-arm cross upon the body of the Medium.

6. **Heart Gateway and Second Invocation:** The Officiant takes the wand and draws a triangle gateway upon the Medium's body, touching the left shoulder, the right, and the groin, centering it upon the heart. Then, the Officiant intones the second invocation, which calls and exhorts the Deity to enter into the Medium and to reside there for the benefit of the worshipping coven.

7. **Ascending Wave:** The Officiant, using the wand, performs the ascending wave as in step two. The Officiant and coven softly chant the name of the Deity for a few minutes and then all become quiet. After a short period of time, if the Medium has not started to speak, the Officiant addresses the Medium as the Deity and encourages them to be present and to speak to their congregants.

At this point, the Officiant and the coven should assess the manifestation of the Deity in the following manner. They will ask the Medium as Deity the following three questions:

1. The Officiant asks the first question:
   "Who are you?"
   The identification must be clear. In a good godhead assumption, the Medium will have already given their identity, so this question can be amended as:
   "You have proclaimed that you are X, is this so?"

2. The Officiant asks the second question:
   "Teach us about yourself?"
   In other words, what are your qualities and characteristics?

3. The Officiant asks the third question:
   "What do you wish to impart to us tonight?"
   This third question is key since what is being asked is the purpose of the working itself, and that purpose was determined by the coven outside of the Medium's hearing.

If the Deity, in the guise of the Medium, answers all three questions correctly and therefore actually divines the purpose of the working, then everyone can be quite certain that the godhead assumption is at a higher than typical level of manifestation. A typical godhead assumption will get two out of three of the questions correct and there will be a sense of otherness about the presence of the Medium. Anything beyond that represents a better-than-average Drawing Down rite, and such an occurrence is quite amazing by itself.

However, if the Medium as Deity is unable to answer any of the questions adequately, including identifying themself, and the Medium appears to be under a great deal of distress and even showing signs of some kind of seizure, convulsion, paroxysm, or physical attack, then the rite should be immediately suspended, and the Medium helped to stabilize.

An exception, of course, would occur if the Medium declared themself as a Deity that is completely different from the one expected by the coven. While this is unlikely to occur because of the focus and the time spent on establishing a link with a specific godhead, it is not impossible due to the fact that Deities are often capricious, and the group must always be prepared to deal with a situation that goes beyond expectations and produces an anomalous result.

Distress and incoherency, however, are the signs of what I would call a regressive trance state, and such occurrences can be mild or severe. The focus should be on the Medium, to aid and assist them, even if it means ushering them out of the temple. Helping the Medium ground should be the first order of business, such as giving them something to drink or even eat. Resting under observation until they stabilize or seeking medical attention if the malady is deemed severe should be the second order of business.

The Officiant, in such a situation, would remain behind, seeking to share condolences with the Deity, and then quietly shut down the magic circle. A regressive trance state is also not common, but it does occur more often than a highly energized and realized godhead assumption. Anything can trigger this kind of experience, and the important thing is to immediately help the Medium to overcome this attack and to stabilize.

If the Medium is successful in manifesting the Deity to some degree, then the working can be continued. What is required is a period of votive offerings to the Deity to be followed by communion, giving of blessings, an oracle, or specific magical workings—all witnessed and consecrated by the presence of the Deity.

We will discuss the various techniques and methods of consecrating sacraments in the next section, so we will now cover the levels of godhead manifestation that may accompany a rigorous Drawing Down rite. It is important to be able to control and judge such an event to validate and authenticate the manifestation of the Deity. Each and every working of this type should be written up in the coven's magical diary, with the date, time, elected Medium, target Deity, the level or quality of the godhead assumption, and any other notable observations that occurred during the event.

Ten Levels of Godhead Assumption

I have written about this in another one of my books, but I feel that it is important to present it here for you to absorb so that you might have the means to judge a particular Drawing Down rite and determine the level of godhead manifestation that has occurred.[8]

It is important to state that the typical successful working of this type will be judged by the coven to be a level three occurrence. I consider this level to be the baseline for a successful working. Anything beyond that would be considered exceptional, and anything above level seven to be improbable. That doesn't mean that a level

---

8 Frater Barrabbas, *Mastering the Art of Ritual Magick,* pp. 271–273.

ten occurrence of a godhead manifestation is impossible. It is that such an occurrence isn't very likely to ever be experienced. In my lifetime, I have only experienced an unverified level six manifestation; but because the controls for that occurrence were not in place, my judgment about even that level could be debated.[9]

The three questions and the coven's secret objective are the controls that help one judge the level of authenticity of a godhead manifestation. The category levels shown below assist in determining how the actual event transpired against the potential of possible occurrences and their incremental levels.

Here are the ten levels:

1. **Level One** is where the Medium is barely able to perceive or project the conscious state of the target Deity. It is characterized by regressive trance occurrences, and further determined by an inability of the Medium to adequately answer any of the three control questions. If the Medium fails to answer the first question—*who are you?*—then everything else is indicative of a failed operation. (I have noted the one exception to this judgment, but the rest of the levels would apply to an unusual appearance of an unexpected Deity.)

2. **Level Two** is where the Medium maintains a deep trance state and adequately answers two out of three questions (questions one and two, but not three). The persona of the Deity is too closely modeled on the personality of the Medium and there is little sense of the occurrence of the otherness that represents the manifestation of the Deity.

3. **Level Three** is where the Medium maintains a deep trance and answers two out of three questions. However, there is a subtle perception of the Deity's personality operating in its manifestation and there is an awakening sense of otherness emanating from the Medium.

4. **Level Four** is where the Medium seems to be in a very deep trance, seemingly unconscious, and also answers two out of three questions. The persona of the Deity is strongly defined

---

9 I have seen or heard of these higher levels, but they are completely uncorroborated and must, therefore, be considered unverified subjective experiences. They are still within the realm of possibility, though.

and appears to act autonomously from the personality of the Medium. There is a strong sense of otherness emanating from the Medium and the facial appearance seems to be taking on the image of the Deity.

5. **Level Five** is where the Medium is very unconscious and deep in trance. The Medium appears to sag somewhat while the image and persona of the Deity are forcefully and tangibly apparent. There may even be a slight illumination emanating from the Medium, and there are also some accompanied paranormal phenomena sensed, such as barely perceptible voices, musical tones, or actual voices. These are only perceived within the minds of the attendees.

6. **Levels Six–Eight** are an ever-increasing manifestation of the Deity and where the persona and even the body of the Medium are vacant and completely supplanted by the Deity. All three questions are answered, and the Deity appears to completely understand the intergroup politics and personal engagements of the coven itself. This begins as a subtle sensibility at level six and grows to become a startling oracular and clairvoyant agency at level eight. The body of the Medium is suffused with a soft inner glow, and the levels of paranormal activity appear to increase and become external. The key to these three levels is that all three questions are answered correctly and without any pause or doubt. Level eight is as amazing and miraculous as level six is subtle and filled with potential.

7. **Level Nine** is where the body of the Medium appears to be covered by a luminescent glow and the image of the Deity coalesces until it appears to be completely tangible. Paranormal activity is increased and becomes obvious to the whole group, and the Deity begins to show signs of omniscience and preternatural insights. There are disembodied voices heard, music and tones clearly discerned, strange and pleasant perfumes, and feelings of bliss and happiness pervade the temple.

8. **Level Ten** is where the body of the Medium has disappeared and is replaced with the image of the Deity. The Medium as Deity speaks with either their mouth opened or

closed, but there is no discernable lip movement. The voice heard is not like any human voice, and the presence of the Deity is suffused with a tangible and glowing light, arrayed with the colors of the rainbow. Any time the Deity either focuses or touches the minds of one of the coven members, it induces an ecstatic rapture. Time dilation is experienced (slowing down or even stopping), and the temple is filled with fragrant scents, mystical sounds, visions, voices, and unearthly music.

As you can see, a level ten manifestation of Deity would likely be a monumental event completely by itself, with absolutely no purpose for performing any further work. Everyone who experiences this level of godhead assumption would immediately achieve the apotheosis of religious and magical ascension. The likelihood of this happening is, probably, never. However, a level four experience would be a tremendous experience and would allow for the sacramental theurgical work to be performed afterward. Above level four is where the Deity has materialized to such a degree that its occurrence represents the absolute and successful outcome by itself without anything further being required except communion and votive adoration.

The Drawing Down rite, as outlined here, is the central Mystery for all subsequent sacramental work and the deployment of sacramental theurgy. It is the highest form of God-Work that a Witch or Pagan can perform. Perfecting this rite and giving it an exclusive focus in the group work of a coven or grove will make the immanent qualities of their pantheon of Pagan Deities fully materialized, and this will greatly aid all magical workings that seek to make changes and initiate transformations in the material world. Godhead assumption and Deity personification are the art forms that allow for sacramental theurgy. However, we should now focus our discussion on the techniques of sacrament generation where the agents of theurgical magic are produced.

CHAPTER FOUR

WITCHES' COMMUNION AND
SACRAMENTATION

"To him who in the love of Nature holds
Communion with her visible forms, she speaks
A various language."
—WILLIAM CULLEN BRYANT

The apex of the Drawing Down rite is the blessing of food and drink, as gifts given by the Deity to the coven members. Similar only in its basic formulation to the Catholic Mass, the food and drink are endowed with the essence of the Deity so that they become like the flesh and blood of that same godhead. Those who eat of this food and partake of this drink are joined in union with the Deity who has blessed and transubstantiated these gifts. It is even more evident when the godhead assumption is more effective than is typical.

How is this act of transubstantiation performed? It is accomplished by the will of the Deity and through the agency of the fully-embodied Medium whose hands and breath (pneuma) make the transformation of normal substances into something that is impregnated with the otherness of the Deity. The act of transubstantiation is performed by the touch, sign-making, and the breath of the possessed Medium. Food and drink become endowed with the essence of the Deity, and those who partake of those sacramental substances join their bodies with that of the Goddess or God. This is a profound magical act

43

where sacraments are generated from normal material substances, and their veneration and use in magical workings are the basis of sacramental theurgy.

When the Drawing Down rite manifests the targeted Deity, the first order of business is to hallow and venerate the Deity. The group performs offertory votive rites such as offering incense, flowers, food, and drink to the Deity. Any jewelry that might be blessed and questions or requests written on parchment scraps are also given as offerings. The questions or requests should be clearly written along with the name of the person making them. These offerings are placed on a temporary table erected to the side of the throne of the Deity.

Additionally, the Officiant may read poetic orisons accompanied by pleasant music with the coven members showing signs of adoration and worship, kneeling and bowing, or standing apart with arms extended in the gesture of offering and heads bowed. The important action is that the offering of food and drink to the Deity occurs before the rite of communion. All of the offerings made to the Deity belong wholly to it, and whatever is given back represents the generosity of that Deity. The votive offerings and veneration establish the tone and atmosphere for what follows.

Once the veneration and votive offerings are completed, the Officiant requests the coven members to be silent and engage in a period of quiet prayer and meditation while the Medium as Deity blesses each of the items placed as offerings. For jewelry, food, and drink, the Deity will make the sign appropriate to their perspective creed (pentagram, ankh, equal-arm cross, etc.). Then, they will touch the items (hold the chalice, touch the bread and jewelry), and gently breathe or blow upon the items, dispensing the spiritual essence of the Deity into them, transforming them into sacraments. A small piece of consecrated bread is placed in the master chalice to represent the mixing of the food and drink to further sacralize it. The Deity will gather the scraps of parchment questions and requests for perusing later. Unlike the traditional approach, the athame is not used to charge the sacraments, since this magical instrument (with a steel blade) would be inappropriate for a living Goddess or God to bless and sacralize substances for the benefit of the coven or group. Their hands are the best tool for this work.

After the consecration of votive offerings is completed, the communion rite begins. The Officiant will assist the Medium as Deity to dispense the sacraments to the coven, particularly in case they are unable to perform the offering of the sacraments to each of the members of the group. A single chalice of wine, mead, or beer holds the liquid offering, and a plate filled with small pieces of bread or cake contains the solid offering of food. If there are hygiene concerns, the single chalice can be replicated with a group of small cups on a tray. There should be a master chalice where the bread and wine or beer are mixed together.

The coven members form a line from before the enthroned Deity, and as each one approaches and bows low to the Deity, they are given a drink from the chalice and then eat the piece of bread or cake by the hand of the Medium. The Officiant stands to the side in case they are needed to help with the communion. To each person who comes before the Deity, the Officiant will say when the drink is offered:

"For this is my blood that becomes one with your blood,"

And when the food is offered:

"For this is my flesh that becomes one with your flesh."

These two phrases indicate that there is a kind of sacrificial offering implied by this blessing, where the flesh and blood of the Deity are given to the worshippers to be consumed. After everyone in the coven has received communion, then the Officiant bows before the Deity and receives the final offering of drink and food.

Once the communion has been completed, the Medium as Deity will make the appropriate sign three times before the group, and the Officiant will say:

"You are three times blessed by the power and authority of the Goddess/God X."

The Deity will handle, make the sign, and breathe upon the jewelry or tokens that were given to them at this point in the rite, and these are then left on the table to be taken up by their owners later.

Then, the Medium takes the pile of parchment petitions, questions, and desires and hands them to the Officiant. The Officiant goes through each one, asks the author to step before the Deity and bow low at their feet, then reads what is written. The Officiant will briefly pause and look to the Medium as Deity, who will respond to what is written in their own manner.

There can be requests for healing, either for the petitioner or for someone close to the petitioner, and the Deity can lay hands upon this person and send healing power to whoever is in need. Then, the petitioner is helped to arise by the Officiant and to back away respectfully, while the Officiant calls the next petitioner. This is repeated until all of the petitions have been read, the petitioners are blessed and answered in some manner, and the business is concluded.

Once this work is completed, the coven may perform a magical working with the Deity acting as their witness and spiritual arbiter, or the rite may be concluded. Liturgical rites might also be performed, such as the naming rite for a child, a handfasting, the conferring of sacral recognition (holy orders), a blessing for a pregnant person, or even a requiem for a recently departed member. At the end of this audience and work, the Officiant will bow before the enthroned Deity, and a coven member will ring the bell three times to signal that the work is at an end. The Officiant will then say an impromptu speech of thanksgiving to the Deity while the coven kneels before them.

Then, the Officiant and the coven will say farewell to the Deity as the Medium allows the godhead assumption to lapse and the Deity to be released. The Officiant and a few coven members will then help the Medium to their feet and assist them to depart the circle through the northwest gateway prepared by the priestess or priest and then head back to the temporary shrine. The gateway is closed, and the rest of the coven will participate in the final closing actions of the working.

This is how I suggest that such a communion rite be performed for the full godhead assumption during a Drawing Down rite. A coven or grove may decide to use this pattern or develop their own. However, there are some important steps for a successful engagement with a Deity that I think should be part of any variation that a group might adopt.

Here are the seven steps or stages to this sacramental rite that follows a successful Drawing Down rite.

1. **Votive Veneration and Adoration of the Deity**
2. **Offertory:** Offerings of food, drink, amulets or tokens, and requests or petitions to the Deity.
3. **Consecration:** Items offered are blessed and charged with the sign, touch, and breath of the Deity.
4. **Communion:** Sharing of blessed and charged food and drink.
5. **Blessings, Oracles, and Magical Sponsorship**
6. **Thanksgiving**
7. **Departure**

Oddly enough, these seven stages are remarkably similar to the stages to be found in the Tridentine Catholic Mass. If you add to them the steps for the godhead assumption, then you would have the elements of what I would call a *magical mass*. Like any magical ritual, this set of steps can be performed by a priestess or priest acting as an agent of the Deity operating under a less demanding godhead assumption and performing a rite that symbolizes what is done in an actual Drawing Down rite.

You might be asking, *why would someone want to do that?* And I would respond that a fully enacted Drawing Down and communion rite is not something that can be done often or regularly. There are limitations due to the preparations and logistics in performing it since it is very taxing for the Medium and requires the coven to plan and organize it. It is a very special rite, one that would be performed a few times in the overall cycle of the seasons.

A mass rite that symbolizes the Drawing Down rite could be performed often and readily whenever needed, even without the assistance of a group. Because what is done symbolically also emulates what is done within the framework of magic, a simplified ritual could stand in for a more involved and complex rite. This, of course, is my intention for writing this book.

While a magical mass would not be able to replicate the oracles and presence of the Deity that would be the provenance of a Drawing Down rite, it would be able to generate sacraments, charge and bless amulets, derive relics, and empower the temple in which it is performed with the tangible manifestation of the Deity or Deities to whom it is performed. Thus, a magical mass would be a formable rite in the repertoire of a Witch coven. We will discuss this rite in much greater detail in Part Two, Chapter Four, but for now, I wanted to make this comparison so that you might understand the basis for building up a set of rituals to perform sacramental theurgy.

Magical Sacraments—Nature and Qualities

A sacrament is anything that is offered to a Deity where it is blessed, charged with the essence of that Deity, and then returned for use by the individual worshipper. All offerings to the Deity represent personal sacrifices made by either the individual or the group. The Deity has no obligation to return anything that is offered, and it is a form of grace that they return to the individual or group what has been offered. Some items that are used in these rites belong to the Deity and are not returned, such as statues, pictures of the Deity, specialized magical tools, the garb and throne cloth associated with the Deity, and other items that are symbolically associated with the characteristics and myths of the Goddess or God. The chalice or cups and the dish used in the communion rite also belong to the Deity or to the pantheon of Deities honored by the coven.

The very first and fundamental sacrament that is produced every time the circle is consecrated is the salt and water mixed together to make the lustral water that is asperged in the temple. As a sacrament, it is used to consecrate and bless other items, such as the magical tools when they are consecrated. The lustral water is produced through the power and authority of the coven Deities where the water is charged and the salt blessed, representing the mixing of water and earth to produce a magical substance, the embryonic fluid of life itself.

This mixing together of salt and water is an important part of the generation of a semi-liquid sacrament. It is called by the Catholics in the Mass rite the *conmixio*, and it is one of the most important steps in that rite. It is also why a piece of bread or cake is placed in the master chalice for the communion rite following the Drawing

Down rite. Mixing elements together that symbolize the joining of the archetypal male and female is the foundational method for the generation of magical power. For the lustral water, the salt is the archetypal male element, and the water is the archetypal female element, similar to the bread and the wine. It is this method in which the two basic sacraments are generated.

Similar to the consecration rite of communion, once the salt is mixed with the water, the Operator will blow their breath over the surface of the cup to imbue it with the essence of the godhead that they have assumed (or is aligned with) so that it is sacramentally fixed. I typically follow that blowing of breath while making a sign of the ankh over the cup as the final step. These extra steps give the lustral water a more pronounced sacramental quality so that it can be more readily used to bless and consecrate anything that the Operator asperges with it.

We have already discussed the sacrament of the food and drink that is used in the communion rite, but I need to point out something that might not be readily understood. While the consecrated drink could be used to consecrate an object similarly to the use of lustral water, it is typically used up and what might remain is carefully disposed to the earth. All sacraments are returned directly to the earth if they are not used.

However, the bread or cake is not as perishable as the drink, so it can be used after and beyond the rite that produced it. The extra sacrament can be saved for later use if it is carefully preserved. Unleavened bread has the ability to remain preserved and inert for long periods of time, so I prefer it as sacramental food. The reason for this is that the fragment of bread can be used in other magical workings. It can be displayed in a reliquary container (similar to the Catholic monstrance) and used to project the powers of the Deity to whom it was consecrated. It can also be broken into fragments, wrapped in silver or even gold foil, and then placed in the four cardinal directions (or the eight directions) of a magic circle, making it continually charged and blessed. As a tool, it is quite potent and magically efficacious, and using the bread in this manner makes sense on a very practical magical level.

A special circle consecration ritual that uses a displayed fragment of bread to charge the magical circle and even connect and awaken token fragments already placed at the circle nodes would be a powerful ritual to sacralize a temple and its associated magic circle. Such an empowered environment would hardly need to be consecrated each time it was to be used, since it would already be in that state.

This ritual of sacralizing the temple and magic circle would be called in the Catholic Church a *rite of Benediction,* but its magical qualities, outside of the religious, make it an ideal rite for any coven or grove. It not only overrides the circle consecration rite but empowers the circle and temple to a degree that is beyond any other kind of charging and empowerment. The essence of the pantheon godhead resonates and is tangible in a temple where such a ritual is enacted. When I employ such a ritual working, I typically perform the magical mass first and then a magical benediction rite. The combination of rituals and their impact within a temple are quite amazing. It represents the most singular, profound energized state to begin any working that requires the tangible presence of the Deities.

Similarly, items such as specialized religious jewelry or religious tokens can be blessed and charged so that they are fully and actively sacralized. Anything that is so empowered and has a religious significance is an amulet. It is a magical sign that the godhead is with whoever wears the jewelry or has the token on their person. I typically use the magical mass to produce amulets, but the alternative is to have it blessed during a rigorous Drawing Down rite if it is to occur when such a need arises.

In the magical mass, other objects can be consecrated along with the wine and bread. This includes containers for sacraments such as reliquaries, amulets, oils, perfumes, ointments, medicines, or even vestments, magical tools, or newly purchased pictures, statues, or busts of the Deity. The priestess or priest would use a combination of lustral water, incense, the already consecrated bread, consecrated oil, an appropriate sign made over it, and the Operator's breath upon it to imbue any of these items with the essence of the godhead. All items, whether to be returned to the owner or given to the Deity as a permanent part of its regalia, should be first fully consecrated. It is for this reason that the utility of the magical mass has its unique precedence.

The production of sacraments and sacralized objects is a central part of the rite of the magical mass, and these things can be used in magical and liturgical operations. An ointment or herbal medicine can be blessed and charged, making it more efficacious. Lustral water and consecrated oils or perfumes can be used to consecrate tools or even people for special blessings, healings, and initiations. The magical mass becomes a kind of ritual factory that can be used to produce every kind of consecrated and sacralized object that an individual or group might wish to use.

While the more rigorous Drawing Down rite is kept as a high point in the magical and liturgical calendar of the coven, the magical mass can be performed by the group or by individuals to generate sacraments and consecrate objects whenever and wherever needed. Both ritual workings are important and integral to the sacramental theurgy that a coven or grove might want to perform, but only one can be performed at any time without much preparation.

Sacramental magic along with godhead assumption, whether individual as the higher self, or as the embodiment of one of the Deities in the coven's pantheon, represent the methodology to manifest the power, authority, and tangible material expression of the magic of the godhead. However, there is another component to this kind of magic, and that is the magic of the placeholder of the Goddesses and Gods. If sacramental magic manifests the Deity to be realized and embodied in the forms of a Medium or sacraments and consecrated objects, another symbolic sign or marker represents that the presence of the Deity is active and manifest at that place and time.

Placeholders for the Gods

Placeholders for the Deities are, of course, consecrated objects, but they are also symbolic forms denoting either a specific Deity or a class of Deities within the pantheon of the group. A consecrated placeholder can also function as a surrogate for an actual Drawing Down godhead assumption. It is consecrated, charged, and imbued with the essence of that Deity, and the symbolic makeup of that object then becomes a place of residence for that entity.

Such ritual and liturgical objects as the Stang, Besom, and Cauldron function as tools imbued with the essence of a specific Deity or class of Deities. Each is a symbolic representation of a class of Deities, or it can be assigned to represent just one. Each is consecrated and set aside for special use, given first as gifts to the Deities and then blessed and charged in their name. These three objects have a history associated with Witchcraft and Paganism, and they have associations that go even further back into the mists of the earliest times.

The Stang is a horned or twin-tinned forked staff with other embellishments that together represent a kind of natural or feral attribute of the Deity. It can be considered masculine or can be considered to be both masculine and feminine. Like all such tools, it has a certain ambiguity making it perfect for a representation tool. Typically, the Stang is used to represent the Horned God, and where it is erected, whether in a temple or an outdoor grove, that is where the Deity resides.

A Besom is a handmade broom constructed of naturally occur-ring components. It is a medium-sized staff with a thatch bristle base. Hidden within the thatch is the end of the besom carved to form a phallus. The consecrated Besom represents the physical joining of the archetypal masculine and feminine in the creation of life. It is, therefore, a representation of both a Goddess and a God, but united as one. This makes the Besom into a lintel or gateway tool, and it is used as both a kind of hobby horse to be ridden between worlds and also as a representation of the trance state that allows for travel to other worlds.

The Cauldron is a large, blackened pot that can be intricately decorated or plain, and it is consecrated and imbued with the essence of the Deity. It is more than just a placeholder since it can be used to make food and drink as well as medicines and various potions. What is produced within it automatically becomes a sacrament, since the Cauldron is fully consecrated. Typically, the Cauldron is a placeholder for the nurturing and mothering class of Deities, which could be a Mother Goddess or even a Crone Goddess. The Cauldron is typically consecrated to a Goddess in the coven pantheon and wherever it is placed, therein the Goddess shall arise and be apparent. However, it is often united with the sacred fire pit to produce sacramental brews, medicines, and potions.

Other placeholders would be pictures, busts, or statues of specific Deities or a family of Deities. These objects would be consecrated and imbued with the essence of those Deities whom they depict. A consecrated bust or statue can be further animated with the intelligence and energy field of a talismanic elemental that would greatly enhance its ability to project and emanate the persona and powers of the Deity. This process is called *statue animation* and it is a part of the theurgy of late classical antiquity, but it likely had earlier precedents. Animating a statue requires the knowledge and use of talismanic magic. I will be sharing a ritual pattern in this book to help you apply this special kind of magic to your work. Having the living and breathing presence of the Deities in a temple or outdoor grove would make any magical operations performed in that space ever more potent and effective.

Another placeholder tool is the sacred Mask of the Deity. Like all other placeholders, it would be consecrated and imbued with the essence of the target Deity that it represents. The mask would be a handmade relic that could be simple or elaborate. I recommend that a gifted artisan with sympathy, or even an alignment, to the subject of the mask, should be employed to create this sacred object. The mask could be made of wood, fabric, or even paper mâché, but it should be crafted by someone who has talent, skill, and experience in making such an object. The artisan should also be paid for their work without haggling or readjusting the price. The completed mask is then offered to the Deity, consecrated, and imbued with its spiritual essence.

Making such an artifact as a mask is only the first stage in an elaborate process where a priestess or priest becomes the living and breathing vessel for the Deity. This process is more involved and time-consuming than what is done to produce an effective Drawing Down rite since it is a fully actualized impersonation of the godhead. It is, therefore, a lifelong commitment, and one that takes years to fully realize. A fully trained, experienced, and self-mastered priestess or priest who dons a consecrated mask to become a living Deity would do so in a periodic event called the *Grand Sabbat*. This event might occur once every three years or more, but it would include the personifications of the Gods and Goddesses of Witchcraft and would thereby represent the highest and holiest gathering that Witches could attend—to meet their Deities and to receive their blessings, marks, signs, and oracles.

I will present in Part Three, Chapter Seven the ritual outline for staging such an event as a Grand Sabbat, which would happen in a very exclusive assembly on private land maintained strictly for that purpose. It would be, then, land given to the Deities and held in their names. Whether the priests and priestesses who would personify the Deities using the artifice of the Sacred Mask would live on this land and be supported by their followers, or whether they would live secret and obscure lives in the mundane world is not important. What is important is that their Craft and abilities be honed to perfection through an exclusive focus on acting and functioning as a Deity at the appropriate time and place. We will discuss what would be required for someone to take upon themselves this onerous duty and strict discipline to be so intensely aligned and deeply connected to their chosen Deity that could slip in and out of a godhead assumption and personification whenever needed.

A final and very important tool, which can be simply consecrated or empowered by use, are the knucklebones or dice that are used to determine the will of the Deity. It is a critically important and significant operation that all groups and individuals know the will of the Gods that they worship. Before any major undertaking, one should consult with the specific Goddess or God to determine if the rite or working is agreeable and permissible to them. Future dates for a major Drawing Down or a Grand Sabbat can also be determined in this manner. The basic premise behind possessing a divinatory tool is that nothing happens that is not in accordance with the will of the Deity. The knucklebones or dice that are used to divine the desires and will of the Gods and Goddesses symbolizes a sacred conduit of communication between divinity and humanity. An example of how to use dice in a divinatory manner can be found in my book, *Spirit Conjuring for Witches*.[10] While I might not mention this operation in the context of the liturgical

---

10   Frater Barrabbas, *Spirit Conjuring for Witches*, pp. 183–185.

and magical rites in this book, I will assume that the practitioners of these rites will consult and be in alignment with their Deities through the use of divinatory tools.

None of these rites and practices are performed in a vacuum. They are and must be performed against the backdrop of the Mysteries of the moon and sun, life and death, and light and darkness. While it is typical for an esbat or sabbat to be performed in the traditional manner, there are additional rites that can lock in the deeper attributes of the Mystery and allow for magical workings that would be hallowed and sanctified by the meaning and significance of the moment. What I am referring to are basic Mystery rituals that can be performed in place of or in addition to what is typically done by the coven. This would include the rites of initiation as it could be extended to include a specialized transcendental transformation. All of these additional rites and practices require a deeper knowledge of the basic Mysteries of light and darkness, and life and death. Therefore, we should examine these Mysteries so we can further discuss the magical Mystery rites of the lunar calendar and the eight seasonal transitions.

CHAPTER FIVE

FIVE MYSTERIES OF
LIGHT AND DARKNESS

"What would be the significance
of the candlelight, if there were no darkness?
What would be the power of the stars over
our minds, if there were no night?"
—C. JOYBELL C.

S acramental theurgy is dominated by the eternal interplay of
light and darkness. As dwellers on the surface of this world,
we are struck by the simple and natural changes of day and night,
the changing seasons, the phases of the moon, and our own stages
of birth, life, and death. Still, within all of these constant cycles of
change is the ever-unchanging fact of beingness and the web that
connects everything together into a fabric of union. There is change
all around the periphery of life on this planet and there is eternal
stillness and *at-one-ness* at its center. That unchanging center, of
course, is not located in the planet's core, but in the heart and soul
of every sentient being. Yet, it is both within and without us and
remains the eternal Mystery at the heart of all religions.

There are Five Mysteries regarding the natural interplay of
light and darkness in our world. These Five Mysteries are also
repetitive cycles that can obscure them from our notice. The
Five Mysteries are the diurnal cycle of day and night, the lunar
cycle and its monthly phases, the annual seasonal cycle of the

sun, the cycle of life and death of all living things, and the nature of spirit and Deity. These Five Mysteries are governed by the cycle of light and darkness, life and death; but the Mystery of Spirit stands both outside and within the passage of change and the endless progression of time. Based on the temporal model of magic, one could say that time is the Greater Mystery that embraces them all.

As Witches, we should engage this changing world with understanding and joy. The Sun and the Moon are our Deities, and the Mystery of life and death is wrapped up in the Horned God and his reign as the underworld lord and the Green Man, representing the fragile and ephemeral nature of life and the finality of death and rebirth. There are also the many Deities of place and location, filling the four domains of celestial, sky, earth, and underworld.

We should most particularly become keen observers of the changing seasons, the phases of the moon, and the night sky in all its glory. Knowing the flora and fauna of the Earth is important, as is the topology of the surface and underworld of the land, but knowing the night sky, the constellations, planets, and fixed stars is equally important. This is a strategic consideration when a Witch is contemplating engaging in the activities of manifesting the hallowed sacral nature of the Deities in all of their worlds to become the material and tangible realization of the coven or the community at large.

Diurnal Cycle of Day and Night

The sun rises in the morning, passes through the sky, sets in the evening, and the night endures until the coming dawn. We are programmed to respond to this cycle of light and darkness at the core of our biological being—our circadian rhythm. We typically sleep at night and work during the day. Before there was oil, gas, or electric lighting, humans typically retired when the sun went down but woke during the middle of the night and then went back to sleep until before dawn. The discovery and mastery of fire changed things for human beings long ago and helped to dispel somewhat our primal fear of the darkness.

The ancient Egyptians believed that when the evening sun had set, it passed through an underground river of connecting gateways and challenging pathways that led from the west back to the east. The Sun God Ra, riding in his solar boat, passed through twelve gateways of connected terrains that corresponded to the twelve hours of the night. At the climax of this passage, he and his helpers had to fight off the great serpent Apep so that the solar boat could gain passage to the domain of Osiris. There, the Sun God Ra would achieve regeneration with Osiris' assistance and be raised up in the east to begin once again his passage across the sky. As the Sun God Ra achieved his apotheosis during his nightly rebirth, so the pharaoh and his devotees might also experience rebirth and eternal renewal when they were properly entombed.

This cyclic passage of Ra through the twelve gates of the underworld was encapsulated in the text of the book *Am Duat* and beautifully represented on the walls of the tombs of the New Kingdom pharaohs. However, the story of the nightly struggle of Ra in the underworld was likely an ancient theme that had its origin in pre-dynastic times. These twelve stages represented for the Egyptians the cosmogonic cycle of life and death depicted in the diurnal cycle of night and day. It symbolizes the five mythic stages of creation, paradise, the age of death, and the final dissolution, all repeated by the endless activities of the eternal source.

Day followed by night has the power to symbolize a daily birth, death, and rebirth. Our sleep cycle is a simile of death, and our dreams are the manifestation of the domain of death and rebirth. When we awaken in the morning, it is like a rebirth or restoration. We engage with our daily activities, hardly aware of the sun's progress when it achieves its midpoint and then begins to recede ever towards the western horizon.

In the religion of Islam, one of the five pillars of that belief is to pray (*Selah*) five times a day towards the city of Mecca. This is done at dawn, noon, afternoon, sunset, and evening. This would also accord with the solar observations of ancient Egyptians and modern Pagans and magicians, although they would be done for completely different reasons and performed in a very different manner. It is just a keen and spiritually engaging observation of the sun at its various stations throughout the day. I have done this kind of observation myself when working magic. It is important for one to align with the passing of the sun and engage magically with the diurnal cycle when working any kind of magic that is focused on the sky and earth.

Lunar Cycle and Phases of the Moon

A keen observer of the night sky cannot help but notice the phenomenon of the moon. Sometimes the moon appears in the day sky, and other times, at night. While the moon makes its passage during a period of twenty-eight days, its shape and appearance change. It ranges from invisible (new moon), a left-facing crescent (first quarter), fully visible with a round sphere (full moon), a right-facing crescent (last quarter), and again, invisible.

The full moon rises in the east when the sun is setting in the west, and the quarter moon rises in the east at either noon or midnight. The new moon rises and sets with the sun, and it can cause a rare eclipse of the sun. Because of these different times of rising and setting with the sun, the moon can appear during the day or during the night. However, it is the appearance of the moon at night that is most dramatic, especially the full moon.

There are many mythic themes connected with the moon and its appearance, and while a few of them might have a scientific basis, many of them are completely mythic. All cultures of the earth have various beliefs about the moon and its phases. The cycle of the moon has been associated with the human estrus cycle, planting and harvesting, and the occurrence of irrational or strange behavior in some individuals (lunacy). The ghostly light of the full moon during the night casts spectral shadows over the landscape, briefly illuminating the ancestral ghost roads between worlds. The cycle of the moon seems to symbolize the burgeoning and diminishing powers of life as it works its mysterious spell on all creatures that are born, live, and die. The moon can also be depicted as the four mythic stages in the creation cycle of a woman, beginning with the estrus inflammation, pregnancy, growing of life, and giving birth, followed by a brief postpartum depression.

Because the moon is associated with the estrus cycle, sexuality, psychosis, and hysteria, the waxing and waning of the powers of the life force, and the manifestation of subtle occult powers of prophecy and cyclic physical transformations shouldn't be surprising. The moon represents all that is good and also evil in life; it is a constant balance of light and darkness that is a part of human nature. It is often, though not always, associated with the feminine archetype and the characteristics of women in general.

Solar Cycle and the Four Seasons

The Mystery of the Sun is twofold—the diurnal cycle of night and day, and the annual cycle of the four seasons. In the northern latitudes, the Sun appears to circle the Earth slanting either to the north, the south, or in the middle of the sky during its orbit. When the Sun is slanting to the north and reaches its maximum movement in that direction, it is midsummer, and when it is slanting to the south and achieves its maximum orbit in that direction, it is midwinter. When the Sun is between those two points, then it is either spring or autumn. The orbit of the Sun is called the *plane of the ecliptic,* and it shifts as much as twenty-three degrees to the north or the south of its equal day-to-night orbit, known as the *celestial equator.* The Sun's apparent shifting of north and south in its seeming orbit of the Earth is what produces the four seasons during an annual cycle of the Sun.

The four seasons are the Spring Equinox, the Summer Solstice, the Autumn Equinox, and the Winter Solstice. The equinoxes are periods in our calendar where the length of day and night are equal. The Summer Solstice is the season when daylight exceeds the night by as much as four hours. Conversely, the Winter Solstice is the time when the night exceeds daylight by as much as four hours. Of course, this depends on how far north one is from the equator since the further north one is, the larger the duration of day or night. In the polar regions, the Summer Solstice is marked by an endless day, and the Winter Solstice by an endless night. Of course, in the southern latitudes, these changes are reversed in their occurrence during the year, where the Summer Solstice occurs in December, and the Winter Solstice occurs in June.

Therefore, the four seasons are determined by the duration of light and darkness and by the relative warmth or coolness of the daily heat from the sun. Plants react to the diminishing light during the autumn when deciduous trees shed their leaves, plants die, and the flora becomes dormant for the coming winter. Animals are affected by the occurrence of autumn as they prepare for the times of diminished food supplies by hoarding or overeating, and the preparation of a place for hibernation or diminished activity. Humans have also followed the seasons, preparing for winter by storing up resources during the summer and autumn and collecting together in a protected space for the winter.

We are genetically programmed to the diurnal cycles of the sun and the annual cycles of the seasons. The four seasons have gained a powerful mythic representation that has impacted every culture on the planet where four seasons occur. Not every place on the planet has four seasons; sometimes there are only two seasons, wet and dry, like in equatorial jungles. Still, the changing seasons and our response to them are represented at a cellular level in all creatures of the earth. These responses vary, of course, but they are most dramatic in the far northern and southern latitudes.

The four seasons represent the four seasons of life and death, where spring is when life is apparently reborn, grows to maturity in the summer, is harvested in the autumn, and sits dormant in the winter. The light is waxing from winter through spring to summer and waning from summer through autumn to winter. Light plays an important mythic part in the passage of the seasons, where it dies and is reborn in the Winter Solstice, and reaches its apotheosis in the Summer Solstice. The seasonal celebrations, in their most basic form, follow the path of light as it expands, contracts, and transforms over the course of a year.

The four seasons of the sun are also exemplified by the stages of life that human beings undergo, where spring is birth and youth, summer is adulthood and the siring of children, autumn is maturity, and winter is old age and death. The cycle of the seasons is intricately tied to the life cycle of all creatures, and so we must discuss the Mystery of that cycle as well.

Cycle of Life and Transformations

The annual cycle of the four seasons is similar to a longer cycle, and that is the cycle of life and death that all living creatures undergo. It is an inescapable fact that everything that is born in our world must, at some point, die. Death is our ultimate fate, and our gift of life helps us to prepare for that fact, particularly if our lives are long and we are in a position to contemplate our end. Still, we can discover through various means, through religion, mysticism, or magic, that death is not the final state of our core being. We leave behind us a rich reservoir of memories, experiences, and beliefs that have touched and affected those who were companions on our path of life. These last for some time, and the impression that we make on the ocean of consciousness can give us a period of existence beyond death.

We live our lives going through stages, both large and small. There are four major stages, which are birth and youth, adulthood, maturity, and old age, but there are other lesser stages as well. Every time we accomplish something significant in our lives, whether it is a graduation or wedding ceremony, a divorce, childbirth, job change, material advancement, location change, acquiring a home, a big seasonal celebration, a special vacation, or meeting with remarkable people, all of these events are significant and represent stages in our life. In order to live fully conscious lives, we should note these passages or stages and properly celebrate them. We need to recognize what we have accomplished and reward ourselves as well. It is all a part of the ongoing joyous celebration of who we are on this path of life.

However, there are times we undergo drastic changes when disasters happen or internal crises arise, and during these times, another kind of process is experienced. This process is not one of the mundane life stages, great or small, which might beset us. This is a profound crisis that we have to endure and adapt to in order to fully resolve. This could be a disaster, such as experiencing an earthquake, a terrible storm, a conflagration that destroys our home and our community, or a flood. It could be a natural occurrence, or one deliberately unleashed by other people, such as a war, a race or class riot, an insurrection, or the complete breakdown of civil society.

An outward disaster has an obvious cause, and its trauma can last for years or even a lifetime. Still, there is also a crisis that can occur wholly within an individual when their normal way of living and coping fails to resolve internal issues and the structure of the self undergoes a complete breakdown. This inner crisis can be involuntary, such as the onset of a severe mental collapse, or voluntary, when change must be embraced, and the self must be dissolved and rebuilt. That latter kind of inner crisis is known as a *transformative initiation.*

All of these kinds of changes, whether by outward catastrophe or inner collapse, follow a process of self-dissolution and, hopefully, the rebirth of a new self. People who have survived disasters have learned to live and thrive again, depending on the harshness of their trauma, but their lives are so greatly changed as to be entirely new lives, representing a kind of psychic death and rebirth. Some never recover, and this can be true whether the trauma they underwent was caused by external or internal events. The one situation where the subject voluntarily submits to the process of transformation and renewal is the magical and mystical process of transformative initiation. The main difference is that the subjects willingly submit themselves to an impending internal ordeal when it becomes obvious that internal change is necessary and optimal.

Those of us who are on the path of Witchcraft and magic will undergo two forms of initiation in the pursuit of our avocation. The first is a social initiation that brings us into the group and confers upon us certain obligations, perquisites, and bonds of brother and sisterhood. Perhaps some Mysteries might be shared or even some secret perspectives, but overall, this is a social elevation.

The other kind of initiation occurs to the individual, and they undergo it alone. There is no group or authority that confers this initiation, and there is no specific training to prepare for it. It just happens that while on the path of magic following the Mysteries of the Gods and Goddesses, a person will discover their shortcomings and find that their normal way of coping and integrating knowledge is no longer appropriate or useful.

At that moment in time, this person will be shown that a profound internal change is immanent and soon after, they will undergo a powerful internal transformation. It may last many hours, days, weeks, or even a year. There will be a resolution, for without it, there would be a collapse into madness and despair. That failure to resolve the internal crisis can and does happen, but typically, the individual learns to submit to the process and gives birth to a new personality. They have a new vision of life and a new mission, but they are not so radically different than their old self.

Luckily for us, there is a powerful mythic pattern that encapsulates this process of transformative initiation. Examining this pattern reveals that it is an age-old paradigm that occurs in all cultures and probably through all times. It is known in literary circles as the *Hero's Journey*. It is a transformative adventure, but it occurs within the mind and psyche of the individual. We can find this pattern in all of the adventure literature, from Gilgamesh in ancient Sumer to the heroic epics of the Greeks to the modern saga of *Star Wars*.

Sacramental theurgy, when performed regularly and consistently, has the power to impact the mind and soul of the practitioner in such a manner that internal transformations periodically occur. This is because sacramental theurgy works in alignment with the Gods, and it is these godheads who can instigate or trigger a powerful psychic transformation in a devotee. It is one of the hazards of working this kind of magic since intermittent contact with Deities leaves a profound and permanent mark upon humanity, and it ultimately leads to a final alignment—union with the One.

Of course, what is behind the transformation of consciousness are the multiple forms of the Deity themself, at once disguised behind their masks and simultaneously real to the experience of individual human beings, and it is this Mystery that we are ultimately drawn towards.

Nature of Deity Within and Without

The various artifacts of sacramental theurgy are powerful signs and symbols that live within our individual and collective minds as links to actualized Deities. Even in our secular world, with its empirical science and monotheistic, religious creeds, the conscious awareness of our immanent godheads represents an edifice of the collective conscious mind that acts and feels like omnipresent Deities. While Christianity declared centuries ago that the old Gods of Paganism are dead and replaced with a new universal truth, Pagan practices have returned and persisted as if such a declaration is both a delusion and a social falsehood. It would seem that the universal truth of monotheism is just propaganda, and that the real truth is that the Deity is so vastly more complex and protean in its form that it can support many different and divergent points of view simultaneously.

While Christians pray and sing hymns in their churches, Pagans and Witches gather in their groups or alone to worship the old Gods and Goddesses in a new way, and people around the world meet and gather in their synagogues, mosques, pagodas, temples, and shrines to worship as they believe is right and true, and indeed, they are all true. In fact, either they are all true or none of them are true, since they are all based on similar mystical and spiritual experiences. The Hindu devotee gives offerings to Krishna in his shrine and experiences a sense of fulfillment, joy, and peace, just like the parishioners of a Catholic church who attend a mass and receive communion.

What this means is that the spiritual context of a religious truth represents the domain of that truth, but it cannot either intrude or contradict a religious truth that resides in another spiritual context. There is, in fact, only the most basic and simplest of truths that could be said to be universal. Explicit sectarian beliefs that have their context within a specific creed cannot be universal. That means that when a Christian says that there is only one true God and only one way to worship that Deity through Jesus Christ, such a statement is not universal. It is highly contextual, and within another spiritual context, it would be meaningless. We need to keep this fact in mind if we fail to realize that judging another faith within our own spiritual context produces the most erroneous and illogical results.

Because the nature of Deity is multiform and appears to conform to our spiritual context, it has become a major source of confusion and even sectarian bigotry when people try to express their faith based on that spiritual context as absolute universals. Monotheistic religions are probably the worst offenders in this type of erroneous behavior, but they are certainly not alone. When religious passion and belief are mixed, a very irrational and toxic form of delusion is created. As Witches, we should understand that our spiritual context is quite unique, but all truths discovered within it must remain within it. This is why secrecy and confidentiality are maintained in covens and Pagan groves. Outsiders typically have no way of understanding what goes on in these groups without that all-important spiritual context to guide them.

We can discover the Deity within us, imbued in our conscious being and pervading all that we are or can be. What the African religious traditions call the "God of your head" is the God Within. It is through that internal Deity that we can, momentarily, be like the Gods. It is also what we realize when we intimately experience spiritual moments and sense the Deity close and intimately within us. It is this internal godhead that acts as the link that connects all sentient beings together into a web of conscious life. At peak moments of consciousness, we can sense and experience this feeling of being connected to everyone and everything.

There is also a Deity outside of us that resides in the collective consciousness of the world's cultures and has many faces, forms, and spiritual contexts. Throughout all of these forms, it connects to us when the God Within perceives and recognizes the God Without. Such an alignment is the basis for what is called *transcendental consciousness,* and it can produce a continuous state of internal self-transformation, called by some *enlightenment.* This mind-state is experienced as the eternal Now, the unchanging and infinite One, which is the primal cause of all meaning and manifestation. It is that ever-present power that can change and transform souls and minds, creating and manifesting new destinies and resolving our internal paradoxes that can block the realization of our full potential selves.

Sacramental theurgy is the magic where we employ the power and authority of Deity within our magical workings. It is where we activate the Gods and Goddesses to play a decisive role in determining our material destiny. Because we know that the Deity wears masks and perfectly impersonates Gods and Goddesses, we as polytheistic magical practitioners choose to engage and expand our religious practices so we can also wear the masks of the Gods and Goddesses and thereby perfectly impersonate them for a true materialization of their beings in the world.

In this fashion, we create a new spiritual context where one may not have existed previously, and we install the component of Deity within our religious and magical workings. This makes our magical workings also liturgical workings, and it brings the power and wisdom of the Deity to bear within our magical goals. It is through the Deity that we are able to change our destiny, through votive offerings, sacramentation, and magical work, as the art of sacramental theurgy makes fully and completely possible.

Part 2

Cultic Practices of the Manifested Deity

CHAPTER SIX

ART AND ORDEAL OF
DEITY PERSONIFICATION

"And Remember Well, that if thou
wert in truth a lover, all this wouldst thou do
of thine own nature without the slightest flaw
or failure in the minutest part thereof."
—ALEISTER CROWLEY, *LIBER ASTARTE*

We have discussed the basic liturgical and magical workings of a rigorous coven or group Drawing Down rite and the associated communion rite. I have shown that these rites can be symbolized by rituals that might also be performed by a single individual, such as the magical mass and benediction rites. I have discussed the place markers for the Deities and talked briefly about the Witches' Stang, Besom, and Cauldron. We will also cover other topics, such as the cultic objects and their associated individualized rites in much greater detail in this part of the book. These are the cultic practices that assist in manifesting the materialized presence of the covenstead Deities and allow for the generation of sacraments to be used in sacramental theurgy. This part of the book will explain the very nature and utility of magical sacraments.

I begin this chapter on the specialized cultic practices focusing first on the Sacred Mask and the greater rigor and expanded life-long discipline associated with Deity Personification. This is the first step in developing a more intensive and profound experience of the godhead, and because it requires so much from the Operator, it also produces a greater manifestation of the chosen godhead for larger groups and intra-community gatherings. Few of our community know about this kind of practice, and fewer can function as a living God for the benefit of others. Still, there is an underlying methodology to this role, and once known, it makes the process seem a little bit clearer and not so challenging.

While the Drawing Down rite can be made into a powerful experience for a small group or coven, the godhead personification assumed by a priest or priestess can be an even greater experience for an expanded audience, such as the Witchcraft community in a region or even a nation. Such a gathering is called a *Grand Sabbat*, but the Officiant of that rite has a long-term commitment and a very rigorous discipline to undergo in order to function in that role.

Many years ago, I watched and enjoyed the British cable series *Robin of Sherwood*, where the title character acted as an emissary (the Hooded Man) for the forest Deity, Herne the Hunter. A central but obscure character in that series was a man who lived hidden in a cave in the Sherwood Forest in Medieval England, and who appeared dressed to his worshippers as a stag-headed man to personify the Horned God Herne, Lord of the Trees. When thus garbed, the humble and unnamed servant of the Horned God became the Deity himself and was the medium of the magical powers of Light and Darkness founded in the forest that fought through the guise of the Hooded Man against tyranny and oppression for the underprivileged peasants and outcasts who lived around and even within the mighty forest.[11]

The stunning visual image of the stag-headed man appearing from out of the misty forest as Herne the Horned God before the gathered woodland folk had quite an impact on me, and it powerfully stimulated my imagination. While I was quite enchanted by this low-budget but brilliantly written TV show, I also saw the practical applications of how someone might be able to achieve this level of union with a Pagan Deity. Yet, I also understood that the sacrifice of one's normal life would be a stringent requirement.

---

11 *Robin of Sherwood*, created by Richard Carpenter, HTV and Goldcrest Films, 1984–1986.

Such a person would have to dedicate their life to this avocation, and as it would be their primary focus, it would limit what they could do as far as earning a living. They would have to get by with very little and live a very humble existence, surviving through the generosity of friends and co-religious backers, and it would likely be a solitary existence, but not at all antisocial. Such a person would be the heart of their community and be well-known and loved.

Decades later, I would meet someone who had chosen for himself the role of priest of the Horned God, and who underwent all of the rigors associated with that discipline to become, when called upon, a peerless and profound personification of that Deity. Yet, there was one very important tool that he had to obtain, and that was a beautifully hand-carved mask of the Horned Deity that he used as a centerpiece to his work as a fully living representative of the Horned God. He later formulated a Grand Sabbat event where certain select individuals were invited to attend, and greatly impressed and overawed all those who participated in this rite.

In this chapter, I will define how a person might become a living and breathing representation of a Pagan Deity. It will not matter what Deity that might be, since this methodology can be used for any Deity. It can also be used to a lesser degree of intensity so that a person might deepen their connection to a specific Deity and forge a more perfect alignment. These steps and stages are also important as teaching tools to help make one a better Witch or Pagan from the perspective of religious liturgy and faith. This is because, from this perspective, Witchcraft and Paganism are systems of religion where liturgy and magic are tightly intertwined, so a greater development of one will also assist in a better capability within the other. Since I have shown that the Deities can be engaged to amplify and extend the magic that a Witch or Pagan performs, it can only aid a Witch to study these stages and to apply them, where necessary, to their religious practices.

Acquiring and maintaining the inhabiting spirit of the god-head within oneself is a lengthy and arduous process. It is a thing that must be continually renewed, and it has a cycle that is set by the passage of the moon and seasons of the sun—the interplay of light and darkness, life and death. The full ordeal spans a lifetime of work, discipline, and dedication. Still, Pagans and Witches can undergo this ordeal for a briefer period of time to test and manifest their ability in terms of their magical capabilities and mystical insights.

For those of our faith, we may share in a brief ecstatic moment what others have decided to undergo for their entire lives. Experiencing this ordeal for a brief time is a challenging but exhilarating undertaking; full of the wonder and awe that occurs with the material revelation of the chosen Deity. However, the longer and more involved version of this ordeal seeks to obtain total union with the Deity, and that kind of ordeal is much more difficult to achieve (if it can be achieved at all), and it even has its perils and delusions, as we shall see.

This is not a new methodology, since it was written about by St. Ignatius of Loyola in his book *Spiritual Exercises*, compiled in the early sixteenth century.[12] St. Ignatius had rigorously studied the lives of the Saints and developed his own method of obtaining union with God as distilled from that study. Although St. Ignatius would not have qualified his methods as a way to seek godhead union, he preferred a more humble and self-denying definition—total surrender to God through meditation, prayer, and contemplation. That he had also started the order of the Jesuits later on will not in any way detract from his mystical writings and the gift of his teachings, which were influential for Catholics and even those of other faiths and persuasions.

It is true that quite a number of occultists and magicians were also influenced by St. Ignatius' writings since any student of the esoteric path must ultimately mix magic and mysticism together. The Eastern traditions also taught how this might be accomplished, and for many, these methods were preferable and seemed more universal and less sectarian. However, for those who were sympathetic to Christianity and who sought a mystical path along with their esoteric practices, St. Ignatius offered a compelling solution. Of course, for those of us who are *not* sympathetic to Catholicism or Christianity and who seek to be divorced from

---

12 Joe Paprocki, D.Min., *What are the Spiritual Exercises of St. Ignatius?* Loyola-Press.com, accessed Sep 3, 2022: https://www.loyolapress.com/catholic-resources/ignatian-spirituality/examen-and-ignatian-prayer/what-are-the-spiritual-exercises-of-saint-ignatius/

those kinds of beliefs, we are left with our own practices and faith. From this alternative foundation, there is a way to achieve this kind of union with the godhead.

I am bringing up this obscure topic about St. Ignatius because Aleister Crowley managed to write his own version of this kind of work, likely using St. Ignatius's book as his model. This brief work was named *Liber Astarte vel Berylli sub figura 175*, and it was included in Volume 7 of *The Equinox*, his monumental series on magic and occultism.[13] It was also included in the appendix of the book *Magic in Theory and Practice*. That is where I first discovered it many years ago. However, I had already begun working on my own version of this methodology when I finally read this work by Crowley. I would be deceitful to say it did not have any effect on what I finally developed, and often, I would refer other Pagan occultists to this work. Still, the foundation of the ordeal of Deity personification is actually based on the liturgy as found in the Alexandrian and Gardnerian *Book of Shadows*.

Crowley's work, although brilliant, is written in a pseudo-archaic manner to give it some degree of ancient provenance. All that did was make the work more difficult to read and comprehend, which was probably one of his conceits.

This work was written for initiates of his order, the Argentum Astrum (A.A.) of the degree of Philosophus, which was the fourth degree associated with the Qabalistic sephirah of Netzach, or Venus. Since love, particularly a higher or idealized love would be the subject of an initiate of the fourth degree, the ordeal of seeking union with a godhead would represent the highest achievement of that degree, or perhaps even the greater harmonic of seventh degree (Chesed, just below the starry abyss).

I understood the factual basis for using this text, and it is why I recommended a variation on this work to be developed by my students who sought some kind of method to achieve the mythic Witchcraft fourth degree. Crowley's work has a huge number of steps and discusses the details of the ordeal in a very verbose and complicated manner, making what is a very challenging ordeal into one that is practically impossible for most readers to follow.

---

13 Aleister Crowley, *Magic in Theory and Practice*, pp. 390–404.

We will not refer much to Crowley's work except a few comments here and there, since this ordeal is practically covered by the liturgical workings that we have already discussed in the previous chapters of this book.

Let us proceed with describing in detail the ordeal and the various steps that are to be followed so we can clearly understand how one might achieve some degree of union with a chosen Deity, whether as a way to strengthen and empower one's religious experience or to become a dedicated priestess or priest for a specific Deity for life.

Witch's Ordeal of Godhead Union

The very first step in this ordeal is to choose a specific Deity to dedicate yourself to and to serve that same godhead in some manner. As a polytheist, what I am proposing here is a form of what is called *henotheism*, a common practice in Hinduism. It is the worship of a single Deity out of many, which is done for a special purpose and outcome. This is not to be confused with monotheism, since that creed denies that there are any other possible Deities, and henotheism is to pick one out of a pantheon of Deities. Since Witchcraft is a better religion if it adheres to a polytheistic outlook, adopting a henotheistic practice doesn't negate the other Deities, it just establishes a precedence and a preference, and this choice can be a temporary one.

Crowley says in his work that it is preferable to choose a Deity that is capable of receiving and giving love and avoiding those who are too intellectual or too stern. What I have seen is that any Deity is capable of showing love and preference to a person who chooses that one for a specialized and focused worship. Giving exclusive favor to a God or Goddess causes a softening and affection to arise, no matter the baseline characteristics of that Deity. Even a saturnine and strict parent will show favor when justified flattery and filial love are given along with obedience and rectitude. Still, the Gods and Goddesses of modern Witch-craft and Paganism can be elected for this kind of work, whether it be the Horned God, the Moon Goddess, the Solar God, or any variation, whether from celestial, earthly, local, or even the underworld; all of our Deities respond to favor, worship, and love from one of their hidden children.

As faithful idolaters, Witches and Pagans will practice their religion surrounded by depictions of their Deities, whether as paintings, illustrations, statues, or some other material representation. A Witch practicing a form of henotheism will construct a temporary (or permanent) shrine where this one Deity will be favored with images, pictures, and statues. It will be a nicely decorated space that will be kept private, clean, and ordered. The cleaning and ordering will be the work of the Operator who will be performing the work. While this work is proceeding, this space should be kept exclusive for this work and supplied with everything required, such as candles, votive lights, incense, perfumes, consecrated oils, and plates and cups for offerings. The vestments should be kept clean and freshly laundered, and they should consist of a robe and stole or scarf of a suitable design and color that the Deity would find pleasing. All of this effort to fashion a shrine, vestments, and tools should be dedicated to this work alone, and it should consist of colors that are symbolically aligned with the tastes and choices that the Deity would make. These selections are based on a deep study of the characteristics, personality, and mythic actions and adventures with which this Deity is particularly associated.

This practice of choosing things based on the tastes and predilections of the Deity also concerns the Operator of this ordeal who shall take great care of themselves. Bathing often (ablutions), wearing beautiful robes and vestments, jewelry, makeup (if appropriate), and becoming an object of desire is an important part of this working. If you cannot engage in self-love, then you will likely fail to be capable of loving another or eliciting passionate love from the Deity. The whole purpose of this work is to make yourself into an object of love that will attract and enflame desire within the heart of the Deity as you summon and stir the passions of yourself and your God simultaneously. This ordeal is a magical love spell that you are going to cast on your God, and it will powerfully affect both you and your Deity. So, self-love is a very important part of this ordeal, especially in the beginning.

Once the Deity is chosen, the shrine is built and decorated, the vestments are acquired, consecrated, and all of the necessary tools and supplies have been collected, then the Operator is ready to begin this ordeal. There are just a few other items that the Operator must consider and employ so that this working will be successful and complete.

There are four important keys to making this ordeal successful and rewarding. The first is the duration or period chosen to do this work. The second is the oath of fealty formally given to the chosen Deity. The third is the magic and mystery associated with the mask that is to be worn when assuming the godhead. The fourth and final key is the invocation, which is a lengthy multipart series of callings to the chosen Goddess or God that are written by the Operator. We should discuss each of these keys since they will shape and organize the working.

Duration of the Ordeal: In organizing this ordeal, I have found that the lunar cycle is the most important measure of duration for this working. This is because Witchcraft is a religion where the cycle of the moon is most important for liturgical operations. It is no less important in this kind of working. Therefore, I determined that three cycles of the moon represent a full period for the duration of this working. A dedicant would perform this ordeal during the whole three-month cycle, then pass through a dormant period of normal religious activity for three months, and then pick it up again for the following three months. A Witch seeking to maximize their ability to assume their chosen godhead for a Drawing Down rite might only perform this ordeal for a month instead of three months. The pattern of the events in the working is then scaled down to accommodate a shorter period.

This ordeal is broken into three parts, where each part represents an ever greater and more focused activity. The first part lasts for two months and is the basic operation of liturgical rites and workings. The second part lasts for one month and represents a more intense and focused working to connect and engage fully with the Deity. The final part lasts for a week and requires a complete sequestration from all public activity, including one's work or vocation. The final week is where the work culminates in a kind of climax of focused activities. All of these parts require a daily regimen of religious rituals, meditations, and observations, which can consist of one period or three, depending on the availability of time and social responsibilities, such as one's job or vocation. The ordeal begins at the new moon of the first month and ends at the new moon of the third month. The three-month period should also encapsulate an entire season, from its beginning, midpoint, and end, yet it is the cycle of the moon that governs this ordeal.

For most of the period of the ordeal, the Operator will conduct their normal life as they typically would with the exception that they now have important religious responsibilities that will curtail some social activities and extracurricular engagements. To outward observers, there doesn't appear to be anything happening other than being a bit less available. The Operator must, however, ensure that they are governed and constrained by their behavior so as to avoid social entanglements, stress, and pressures from those outside of this working. Equanimity is a mental state that the Operator must strive to achieve at all times. A real crisis, however, will necessarily interrupt the ordeal, and that is completely allowable. The Operator will quit the working and re-engage at a later time when the crisis has passed.

Oath of Fealty: The beginning of the ordeal starts with a working where the Operator formally states their intentions and swears an oath of fealty to the chosen Goddess or God, gives an offering (an expensive gift) to it, and then makes a shallow cut or incision on their body that will bleed a small amount of blood to seal the oath, capturing the blood on a clean white cloth.[14] The gift becomes the property of the Deity and it is placed in the shrine on the altar, along with the bloodied cloth. The Operator should write up a formal oath that dictates the terms of the service, its duration and purpose, and the depth of fidelity that they are offering exclusively to the Deity. The oath is the starting point for this working along with the gift and the bloody cloth. I would recommend using a sharp knife to do the cutting so that it is precise and painless and to exercise great care in using it on one's person.

---

14 During this procedure or any others herein, please use the utmost caution and care whenever skin is broken. Follow basic first aid practices of cleaning and dressing wounds, use sterile materials, and always dispose of blood and other bodily fluids responsibly. If bleeding ever becomes uncontrollable, promptly seek medical advice.

Mask of the Godhead: Before this work can even commence, it requires that the Operator has obtained a charged and consecrated mask representing the image of the chosen Deity. As I have stated previously, the mask should be constructed by someone highly skilled in that craft, unless, of course, the Operator has that skill. The mask then becomes a perfected tool representing the Deity itself, and most importantly, it is what the Operator wears when performing the rite of godhead assumption. The mask should be consecrated three times through the intercession of the God or Goddess before it is ready to be used, representing the maximum charging and blessing to make it a sacralized and holy instrument. When not being used, the mask should be placed in a prominent location on the altar of the shrine, as close visually to the image of the Deity as possible.

Godhead Invocations: Prior to the ordeal, the Operator should spend some time carefully constructing a series of invocations that will summon, inspire, cajole, align, merge, and impassion the targeted Goddess or God. I would recommend that the Operator write up three lengthy invocations to use in this working. The first invocation should focus on all of the beautiful, loving, giving, compassionate, and righteous characteristics of the Deity. This invocation should be one that is full of flattery, adoration, praise, love, and exaltation for the Goddess or God. The second invocation should define the basis for the Operator to seek union with the Deity, so it should describe the compassion that this God or Goddess has for the Operator to sanction their approach to service and to be absorbed into the great being of that Deity. The second invocation describes the Operator's surrender to the godhead and the negation of the egoic self for the sake of perfect service and representation. The third invocation is a reduction of the previous invocations into a short phrase or mantra that can be repeated over and over again. These invocations are used in the ordeal at strategic times. Additionally, the Operator should collect hymns and sacred tracts, prose or poetry that are fitting to express one's love of the Deity and the rapture and ecstasy of that love.

Here are some examples of the three invocations, although they are short and brief, the Operator may seek to write something grander or of greater length. The first two invocations can be read from a script, but the mantra is, of course, short and easily

remembered, emphasized as it is by constant repetition. These are representations only, since to present anything that I or anyone else has actually used would be a violation of the oath of secrecy. I have chosen the Goddess Nox as a suitable target Goddess for a priestess or priest seeking her healing powers.

Invocation One

O Great Goddess of Darkness, Nox, I seek you in my heart and soul.
The night is full of peace, rest, dreams, and the regeneration of all living things.
You stand at the beginning of creation and are the gateway to its final end.
You are that enveloping stary body whose soul is the moon in all its variations—
You hold all of the Mysteries of life and death in your heart.
Peace, love, sleep, and rest; rebirth and dreams are your powers which I seek to emulate.
O raven-haired lady, whose colors are black and silver,
Clad with the diaphanous veils of stars, nebulae, and galaxies,
Whose blue-lidded eyes are all seeing orbs of scintillating light,
I yearn for you and seek to join you in the forever night.

Invocation Two

O Great Goddess of Darkness, Nox, I kneel before your shrine and image,
Naked and defenseless, full of remorse and dejection, seeking your favor and gentle touch.
My heart is open and given to you alone.
You, I shall serve, and I abase myself before you.
O Lady, I am unworthy, I am unworthy and scorned, I am so unworthy of your love and favor. Yet you see the core of my spirit within me, and that I have promise and potential.
You raise me up to meet you, and I feel the rapture and embrace of your love.
I am your gift and your obedient servant.
Take and guide me to do your work, and I shall serve you faithfully for a year and a day.

Invocation Three (Mantra)

Nox, Hypnos, Thanatos, Erebus, peace, love, and rebirth—I adore you.

These are the three invocations that the Operator needs to develop. They can vary them or even rewrite them while undergoing the ordeal. Also, spontaneous expressions of piety, love, and passion can be incorporated as well.

Once these four keys are fully developed, then the ordeal can be performed. The Operator chooses a new moon phase to begin the working and, on that day, they will also perform the oath of fealty that properly begins the ordeal.

Rituals of the Ordeal

The Operator will use the basic liturgical rites that are a normal part of their Witchcraft practices, except that they are performed for a very specific purpose and that the operation consists of contiguous daily and weekly practices. There are nine types of rituals that the Operator will perform during the ordeal, and all of these should have already been developed as part of the basic religious discipline that the Witch or Pagan will have as their liturgical repertoire.

1. **Votive offerings:** The Operator will offer votive candles, incense, food, and drink to the Deity within the shrine.
2. **Meditation sessions:** Prayers and focused appraisal of the shrine, images of the Deity, and the Sacred Mask.
3. **Invocations, orisons, and calls to the Deity.**
4. **Reading of hymns and offering worship to the Deity.**
5. **Godhead assumption of the chosen Deity, including wearing the mask.**
6. **Communion:** Charging, blessing, and sacralizing of food and drink to be shared.
7. **Blessings (healings):** Receiving and sending blessings to the collective and individuals. Ointments, medicines, or tokens can be blessed and given to people in need.

8. **Offerings of thanksgiving for the reception of gifts and blessings.**
9. **Community work:** Giving back to the community without acknowledgment. This can and should include giving money or service to charities and organizations that help people.

There are three types of liturgical events that are performed during the ordeal. These can be shown to use the following selection of liturgical rites.

1. **Daily Practices:** These are done once or three times a day, consisting of meditation and prayer, reading of hymns, and offering worship to the image of the Deity.
2. **Bi-weekly Practices:** These are done once every three days—daily practice joined with votive offerings and invocation (first of three).
3. **Weekly Practices:** These are done once every seven days—daily practice, bi-weekly practice joined with godhead assumption, communion, blessings, and offerings of thanksgiving. Since this is a very involved working, I have found that it is best performed on a weekend evening; I will juggle the bi-weekly practice so that the weekly can occur on the weekend, at least for the first week, and once that is done, then the rest of the practices should fall within that schedule.

The second month will use the second invocation, and the third month will use only the mantra. During the first and second months, the Operator will engage in community and volunteer service, to be ceased for the third month. During the final month, the Operator will perform the thanksgiving rite for each meal, upon waking, before going to sleep, and before performing the ablutions. For the last week, they will offer thanksgiving internally and continuously, centering it on each breath during meditation.

If you choose to perform this rite in a single month, then you would divide the working into three parts that would span these four weeks. The first part would last for seven days, the second part for ten days, and the third part for eleven days. The schedule of practices would not vary, of course, but the special occurrences and the starting of the second and third periods would be placed during one of those three practices and would have to be adapted in order to work. However, the same pattern would be used overall, only that the durations and boundaries would be different.

Now that we have covered all of the components, we can show the pattern to be followed for the ordeal of godhead personification.

Ordeal of Godhead Personification

First Month

1. On the first day of the new moon, begin with the daily practice performed three times. On the third time, perform the rite of the oath of fealty.
2. For the following days, perform the daily practice at least once a day.
3. Plan and engage in community and volunteer work during the first two months.
4. After three days, perform the bi-weekly practice. This should be done two times a week.
5. After seven days, perform the weekly practice. This should be done four times for the first month.
6. On the day just before the next new moon, a special observation is performed during the weekly practice that will mark the end of the cycle. This is where the Operator will announce their intention to seek union with the chosen Goddess or God.

Second Month

1. On the first day of the new moon, begin with the daily practice performed three times. On the third, renew the oath of fealty by re-reading it with solemn intent. During the second month, the practices will be performed with greater intensity and desire.
2. Daily practice is performed at least once a day.
3. Community work continues to be performed.
4. Bi-weekly practice is performed, using the second invocation.

5. Weekly practice is performed. The period of godhead assumption is lengthened and intensified through a greater focus on the Deity and a diminishment of the personality of the Operator.
6. On the day just before the next new moon, a special observation is performed during the weekly practice that will mark the end of the second cycle. This is where the Operator will completely abase themself, announcing all of their faults, failings, and mistakes in life, and seeking to be absolved of them through the blessings and grace of the Deity.

Third Month

1. On the first day of the new moon, begin with the daily practice performed three times. On the third, renew the oath of fealty by re-reading it with solemn intent. Then, the Operator will focus on the gift that was given to the Goddess or God, touching it three times and acknowledging it as a means of their salvation—a compensation for all of their flaws and failings. With the final lunar cycle, all of the practices will be done in complete silence, with the exception of the third invocation or mantra. Any music that was previously used will no longer be played.
2. Daily practice is performed at least once a day in complete silence.
3. Community volunteer work ceases.
4. Bi-weekly practices are performed using the third invocation. This practice is done in complete silence except for the mantra, which begins with a vocalized intoning that becomes ever softer with repetition until it is merely whispered.
5. Weekly practice is performed. The period of godhead assumption is lengthened until it is the primary and only rite performed, omitting the other steps entirely. The Operator seeks to function as the living and breathing representative of the Deity, eliminating any kind of emergence of their persona or character from the performance.
6. The final week of the third month is when the Operator will perform a kind of hand-fasting rite that binds them to the chosen Deity. This is done at the final weekly practice,

just before the godhead assumption. It can be an elaborate ceremony or one that is very simple, consisting of saying the marriage vows, standing before the image of the Deity, and then placing on oneself a token of that union, whether it be a ring, medallion, or bracelet that has been sitting on the shrine and absorbing the energies of the ordeal. After this binding is completed, the rest of the weekly practice is performed.

7. The next day is the newly arrived new moon, and the Operator performs a vigil in the shrine where all is dark and silent, except for a single votive candle. The Operator will perform the mantra endlessly in silence for a few hours and seek to fully encounter the Deity without the aid of a mask or any other prop or artifact. They will then sleep in that space, allowing the spiritual powers unleashed to be fully incubated within their core. It is very likely that the evening will pass with a monumental visionary experience, and they will feel the Deity residing in their very being.

It will be quite obvious to the Operator if this ordeal has been successful, but having performed such an extensive and rigorous series of workings will doubtlessly achieve some degree of success, and, in fact, it will likely exceed expectations. When I performed variations of this ordeal, the result has been completely mind-blowing, and it had a permanent effect on me. A true dedicant, however, will perform this ordeal twice a year and continue to perform it year after year.

After several years of consistent work, the priestess or priest who has engaged with this work as a singular dedicant will be a powerful and fully active representation of the Goddess or God with whom they have chosen to become one. You can see, though, that such an avocation would limit what a person could do with their lives, such as building a career or raising a family. It becomes important for the dedicant to reduce or eliminate distractions without also disconnecting from their community. A dedicant is devoted to a God or Goddess for the purpose of a greater spiritual service and that would include service to the spiritual community at large.

To complete this ordeal, it is important for the Operator to perform a Drawing Down rite for the chosen Deity using the empowered and consecrated mask so that a group may partake of this divine blessing. What has been done in secret needs to be revealed to those privileged and prepared for such an encounter. An experienced dedicant should plan for a Grand Sabbat once every few years to share with their community the sacramental blessing of the Deity, residing, living, breathing, and sharing space with the worshipful community.

There is a risk in performing this type of working in that it will cause the Operator of the ordeal some difficulties in maintaining objectivity. This is why performing a Drawing Down rite with a group afterward will help to mitigate any erroneous assumptions or delusions about the role that a person who has undergone this rite might otherwise possess. Without being objectively tested as to the veracity of the achievement that the ordeal has conferred, it remains wholly within a subjective realm, and it could lead a person to believe all sorts of unproven or unsubstantiated affirmations about themself. It is also possible that the ordeal may fail to be completed because of the intervention of fate or the Gods having willed it so, and the Operator has not been able to adjust to that fact. However, objectifying this kind of ordeal is the type of verification that is needed so that the group or the community will know that the results of this process are authentic and that what is delivered is a truthful representation of the elected Deity.

The greatest sacrament that a Witch or Pagan can receive is the manifestation of a specific Goddess or God for the benefit of the group or the community. It is our place and role to do the work of the Deity in the material world. Yet, we must be thoroughly tested and transmuted to perform that holy work.

CHAPTER SEVEN

PLACEHOLDERS OF THE DEITY— STANG, CAULDRON, BESOM, AND STATUARY

"The human heart is an idol factory"
—JOHN CALVIN

Secondary to the materialized realization of the Gods and God-desses, which is primary, is the means and method of marking a specific place and using a sacramental object as the resident point of divine emanation. What I am referring to here are the various placeholders of the Deity that act as stand-ins for the actual representations. It is a feature of idolatry that makes Witchcraft and Paganism so compelling because it touches something that is intrinsic and dear to human nature.

Eliminating all representation in religious décor and presenta-tion, while faithful to true monotheism, is actually alien to human nature. Catholics understood that quite well, dealing as they did with a converted Pagan population. Using religious representations is helpful and meaningful to the way human beings are wired. Witches and Pagans go one step further, in keeping in line with the Pagans of antiquity, to promote that which represents the divine can also mediate it under certain conditions. That is the baseline power associated with consecrated artifacts, such as the variations on the

91

Stang, the Besom, Cauldron, and iconic statuary. I will explain how these artifacts work, what they symbolize, and how they can be used in Witchcraft covens and Pagan groves.

The Stang

The Stang is not an artifact to be found in the Gardnerian or Alexandrian traditions of Witchcraft. In fact, the Stang has been borrowed from what is called *Traditional Witchcraft* (or Old Craft) which was promoted by Robert Cochrane and Evan John Jones.[15] There is no mention of it in any of Gardner's writings or the *Book of Shadows*. It is a complex artifact that has many symbolic attributes, but it is a placeholder for the Deity, specifically the Horned God, Herne, King of the Forest Glade. In Traditional Witchcraft, there is the personal Stang that is used and belongs to each member of the coven, but there is also a single coven Stang that has a greater precedence and utility. This artifact has caught the popular imagination of Witches in Europe and the U.S., and so it has been quickly adopted. It would seem that it is such a powerful symbol of Witchcraft that adopting it seems like a natural thing.

The traditional Stang was a two-tanged pitchfork with a handle made of ash, surmounted by a garland circlet with two arrows crossed over the garland. Its end had either a nail or a metal cap so that it was iron-shod. Sometimes, a candle was placed between the tines, and at other times, the garland was excluded. It was placed at the northern point of the compass round and acted as a bridge between worlds as well as a sign of the presence of the Horned God. There were many variations on this rudimentary theme, and in some instances, the Stang was a wooden pole upon which was mounted the antlered skull of a deer or stag. There was typically a second coven Stang whose handle was made of blackthorn, but this Stang was used for dark workings or cursing, representing as it did the power of darkness and death, and it was rarely brought into the compass round unless it was needed.

---

15 Evan John Jones and Doreen Valiente, *Witchcraft—A Tradition Renewed*, p. 116–121.

In the grove that I had use of when I lived in the countryside in Minnesota, I had two Stangs erected in the compass round. The first was at the northwest edge of the grove close to a thicket that also functioned as a deer path. It was my black Stang of the Power of Death and the pathway to the underworld. The other Stang was placed at the westernmost edge of the grove, standing a dozen yards from the steep banks of a shallow lake. This was my red Stang, which also had a statue of the Maid of the Woods and the bas relief of the face of the Green Man placed before it. The red Stang represented the Power of Life and the pathway to rebirth and renewal. Both Stangs had a deer skull mounted on a post, one post stained black and the other red. I also had a personal Stang that was a staff with deer antlers mounted upon it, and it was also stained red. This Stang staff was transportable, whereas the Stang posts in my grove were more permanent.

There are many variations of the Stang, and I have seen them decorated with many deer skulls that nearly cover the entire staff or pole. I have seen them with straw arms and skirts of straw, looking more like a scarecrow with a deer skull than a traditional Stang. A Stang can even be burned in a sacrifice, representing the passage of the Horned God into the underworld, where he has become the God that dies and is later reborn, so as to give us life and to share in our death.

A Stang, like the Sacred Mask, is a three-fold consecrated artifact, and like the mask, the Stang is associated with the votive rites, invocations, and godhead assumption for the Horned God, Herne. It can also be blessed by the hands, sign making, blowing the breath upon it, and also embracing and kissing it as a lover by a person impersonating the Horned God. This final blessing goes beyond the three-fold consecration, and it can be omitted without making the Stang any less of a potent tool than it normally is. An artifact that is blessed by the Deity to whom it is supposed to represent can only add to its efficacy in the mind of the group or coven who uses it.

Since the Stang is a place marker and only has the association that the individual or group gives to it, then it can also function as a marker for any Deity worshipped in the coven or grove. Modify the Stang's symbolic construction, and it can represent even a Goddess, such as Artemis or Diana. The nature of any place marker is that it is protean and can function for many different purposes. However, once a Stang is blessed, charged, and consecrated in the name and image of a specific Deity, it then becomes the place marker for that Deity.

Therefore, the Stang functions as a symbol for the gateway and pathway between worlds, similar to the World Tree that acts as a pillar that holds the world in a stable state and allows various individuals to pass through it to travel to the three worlds, following the ghost roads of our ancestors. Since it is iron-shod, it is also like a horse or a steed, representing both the point of entry and the method of travel.

Besom—The Artifact of the Traveler

The Besom is a broom that functions as a sacred artifact and is also a place marker for a Deity, except that it functions as the medium of travel between the three worlds. Thus, the Besom would represent any Deity that travels between the worlds, such as Hermes, Mercury, Khonsu, Lugh, Meili, Xandria, or Abeona, to name a few. A ritual besom is a hobby horse that Witches ride to and from the sabbat. However, that broomstick ride is more of a trance-based type of travel like astral projection or spirit traveling.

Like the Stang, the Besom is a composite of various symbols that can be disguised as a simple household working tool. In the previous epoch, it was believed that the Besom had a disguised phallic end hidden by the rushes or twigs from various trees bound to its lower half, signifying the image of sexual union as the phallus immersed in the pelvic bush of a woman. As an instrument that represents the lintel doorway (as a symbol of union) and its key, the Besom functioned as the personification of the most famous of Witchcraft events: the flight of a Witch into the underworld and their successful return. The shamanic qualities of the Besom are quite plain since variations have been attested to as an instrument used by shamans to fly through the gateways of the world tree, descending and ascending through the three worlds. It has been used as such in the distant past before history was even written, and it is used today by the adherents of modern Witchcraft.

The characteristics of the magic broom will vary considerably from coven to coven or individual to individual. The obscured phallic end is not always employed in the construction of the broom, but twisty and shaped poles of wood and natural rushes bound to it are a typical feature. The size will vary, but it will be of a size that makes it easy to wield by coven members if it is the coven Besom, or by the individual Witch who owns it. What a magic broom is *not* is a commercially off-the-shelf broom, since it doesn't have the more natural look of a handmade Besom, nor its esthetic qualities. Like the Stang and the mask, the Besom is thrice consecrated, and it can be blessed by an individual personifying a Deity.

The Besom has a number of uses in modern Witchcraft. It is used to sweep or purify an area in a temple or grove to remove debris or unwanted and distracting thoughts and attitudes and to make a clear pathway to follow. It acts as a bridge for the coven to enter into a grove or temple, and it is used as a barrier for a handfasted couple to leap across, symbolizing their leap of faith into a new life. Yet, the Besom is used for traveling, and this is its most potent use as a means of spirit travel.

Flying ointment is typically associated with the Besom and its ritual use as a traveling tool, and this ointment is also charged and blessed for use. It should have some psychotropic qualities, but it need not be strong in order to be effective. A Witch will smear the ointment on their naked body and also anoint the Besom to begin this work. As a form of a hobby horse, the Witch will mount the Besom seemingly backward with the bristles pointing out in front, while the handle will be dropped to the earth. The handle can be iron-shod at the tip with a metal cap or a nail like the Stang. As it is iron-shod, it also symbolizes the iron-shod hooves of the mythic steed of Witches that was depicted imaginatively as a skeletal horse. I have heard of a coven that had a black cloth cover placed over the broom handle that had a skeletal horse drawn upon it. It sounded so very intriguing that I would recommend it here in this work.

Spirit traveling requires achieving a deep trance, so it is necessary for others to assist the traveler in handling the Besom and maintaining an erect stature while straddling it. It should take the traveler a couple of hours to enter into such a deep and altered trance state, so the travel should be sequestered for a time when they seek to gain that deep state of trance. The trance state should

not be so deep that they would be unable to manage the mounting and riding of the Besom, but to safeguard them, two helpers stand at either side to ensure that they don't fall.

What is most effective is that the traveler should have a destination in one of the other worlds to achieve and a purpose or quest to accomplish. What is sought is typically knowledge of unseen things or meeting a mythical personage or someone who recently died and has a connection with the traveler. Here are the steps that can be taken by the traveler and their coven when they seek to ride the Besom to fulfill their quest.

Rite of the Besom Flight

At the beginning of this working when the circle has been consecrated and empowered, a Goddess or God of travel is invoked in the normal way with cakes and wine. Once the priestess or priest has made a gateway in the north, the traveler will be guided and helped into the circle in the traditional manner, and then the northern gateway is closed. The rider will sit in the center of the circle and someone will hand them the holy Besom to hold. The priestess or priest will perform the ritual to establish a western gateway into the underworld—it is this gateway that the traveler can enter to access all of the three worlds.

1. The priestess or priest proceeds to the southeast angle from the east using their wand and draws an invoking spiral at that point. They say:

   "Before me stands the Guide of Light who will guide and watch over our sacred traveler."

2. The priestess or priest proceeds directly to the northeast (going widdershins) and draws an invoking spiral at that point. They say:

   "Before me stands the Guardian of Darkness who will guard and watch over our sacred traveler."

3. The priestess or priest proceeds directly to the west and draws an invoking spiral in that watchtower. They say:

"Before me stands the Ordeal and its trials, may our traveler be found worthy and achieve their quest."

4. Then the priestess or priest proceeds around the circle widdershins until they arrive at the east and faces the west.
5. The priestess or priest draws the southeast and northeast angles in a line, and then draws those two points to the west, forming a triangle. They then slowly walk from the east to the west and once there, they will make the gesture of opening a curtain or veil. They will step forward and then turn around to face the east, imagining as they do a golden light cascading down upon their head and body. They will slowly walk to the center of the circle imagining that they are walking down a stairway leading to a basement of the underworld. They will turn to face the west and bow—the rite is completed.

Once the gateway is established, the traveler will stand up, take the Besom with both hands and stride it with the bristles facing up and out with the iron-shod handle on the ground. Their two helpers will be at their side. They will face the magic gateway established in the west.

Once mounted, the traveler will begin a period of cool breathing and moving back and forth on the Besom, and when they feel the energies achieve a heightened level, they will cry out, begin to briefly hyperventilate, and the coven will then proceed to beat on drums, shake rattles, ring bells, and shout *Evohe! Evohe! Evohe!* Then, when the traveler feels themself achieving a kind of ecstasy, they shout out a second time, and everyone will become immediately quiet. Then they will ride the besom (with eyes closed) in their visionary quest while everyone watches.

When the traveler tires or seems unable to remain upon the Besom, the helpers will assist them to gently recline on the ground and will place the Besom in their hands with the bristles down to their feet. They will remain in trance as long as they are able and the helpers will sit closely by and monitor their progress.

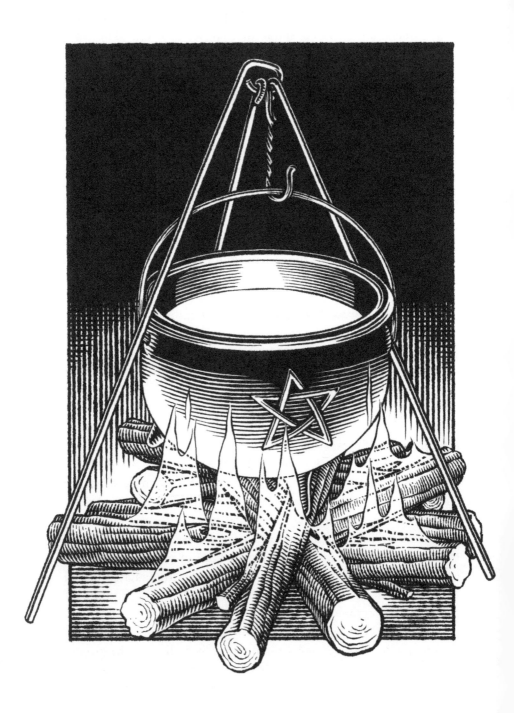

Once they have returned to full consciousness, their helpers will take the Besom and hand it to the priestess or priest and assist the traveler to rise. They are given wine and cakes as a form of communion with the godhead of the coven for that night, and then the priestess or priest sets sealing spirals to the gate nodes. The priestess or priest then opens a gateway in the north and the traveler is helped out of the circle.

Before the traveler is given more food and drink to help them ground, they may recite what they experienced to someone who will take notes, or they can write it down themself. Performing a full grounding exercise will be very necessary to help return to the waking world.

I have seen many variations on this kind of working, and because it is so iconic and imbued with a compelling historical provenance, I have seldom ever seen this rite produce anything but remarkable effects. The thrice-consecrated Besom is a truly mighty magical artifact—and one that can be used in many different ways. I have shared but a few, and many more wait to be discovered by you.

Cauldron of Life and Death

The Cauldron, or the black Witches' Cauldron, as it is typically depicted, is also a placeholder, thrice consecrated, and an important tool. It is modeled after the mythic Cauldron of *Pair Dadeni,* or the Cauldron of Rebirth, which is featured in various Brythonic and Celtic mythologies, also called the Cauldron of Cerridwen of Taliesin fame. It can also be compared to the later alchemical alembic, where the elixir of life is prepared. In Caribbean traditions, it would be the *Premba,* the pot of graveyard earth where spirits are kept. In all of these depictions, the Cauldron or magical container has the power to forestall death, cause rebirth after death, or brew elixirs of wisdom and enlightenment. In all of these examples, the Cauldron is a placeholder for the Mother Goddess of ancient renown, and the Cauldron itself symbolizes her womb and belly. It is, therefore, a container for all sacred actions that the coven might engage in.

The Cauldron is very much a utilitarian kind of placeholder since it has so many uses, and is, therefore, not used in the same fashion as the Stang and the Besom. It is more integral to a coven's magical work, being used in an endless number of ways. Still, the Cauldron is the foundational artifact representing the power of the Goddess in all things that the coven might do, and it is often, but not always, associated with a specific Deity in the Witches' pantheon. When it is thrice consecrated, it is done in the name of the coven's Mother Goddess.

Like the dagger to the sword, the cup or chalice is the sister of the Cauldron, and when dispensing out a potion to the group, it is the cup that is used to share in the completed mixture. Along with the Cauldron and the cup are the stirring spoon and ladle, or a bowl, which form a part of the tools that accompany the use of the Cauldron. If a heated drink or stew is to be made, then the Cauldron is united with the sacred fire, and a three-legged stand is used to keep them separate and to control the heat.

While the Cauldron does not often feature as the focus of a religious rite like the Stang and Besom, it is more often the foundation and container for many ritual actions. It should be kept clean and pristine after any such use since it can be used to brew drinks and potions, and also cook food. Here are some of the uses that I have witnessed where the Cauldron is featured in rituals:

1. **Holder of secrets:** Writing wishes or desires on scraps of parchment can be collected into the Cauldron where they are then burned. Also, the container of white and black stones can assist a selection process or the tallying of a secret coven vote consisting of white (yea) or black (nay) stones.

2. **Dispenser of sacred spices and incense:** Special incenses can be burned in the Cauldron, and this smoke can be aromatically appealing or even mildly intoxicating.

3. **Well of dreams and visions:** Water can be put into a Cauldron and then its surface can be gazed upon. This creates a black mirror, but since it is a holy artifact, an entranced seer can peer deeply into it to divine the answers to questions.

4. **Container of potions:** This can include medicines, sacramental drinks (such as wine or mead steeped in herbs), or poisons (hallucinogenic herbs). It is united with the sacred

fire to help meld the various compounds together into a liquid base.

5. **Container of feasts:** The creation of soups or stews that function as a sacred meal blessed and charged by the Goddess for communal consumption.

When deployed in a temple, the Cauldron is placed on either side of the altar, but in a grove, it is placed at the base of the Stang, representing the joining of the God and Goddess. When the Cauldron is to be used in a ritual, an invocation to the coven's Mother Goddess is appropriate, along with the brief telling of the stories and myths that are part of its sacred nature. Apprehending the sacred nature of the Cauldron is important because as a tool, it is often taken for granted.

Statues, Busts, and Icons of the Gods

Perhaps the most obvious placeholders are the statues, busts, and icons of the Goddesses and Gods that are part of the Witches' pantheon. While these kinds of idols would have been hidden, obscured, or nonexistent when the Craft was persecuted, they have become a favorite representation of Deity in modern Witchcraft. We are natural born idolaters, so collecting artwork that represents our Deities is a pleasurable pastime. However, a piece of artwork, no matter how lovely or esthetically appealing, does not automatically become a placeholder for Deity unless and until it is dedicated (gifted) and thrice consecrated in the name of that godhead.

An icon is a painting or illustration that is suitably framed and prominently displayed in a temple or a covenstead meeting room that acts as a temporary temple. A statue or bust is a stone, ceramic, or resin-cast depiction of a Deity, and it can be placed in a temple or an outdoor grove. Yet, all such representations are to be considered a form of icon of the Goddess or God. A thrice-consecrated artwork representation of the Deity should be considered not only a likeness or representation but also treated and venerated as if it were the very Goddess or God itself. Like all placeholders, to the idolatrous Witch or Pagan, such an artifact is not an empty receptacle or merely a symbolic representation. It is the thing it represents in materialized form, and it is treated with love, awe, veneration, and devotion, just as one would treat a manifestation of the Deity.

While this process alone should suffice to awaken and activate an icon, there is an additional step that can be taken to fully animate an iconic artifact. If the coven is well versed in the art of talismanic magic, then they might use this knowledge to place within the icon a perpetual charge and planetary intelligence to merge with the spiritual essence of the Deity. This ensures that it becomes a powerful magical foundation or nest that will affect everyone who might encounter it.

Similarly, an iconic representation should receive votive offerings and be focused upon when offering prayers or invocations to the Deity that it represents. These associations, and the fact that the artifact is thrice consecrated, cause the representation to become activated and alive in the minds of the devotees. An iconic representation need not be a picture or statue, since I have had icons that were large carved images of the phallus that represented the regenerative powers of the masculine archetype as godhead. I have also had icons of stone eggs that represented the archetypal feminine godhead. This kind of icon can be a token or symbolic representation and still stand as a powerful placeholder for an attribute of Deity.

One of my favorite TV movies that appeared in the 1970s, *Ritual of Evil* (1970), had at the center of a group of occultists an immortal priestess of ancient provenance and a statue of the Horned God, attributed to be the Devil. When approached and activated, the eyes of the statue would glow with a fiery reddish-golden light, and the statue, thus activated, became the source of power for the priestess and her presumed coven. Of course, the hero, who is a psychiatrist, manages to overcome the powers of the priestess and the statue by virtue of his steadfast goodness and scientific mind, and breaks the statue, ending the frightful conflict; but the priestess merely slips away into the time stream from which she emerged, promising to return someday.[16]

I have always been intrigued by that movie and sought for some years to replicate it in my Witchcraft workings. In determining

---

16 *Ritual of Evil*, Directed by Robert Day, Universal Television, 1970.

how to animate a statue or bust with a talismanic elemental, I have found a suitable surrogate for a fun but fictional tale. I will show how such a thing can be accomplished on page 113.

Once an icon has been thrice consecrated, it should be introduced into coven use through a dramatic unveiling. As this action implies, the coven convenes, and the icon is covered or veiled so it cannot be seen. Then the Officiant, or whoever is an intimate representative of that Deity, stands in front of the group and relates the stories and myths of that godhead. Then, they will recite a short invocation, at the end of which, they will carefully remove the veil from the icon. The coven will bow before it while the Officiant says,

"Behold your Goddess/God, whose name is X!"

The coven will then perform a simple extended invocation of the Deity, bless cakes and wine, and then share the communion with the icon, leaving offerings before it. From this point onward, the icon will partake in the liturgical rites and be a present godhead for all magical and religious undertakings.

Rite of Threefold Consecration

I have mentioned the act of consecrating a placeholder artifact three times instead of the typical one time, and I should therefore define what that is and how it is done. A threefold consecration is a single consecration rite done three times on three different consecutive days. The aim is to perform this rite in three days, but sometimes that is not possible, so it is in the mind that each consecration follows the one previously done in a seamless manner. The materials that make up the artifact can determine what sacraments are used to consecrate it.

Sacraments that are used to consecrate are lustral water, incense, consecrated oil, wine, and a fragment of a consecrated piece of bread. A painted icon or a poster would not lend itself to being consecrated by any sacrament that is wet or could stain it, such as wine. So, the medium of consecration should be able to bless and sacralize an artifact without ruining it. For such delicate representations, a consecrated fragment of bread touching it along with a few passes of an incense stick should suffice.

An Officiant personifying a Deity could also touch, make a sign over, and breathe their breath on the artifact to further consecrate it, but that would only have to be done once. The Officiant who is to consecrate the artifact to a specific Goddess or God should also be the one who has a close relationship with that Deity and perhaps has taken on the role of personifying that godhead for a coven gathering. The important consideration is that whoever is going to consecrate and awaken an artifact and imbue it with the essence of a specific godhead should be someone who has an alignment with it. This connection grants the Officiant the authority and vests them with the capability to sacralize an artifact in the name of a Goddess or God. That means that not just anyone in the group should seek to consecrate an artifact; it has to be someone who has specialized in acting as a mediator for that Deity.

A consecration rite consists of four steps: invoking the Deity, offering the artifact, sacralizing it, and then naming it (making it specialized as a possession of the godhead). The sacralizing will use a sacrament to touch or apply to the artifact. Here is a list of sacraments to be used for specific artifacts.

1. **Stang:** Oil, lustral water, incense, wine, and bread
2. **Besom:** Oil, lustral water, incense, wine, and bread
3. **Cauldron:** Oil, lustral water, incense, wine, and bread
4. **Iconic Painting or Poster:** Incense and bread
5. **Statue or bust:** Oil, lustral water, incense, and bread

The ritual steps used to consecrate one of these artifacts is a simple process, but it is done three times consecutively. There is no special time, season, or phase of the moon for these rites to be performed since the Deity is everywhere and immediately accessible to the one who calls it.

1. The Officiant invokes the Deity while kneeling before the artifact. If the artifact is not free-standing, then a helper should hold it upright.

2. The Officiant stands and holds their hands out to the artifact, touching it, and saying:

   "I present this artifact X to you, O Goddess/God Y so that it may act as an instrument of your will and be a representation of your presence."

3. Then the Officiant will sacralize the artifact, using the appropriate sacraments and applying them to it, each in succession. They will sprinkle the artifact with lustral water if that sacrament is to be used. Once the succession of sacraments is applied, they will then make an appropriate sign (pentagram or ankh, depending on if it is for an active or passive Deity), and finally, use a cloth to wipe off the excess sacrament.

4. The Officiant then kneels before the artifact, saying:

   "Here is the artifact X blessed and charged in thy name, O Goddess/God Y, and I shall name you Z, you are Z!"

   The Officiant can either think up a name well before performing this rite for the first time, or they can allow it to emerge spontaneously. However, they must use that same name on the second and third consecration.

The letters X, Y, and Z are, of course, the names of the artifact, the Deity, and the artifact's secret name, to be shared with the coven. You can remove the word "artifact" from the statements made if it seems cumbersome or redundant. Once the artifact has been consecrated three times, then it is used in the next ritual and takes its place in the workings and liturgical rites of the coven or grove.

Chapter Eight

Art of Talismanic
Statue Animation

"Sometimes we all want to be like a statue:
Always calm; always observer; always listening;
always fearless and always inspiring!"
—Mehmet Murat Ildan

One of the most magical acts of theurgy as reported by the
legends about the Neoplatonic philosophers was the animation of a statue or bust with a Deity. It was considered one of
the more basic types of magic that a philosopher could attempt.
It was amazing because the actual methods of performing this
kind of Neoplatonic magic were secrets that have been lost over
the centuries, although there are fragments and hints in how it
was done, you can find out more about the traditional approach
and a reconstruction of that methodology by checking traditional
Hermetic websites.[17]

What ancients believed, however, was through the magical
arts of *telesma* and the god-like powers vested in a philosopher
magician that a bond or connection could be made between a
statue or bust and a particular Deity. It is not so much as the
Deity would dwell in that statue once it had been charged,

---

17 *Animated Statues* at Hellenic Faith, accessed on January 1, 2022: https://hel-
lenicfaith.com/animated-statues/

empowered, and the Deity had been summoned forth; rather, it was that a magical connection or association existed between the Deity and the artifact, and that connection was readily sensible to those who encountered it under the right conditions. What the ancients were discussing when they talked and hinted about this mysterious philosophic magic sounded a lot like some kind of talismanic magic to me. So, years ago, I decided to try to emulate this magical operation using a talismanic charge as a base. What I discovered back then was that it worked quite well, much to my amazement, but not unsurprisingly. The key is knowing how to set a talismanic field on an object.

The real secret was to integrate a godhead summoning into some stone or ceramic artifact where a talismanic charge had already been set. The perpetual charge and intelligence of the talisman would act as the perfect base or container to house a bond or connection with a Deity. Once established, then the statue would be perpetually charged and embodied a spiritual connection with that Deity. It would seem that the statue or bust had actually become a residence of the Deity, but that was only the appearance. Still, such an artifact would be an enormous gift or relic to be kept in any temple, sacred home, or covenstead of a Wiccan or Pagan group.

Since this was such a simple project, although the results were quite amazing, I went through the steps and animated three statues of three Goddesses for my temple, and they have been a living part of my religious life and magic for decades. I am certain that they have intervened at certain strategic times and made the pathway of my life easier and deflected, where possible, those events and people who would have hurt me or damaged my reputation. It didn't mean that I was immune to my own stupidity and the deceit of others, but it helped to make events turn out better in a meaningful and positive manner. Having living Gods or Goddesses in your temple home can make that place more sacred and protected.

Modern magicians have tossed around some ideas and tried to fill in the unknown parts regarding the methods for performing this magic, but I will assume that they came up with a similar idea that I discovered years ago. Still, having gone over the techniques of talismanic magic in my book *Talismanic Magic for Witches* and discussing the theurgic magic of animating a statue in this work, I thought that it would be optimal to produce a ritual pattern here so that you, my readers, might also know how to perform this kind of magical operation.

To perform this working, you should approach it just as you would any talismanic and theurgic working. The only difference is that you need to select a talisman that works with the godhead that you intended to summon and call it into the statue or bust. You can use any of the three talisman types that I presented in my book on talismanic magic, such as a talismanic elemental, a decan, or a septan. Any of these will make an excellent foundation for the theurgic container.

What I have done is build up a character profile for the Deity that you want to link to the artifact, and once you have done that, you can look at the chosen type of talisman and find the one that would best characterize your Deity. I had three Goddesses, so I decided to set a talismanic elemental of Venus of Air, Venus of Water, and Venus of Fire into the three Goddess artifacts. Then, I wrote an elaborate invocation for each of these three Goddesses and bound them to the three statues. What I had done was create the perception that the three Goddesses inhabited these three statues, and so it seemed to those who also encountered them.

The preparation steps for this working include the following steps. You will not only have to give offerings and worship to the planetary Deity, but you will also need to connect that Deity to the one that you are going to invoke, thereby creating a powerful link in your mind.

1. Take the statue or bust and consecrate it in a magic circle with lustral water (salt water), gently wipe it dry, and then consecrate it lightly with a scented oil. The scented oil should be associated with the target Deity. This will be done three times.

2. Perform the full spectrum of devotional liturgies with the combined planetary Deity and the target Deity. This would include votive offerings, prayers, hymns, godhead assumption,

and communion. It might also be a good idea to do some good workings in the community in the name of this target Deity. All of these efforts are to be directed to the statue or bust as if this were the Deity in the flesh.

3. Perform all of the other normal preparation tasks up through the date of the elected magical event.

Choosing a date and time becomes an important step, more so if you are going to incorporate a lunar mansion. However, my advice is to perform the celestial working a few days before the full moon. This will allow the artifact to be ready for use after the seventy-two hours of incubation so that you will be able to perform a lunar esbat to celebrate the installation of the Deity into your temple and household. It should be a joyous occasion with a feast after the religious ceremonies are completed. Offerings from this feast should be officially made to the Deity, and you should invite others of like mind to attend.

For this kind of working, you can use a metallic talisman or not, but you will need to create and consecrate the parchment sigil. The statue or bust artifact will be sitting on the main altar until it is to be charged. If you choose to forge the talisman, it will become an artifact placed on the statue or bust in some manner. If you don't want to bother with a metallic talisman, then you will use the stone or ceramic artifact as the talismanic receptor.

In this example, I will use the *Invocation for the Talismanic Elemental* as I did decades ago to create the three living Goddess artifacts.

Refer to Chapter Thirteen in the book *Talismanic Magic for Witches* and perform the *Invocation of the Talismanic Elemental Ritual* through step 30, using a parchment sigil and the metallic talisman (if required) to focus the charge or just the parchment sigil.[18]

Then, taking the statue or bust, place it on the septagram icon on the central altar, bow before it, and then perform the *Stellar Vortex for Talismanic Charging Rite* in the same chapter, and perform the first seven steps (31–37).[19] Instead of step 38, perform the following six steps.

---

18 Frater Barrabbas, *Talismanic Magic for Witches*, pp. 206–210.
19 Ibid., pp. 210–212.

Animating a Statue with a Godhead to a
Talismanic Charge Ritual Steps

1. Take up the wand and draw a great rose-ankh in the zenith, imbue it with a deep purple energy, then place the wand on the septagram icon.
2. Intone the invocation of the target Deity while kneeling before the statue and gazing to the zenith. This invocation should describe the Deity based on its character profile, and the Operator should urge the Deity to descend and animate the statue. This action should be done with all of the emotional passion and desire for the Deity that the Operator can muster. Repeat this invocation two more times, then kneel in silence.
3. While still kneeling, take the wand and draw an invoking spiral in the zenith, and then draw the energy down into the statue, touching the statue with the wand three times.
4. Lay down before the statue while covering the face, not looking at it. Stay in this prone position for several minutes, listening and sensing for contact from the Deity.
5. Once you sense the Deity in the statue, carefully take the statue with your hands covered by the stole and carry it in a slow and stately procession to the main altar. Then make offerings to it of incense and votive candles. After a short time, take a colored veil cloth and cover the statue. It should remain covered for seventy-two hours. During this time, make offerings of incense and votive lights.
6. Continue with the ritual steps 40 through 48 to complete the rite appropriately.

This completes the steps needed to animate a statue or a bust with the talismanic receptor and the link or association with a Deity. The most important part of this working is the preparation. You will need to get so deeply involved with the liturgical work associated with the Deity, not to mention assuming its godhead, that there will be no chance that the invocation to it will fail to draw it down into the statue. In fact, you will know just by performing the preparatory devotions if the statue animation will actually be successful, delaying it as necessary until you have a solid connection with that Deity.

CHAPTER NINE

MAGICAL MASS OF THE GREAT MOTHER GODDESS

"The Mass is the most perfect form of prayer."
—POPE PAUL VI

As I have shown in Part One, Chapter Three, the rituals of the rigorous Drawing Down rite and the communion rite that follows can be symbolized and performed by a single person and still retain all of the power and glory of the more involved and complex rituals. It is the nature of magic that elaborate ritual actions can be symbolized and condensed but still produce the same results. It is a rule that I have successfully used in a consistent manner, and it is not a new idea.

The early Christians realized this fact and, over time, they produced a very powerful ritual that emulated both the bloody sacrifice of their Savior and the Seder meal that he performed as the Last Supper. It is, however, not part of the practice of Judaism to equate the wine and bread of the Seder meal with the blood and flesh of a living God.

What is actually occurring is a two-fold process of symbolizing the bloody sacrifice with the surrogate of consecrated wine and bread that stand in for the cannibal feast where the God-man is consumed after his ritual sacrifice. This is obviously a very ancient Pagan rite that is made much more amendable to the Christian pallet that refused to eat the meat of Pagan sacrifices. Instead of sacrificing an ox or a goat (or a human), the Christians symbolized the sacrifice of their Savior and partook of his blood and flesh in the form of wine and bread.

The fact that their Savior, in the form of Jesus Christ, was executed by being crucified, the last Seder meal with his followers became the sacrificial meal of his blood and body as a proto-Deity. It was meant to replace the animal sacrifice that was a liturgical part of the Jewish religion of the Temple period. It was also a part of most other religions in the Near East and Europe at the time. The mass rite was a symbolized version of this sacred animal sacrifice, and it represented both the magical action of godhead assumption and the transubstantiation of wine and bread into the blood and body of their Savior.

We can, as Witches and practitioners of magic, also take our sacred rite of godhead assumption and communion and encapsulate it into a ritual that is celebrated by a priestess or priest for the benefit of the coven or group, or just for the individual who celebrates it. What this does is produce a ritual that can be used to create sacraments whenever required, and also to bless and consecrate anything that needs to be charged and blessed by the symbolic hands of the Deity in the guise of the ritual celebrant. The whole science of sacramental theurgy proceeds from symbolic rituals that make the deployment of sacramental powers and blessings simple to perform and capable of being performed with little or no preparation, and at any time.

The combined actions of the assumption of godhead and communion have the following steps, and I would assume that any mass rite would have the same steps, although done by a single celebrant acting in the role of priestess or priest. The steps are the same, but instead of the actual periods of preparation, sequestering, and deep trance adoption, these actions are symbolized and performed by a person with an ordinary conscious state and without any long-term preparation.

Here are the steps as we have determined them for a Drawing Down rite and the follow-up communion rite. These are the eleven steps with both rites combined.

1. **Introduction or Introit:** Set the temple for the working to commence.
2. **Purification of the temple area:** Circle consecration, incensing, meditations, etc.
3. **Votive veneration of the Deity**

MAGICAL MASS OF THE GREAT MOTHER GODDESS

4. **Invocation of the Deity**
5. **Godhead assumption**
6. **Offertory:** Offering of sacraments.
7. **Consecration and conmixio:** Sacraments blessed, charged, mixed (wine and bread fragment).
8. **Communion**
9. **Blessing, oracles, and wisdom teachings**
10. **Thanksgiving**
11. **Final blessing and departure**

We could expect that a proper mass rite would have all of these steps included in it and applied in this sequence. The magical mass rite that I am including in this book as an example has just these components written into it. I believe that these steps represent the most efficient symbolic representation of the combined rites of the Draw and the communion.

While the mass rite generates the sacraments and creates the powerful holy atmosphere of the charged and blessed temple, it is the benediction rite that deploys these sacramental energies into a vortex where other items might be blessed and charged, such as vestments, oils, ointments, medicines, ancillary tools, and amulets.

We will now examine an example of a mass rite, and I have included here a rendition of my Mass of the Great Mother Goddess, which I have used in various forms over the last forty years.

Mass of the Great Mother Goddess

The Mass of the Great Mother Goddess is performed in a temple that has a veil suspended before the altar, creating a barrier between the inner sanctum and the outer court of the temple. If there is no actual veil, then the Celebrant will act as if there is an invisible veil set before them. They will begin this rite while standing before the veil and performing their actions before it. As this is the Mass of the Great Mother Goddess, the celebrant should be either a priestess or someone taking that role. Since this rite is very verbose, it is expected that the Celebrant will read from a book that is placed on a lectern or held in their hands, as needed.

This mass rite is very elaborate with elements of ritual magic written into its texts, particularly the barbarous words of evocation as taken from the *Sworn Book of Honorius*.[20] I have been using a form of this mass for a few decades now, and it is always profoundly effective. You may want a mass rite that is less verbose or wordy, and you might want it to celebrate a different set of Deities. You can use this mass rite example to formulate your own variation, perhaps making it simpler with fewer actions and less wordiness.

1. Introit

The Celebrant kneels before the altar. Bowing their head, they align their physical, emotional, mental, and spiritual bodies through meditation before intoning the following dedication:

In the infinite and numberless names of the Great Goddess,
I begin this celebration of the Mass,
To give honor, love, and devotion to the Idol of She
Who is the object of my highest veneration,
The Cosmic Goddess of Greatest Renown!

I give worship to you and the full service of my spirit, mind, and body.
Let there be no distance between us,
Let us be as One—the Goddess as Avatar,
Living Spirit of all Womanhood
Embodied in the sanctified and holy flesh of Woman as Priestess.
Unto this great Mystery and its profound manifestation,
I begin this sacred work.

[The bell is rung three times]

Three is the number of the Deity. Creation, Preservation, and Dissolution.
Let us meditate on this great wisdom.

---

20 Joseph Peterson, *Sworn Book of Honorius – Liber Iuratus Honorii*, n.d.

[Pause for meditation]

The Celebrant raises their arms to the heavens and says:

Hear me, O Great and Powerful Goddess of the Celestial Veils of Heaven.
I entreat you with gifts of love, devotion, and offerings of incense, wine, and bread.
My heart lifts up to you with love and adoration.
Through this gateway of divine love, I summon and call you
Into this sacred rite of consecration and communion.
Bless us with your sagacity and reveal to us the truth about Light and Darkness—
Twin pillars of your divine wisdom!

Then the Celebrant rises and approaches the altar with a humble countenance. The lights are slowly brightened, but the Celebrant does not yet draw the veil around the Holy of Holies.

2. Purification

The Celebrant anoints themself with Holy Oil and Holy Water, bows before the veil, and intones:

O most High and Infinite Queen, I humbly stand before you and seek your blessings and empowerment to perform this rite with truth and love. I utter the sacred words of power to build a temple of light, darkness, and glory made fit for your presence. I purify myself to take on your spirit and body as my own.

Ielominctos, Gadabany, Zedabanay, Gederanay, Saramany, Lomtety, Loctosy, Gerohanathon, Zahamany, Lomyht, Gedanabasy, Setemanay, Henlothant, Helomyht, Henboramyht, Samanazay, Gedebandy.[21]
—Prayer 24

---

21 Joseph Peterson, *Sworn Book of Honorius – Liber Iuratus Honorii*, p. 101.

The Celebrant makes the sign of the ankh ☥ upon the veil and says:

Hielma, Helma, Helymar, Heuina, Hytanathas, Hemyna, Hitanathios, Helsa, Hebos, Hiebos, Helda, Hagasa, Hoccomegos, Raitotagum, Coictagon, Myheragyn![22]

—Prayer 32

Aum-Ha!

We pray, dear Lady, that with illuminated minds, we may enter this Grove of Sacred Life.

The Celebrant then kisses the veil.

3. Veneration and Invocation of the Goddess and Her Son

The Celebrant stands before the veil and with a profound bow she raises her arms in adoration, she says while making the sign of the ankh:

Glory to the Goddess on high
And on Earth peace to those of good will.
We Praise You!
We Bless You!
We Adore You!
We Glorify You!
We give you thanks for your great love!
O Adorned Goddess, Heavenly Queen,
Goddess the Mother All-pervading!
Take away the blindness of the World!
Have mercy on us and receive our prayer.
Together with your daughter Earth, Your Only Son, and the Holy Spirit [☥]
Unity in Eternal Creation!

Aum-Ha!

---

22 Ibid., p. 107.

The Celebrant blesses the incense and feeds the charcoal in the thurible. They will then say:

Receive these burning herbs,
Oils, and resins from your sacred trees and bushes,
Pure offerings without blood or flesh.
(For we shall make a more serious offering later.)
These offerings give forth a pleasant aroma of spices from the good earth,
To purify and sanctify this holy temple,
Making it a fit place for your descent—
O, living power of love and light.
These offerings of scented smoke are made to you in love and devotion.
May it enliven us with your eternal grace and holy presence.

The Celebrant then moves the thurible in the form of an ankh before the veiled chalice where indicated, saying as they do so:

May this incense ☥ blessed by You ☥ Arise in Your Sight;
And may Your Light ☥ descend upon us.

The Celebrant then incenses the rest of the altar. The Celebrant faces the congregation with outstretched arms and says:

I summon forth the power and majesty of the Great Goddess,
Seeking from her the first sign in this Mystery of the Mass.
The appearance of her spirit causes apparitions, visions,
And the realization of prophecy.
The Feminine Spirit knows all things—past, present, and future.
Ask. Listen to the depths of your inner heart and soul.
There, you shall be instructed.

[Pause]

O, Listen to the Words of the Great Goddess, who reveals all things:

As the Vine, I bring forth a pleasant aroma. My flowers are the fruit of honor and wealth. I am Holy Hope, the Mother of Fair Love, strength, and knowledge that grows to understanding.

In me flows all grace of the Way and Truth—knowledge of Eternal Life. In me is virtue and faith.

Come, all you who desire me. Take your fill of my fruits. My Spirit is sweeter than honey and my dowry richer than the honeycomb.

On Earth, I am Pangaia, the life of the wild woods, domestic crops, and placid orchards.

I am the fertility that never ceases, the night dew, and gentle rains that nurture. Rivers, creeks, and aquifers bestow the water of life on all living things. The lifeblood that flows are rivers of vitality, fulfilling my passions and singing of eternal ecstasy! Joy in life is my eternal gift.

In the heavens, I am the celestial rings of the starry arms of the Galaxy. I am the Sun and Moon, the mists of dawn and the evening fog. I am the rainbow that gives vibrance beneath the dark, gloomy clouds. I am the promise of passionate beauty as the budding roses of spring.

As the Womb of the Cosmos, I am She who gives life to the bright stars that glimmer as jewels upon the blackness of my body. I am as fathomless as the vast universe, infinite and eternal.

My memory is unto everlasting generations. They who eat my sacred bread shall not hunger and they who drink of my holy wine shall not thirst—for these are the flesh and blood of my only Son. They who harken to me shall not be confounded and they who work by me shall not wrong. Listen intently, oh my hidden children, for you who accept me into your life shall have everlasting joy.

Thus is the Wisdom of the Great Mother!
So Mote it Be! Aum-Ha!

The Celebrant deeply bows and meditates for a few minutes, breathing in the powers emanating from the Great Goddess into their body, then they will stand again, facing the veil, and then say the following invocation.

I call to thee, O Dionysus, Son of the Great Goddess, to hear my call and to heed my entreaty. Come before me. I am filled with the spirit of the Great Goddess, your Mother. I ask that you submit yourself to me to bless this rite and to fill the sacrament with your sacred essence. We, your hidden children, are the benefactors of your eternal sacrifice and carry in our flesh, blood, and spirit your secret source. Come forth to us and celebrate the life, death, and rebirth of the eternal cycle, of which we are all a part.

Aligned to the Great Mother and in association with her Son, who shall be the gift of life that restores us from death, I assume the mantle of her Spirit and offer her Son as a blessing to the celebration of life, as it has always been.

The Celebrant deeply bows again and meditates for a few minutes, feeling the emanations of the Great Mother and her Son touch their soul with their emanations.

4. Mantle of Glory and Godhead Assumption

The Celebrant makes the sign of opening the threshold as they part the veil and steps up into the Holy of Holies. Once within, they will draw the sign of the ankh ☥ and say, while drawing a line downwards from on high to the altar for each Goddess aspect:

I reveal the Five Goddesses of the Greater Cycle of Rebirth—Womanhood in all its variations.

I summon the imago of the Maiden, pure with child-like innocence, curiosity, and wonder, full of song, beauty, and optimism. The flowers dance at your gentle footfall. All nature is tamed and made sweet, kind, and good because of your endearing disposition. Shower us with the simple gaiety of your laughter and the sweetness of your smile.

I summon the imago of the Lover who experiences divinity through ecstasy; passionate, inflamed, full of vitality and eagerness. Alluring, naked, bold, devoted, and full of adventure, you open yourself to be taken and possessed so that you might obtain and acquire unlimited potential. To be penetrated by the God and writhe in ecstatic waves of consummate pleasure—to enfold, hold, and possess, to receive the gift of the silver stream. You are the teacher of the little death and the promises of things yet to unfold.

I summon the imago of the Mother, life-giver, nurturer, empowered creator of all living things, from whose loins are birthed all living creatures. You are the maker of civilization—the drop spindle, oven, and butter churn are your tools of the Mysteries of life. From the womb of your being is new life formulated, and your love masters the world and makes it a domesticated home.

I summon the imago of the Crone, experienced keeper of wisdom and teller of tales. You are full of years, remembering past trials endured and life persevered. Death is your Mystery, but eternal life is found in memories, legends, and histories—the Mysteries of the clan and the names and stories of the ancestors.

I summon the imago of the Cosmic Goddess, who contains all the forms of Womanhood and more. Thou art the Great Spirit that gave birth to the universe, who reflects life in the mirror of death. Thou art the womb and the tomb. The Mystery of the Light and Darkness is forever spiraling in your arching body that illuminates the night sky.

Thus are the five aspects of the Divine Feminine—let us know their names and celebrate them in this rite.

The Celebrant makes the sign of the equal-arm cross on their body, touching their left shoulder, right shoulder, groin, and head, and envisioning a cross of light glowing on their body. They will then kneel before the altar and say:

I summon the Goddess of Love, known by many names—Aphrodite, Venus, Hathor, and Rhiannon. I call upon the powers of ecstasy to fill my heart with desire and bring me to that place of Oneness and Union. Let there be love, light, and laughter. Let there be passion, celebration, and revelation. I summon the Only Son of the Goddess of Ecstasy—who is her emissary and worthy sacrifice, known as Dionysus Zagreus.

I call upon loud-roaring and reveling Dionysus,
Primeval, double-natured, thrice-born, Bacchic lord,
Wild, ineffable, secretive, two-horned, and two-shaped.
Ivy-covered, bull-faced, warlike, howling, pure,
You take raw flesh, you have feasts, wrapped in foliage, decked with
grape clusters.
Resourceful Eubouleus, immortal God sired by Zeus
When he mated with Persephone in unspeakable union.
Hearken to my voice, O blessed one,
And with your fair-girdled nymphs, breathe on me in a spirit of
perfect agape.[23]

—Orphic Hymn to Dionysus

She has chosen beloved Dionysus as her emissary and offers up his blood
as wine and his flesh as bread so that when we consume these gifts, we
might be one with the Gods.

The Celebrant then stands before the altar and makes the sign of the gate on their body. They will touch their left shoulder, right shoulder, and then their groin, focusing the energy on their heart, while silently inviting the Great Mother to enter into their body. They will then kneel again and say the following invocation:

Divine Goddess of ten thousand names,
Mother of the Gods that do homage unto thee,
You who are called the Great Deep, the Celestial Abyss Nuit,
Protect us as we face your Mysteries.
Aid us who dread the darkness and the unknown;
Wrap your starry mantle of light about us.
You, who arches the heavens with your body that holds the Milky Way
as your veil.
You, who holds all time and space in your darkness,
Bring our souls into their true fruition of eternity.

On Earth, we know you through your daughter, Nature.
At your feet, the flowers bloom and grasses grow,
By your voice, the spirits of the Earth rejoice

---

23 Orphic Hymns are public domain unless recently translated. This is a version from the early nineteenth century.

And the Elements obey your natural rhythm of the universe.
At your breath, the winds blow,
And through rain, dew, and mist, you bring forth new life to all.

We know thee through your only mortal Son, whose essence
Is in our flesh and blood, and whose Spirit ensouls us.
We are offered his blood and flesh to drink and eat,
As the cup of foaming wine and the plate of unleavened bread,
So, partaking we might be like unto the Gods.

We call your Spirit, O Celestial Queen,
To rest in this temple properly prepared for you.
Abide herein, sweet Mother, and commune with our souls.
May your divine presence touch our spirits.
May your divine will inspire our minds.
May your divine love imbue our hearts.
Intercede for us and through us as you will,
While proceeding with your most Holy Work.
Not our petty designs but your eternal destiny shall unfold.

After a short period of kneeling and feeling the power and glory of the Great Mother enter into their heart, the Celebrant slowly stands before the altar to begin the mass rite proper.

5. Offertory, Consecration, and Conmixio

The Celebrant unveils the chalice and takes up the host upon a silver paten, and offering it to the Goddess, they will say:

Receive, O Living and True Light of my Soul, Divine Principle behind the Sun, Matriarch of all humanity, this offering of bread as the flesh of your Son which I make to you. Grant that it provides for us the means to a higher awareness.

The Celebrant then pours the liquid sacrament into the chalice, blesses it, makes the sign of the ankh ☥ then holds it aloft, offering it to the Goddess, saying:

We offer to you, O Spiritual Sea, the Chalice of Life from whose womb all living things arose. May the holy elixir contained herein, the blood of your Son, be our deliverance and that of the whole world.

Then the Celebrant sets the paten on the altar before the chalice and bows over it, breathing the life of the spirit into the sacrament. They will then invoke the name of the Highest:

Agla, Monhon, Tetragrammaton, Ely Deus, Ocleiste, Amphynethon, Lamyara, Ianemyer, Sadyon, Hely, Horlon, Porrenthimon, Ihelur.[24]
—100 Names of the Living God, 1–13

Thou art the Flesh of the Son of the Holy Mother.

Then, the Celebrant holds the chalice close to their lips and breathes the life of the spirit into the Elixir. They will then invoke the names of the Highest:

Adonay, Achionadabir, Omytheon, Hofga, Leyndra, Nosulaceps, Tutheon, Gelemoht, Paraclitus, Occynonoryon, Ecthothas, Abracio.[25]
—100 Names of the Living God, 52–63

Thou art the Blood of the Son of the Holy Mother.

The Celebrant then replaces the chalice veil. The Celebrant deposits the host in front of the chalice and places the paten on the right side of the altar.

The Celebrant bows profoundly and, while making the sign of the ankh over the host and veiled chalice, says:

Come Oh Glorious Goddess and bless ☥ this offering prepared in your honor.

O Merciful Mother, we humbly entreat you to accept and sanctify ☥ these gifts, the flesh and blood of thy Son, which we first offer to your

---

24 Joseph Peterson, *Sworn Book of Honorius – Liber Iuratus Honorii*, p. 185.
25 Ibid.

daughter Earth, that you may grant her peace and preservation, unity and direction; together through us, your servants, and all your devotees, aspirants, and initiates.

Remember, dear Lady, your servants in need [pray now for those who need a blessing] *Give blessings to those who are in dire need; healing to the sick and alms to the poor. Let all be made whole, full of life, and inspired by your love forever more.*

The Celebrant takes up the host in both hands and, where indicated below by the numeral, breaks it first in half, then breaks a small segment off from the bottom of the right half where indicated, saying the following prayer:

We harken to the time when the only Son of the Great Mother gave up his life so that we might be ensouled.
That he was ripped limb from limb by the Titanic Forces of Mortality ❶
and thereof they became drunk after consuming his flesh and blood ❷ .
Then they were destroyed by the Thunderbolt of Necessity, and from their Mingled Ashes were made the Blood, Flesh, and Spirit of the human race which begins the process once again:

Throughout all Aions of Aions. So Mote It Be.

The Celebrant removes the chalice veil and bows. They then will take the small host particle and draw three ankhs inside the chalice rim at the points indicated. They will say:

May the Potency ♀ *of the Lady* ♀ *be always with* ♀ *you. And with your essence.*

Then the Celebrant drops the particle of host into the chalice. They will say:

May the mingling and hallowing of the Body and Blood of the Son of the Great Goddess be for us who receive it a source of Eternal Inspiration.

The Celebrant returns the veil over the chalice and bows.

6. Communion

The Celebrant then communicates with deep contemplation of the Divine Osmosis transforming, blessing, and penetrating their every fiber of being. The Celebrant then gives silent inner thanks to their Beloved Goddess, yet aglow with the power of her Holy Feminine Spirit. They then will turn to the congregation, and all will bow low as the Celebrant parts the veil of the Holy of Holies and stands in the dimensionless space between worlds while holding the chalice and the paten. They will then summon the congregation to approach, saying:

Come forth unto me, O thou chosen ones. Behold the Life Essence of the Holy Son of our most High and Venerable Lady, the Great Goddess. Come forth and be illuminated. Say unto your heart and Soul:

The Celebrant and congregation will say the following together:

Let good thoughts reign over my mind. Let good feelings emanate from my heart. Let good words come forth from my lips, filled with Truth and Inspiration. Let my life's path be guided by one objective, union with you.

Then, as the Celebrant administrates the host, they will say:

May the Body of the Son of the Mother of All
Awaken and nourish the Divine Fire
That lives within you (me).

Then, as the Celebrant administrates the wine from the chalice, they will say:

May the Blood of the Son of the Mother of All
Awaken and nourish the Divine Fire
That lives within you (me).

So Mote it Be!

Then, the Celebrant performs the Ablutions, cleansing the paten, and rinsing the chalice first with wine, then wine mixed with water, then finally, with only water. The chalice and paten are then dried off and replaced with a purificator and chalice veil.

7. Blessing and Wisdom Teaching

The Celebrant, having returned to the Holy of Holies, standing with their arms raised in supplication to the Goddess, says:

I heard the voice of Goddess sing, and this is what she said in a sighing and sonorous voice to her only Son and Lover:

"As a rambling rose grows upon the temple wall,
So, like a rose does heart join with heart
Within all-embracing love.
For the love of the Great Mother penetrates all spheres;
The hearts of all creatures, of all atoms, of nothingness itself.
Where there is heart, there is life, and there I am also.
Therefore, worship me with hearts of joy;
For all acts of love and joy are my rituals.

Fear not the unknown lest you fear me;
For I am the Great Unknown.
From my womb shoot forth the Suns and their children, the planets and moons.
When time has rounded its cycle to my call, I embrace them in my darkness,
For I am both Birth and Death.
The Sun that dies in the depths of my abyss
Returns to greater life in other dimensions.
For I am Mistress of the Spheres, and nothing is lost.
From the space within each atom, I give birth to new universes.
I bring death to transform unto greater life.

So, it is with you!
Each sun, each tree, each spark is my emanation.
Without you, I am incomplete.
Therefore, come to know me, for I am you.
Seek me within yourself, seek me all around you;
For here I am and I wait patiently
For your revelation of me!"

The Celebrant turns with arms raised to face the congregation, and they continue:

"I gave you Birth from darkness to walk in the light of day.
As you grow in thought and action, I put you from me.
You turn to the Horned Father, and from him, learn the Laws
And how to enforce them through discipline.
When you reach the end of this schooling and turn from the father,
You come again unto me.
I lure you with strange enchantments of the Moon.
I draw you through the Worlds of Shadow to teach you my Mysteries.
When I shine upon you with the warmth of my love,
You long for the Alchemy of Divine Marriage of Twin Souls in Deathless Love.
When darkness falls and loneliness enters,
You long for me as I long for you.
In my azure-lidded eyes, I hold the Mysteries,
in my arms, I hold you in eternal embrace.
In the sleep of death, I shall awaken you.
Come! Answer my call and die with me to a life within ecstasy!"

Aum-ha!

Then the Celebrant pauses and bows before the congregation, meditating for a moment of silence. They can continue the mass with a special wisdom reading or end it here with the final blessing.

8. Thanksgiving and Final Blessing

The Celebrant departs the Holy of Holies via the "Closing of the Threshold" gesture and kneels in front of the veil. They will say:

O Supernal Mother,
We depend on your Divinity for life and our perception of its purpose,
In you do we perceive a promise of Eternal Being.
Teach us to accept you in your absolute state.
Teach us to contact you first and harness our will and activity to your own.

Fully touch and grace our thoughts,
For it is your magic power that courses through our living bodies,
Our hands are guided by your hands, our feet are directed on your sacred path,
And our souls are joined together in love as your One Illuminated Spirit,
To perform all of your Holy Works of Deliverance and Resolution.

The Celebrant turns to face the congregation and makes the sign of the ankh ♀ upon themself, and then to the congregation ♀ and says:

We have been chosen and sanctified by You
That our names dwell here with you in this Sacred Grove,
That our hearts have become like holy grails to hold your eternal love,
And our bodies are the temples that emanate your eternal passion.
May you all—Blessed Be!

Aum-ha!
YASTARRE!

The Celebrant silently gives holy thanksgiving to the Great Mother and her hosts for their blessings and aid, then bids them farewell. They will give the sign of the ankh ♀ as the final gesture.

The Mass is ended—go in peace!

CHAPTER TEN

RITUAL OF THE
TEMPLE BENEDICTION

"Tantum ergo Sacramentum Veneremur cernui."
(Down in adoration falling,
This great Sacrament we hail.)
—BENEDICTION RITE AT
ST. ANTHONY AT PADUA[26]

Now that we have discussed and examined the magical mass, and particularly, the Mass of the Great Mother Goddess, we can discuss and examine the next ritual that typically is used in conjunction with it, which is the benediction ritual used for super-charging and blessing a temple and any other artifact.

While the mass is used to generate sacraments, the benediction is used to project the power of the sacrament of bread, as the host or body of the Dying God, into the octagon (or quaternary) structure of the magic circle in the temple. Within that sacralized environment, the Celebrant can charge and empower ancillary objects, such as amulets and medicines. If a coven's magical working or the working of an individual requires a foundation of sacramental power to give it an enhanced boost,

26 Author unknown, *Rite of Eucharistic Exposition and Benediction at St. Anthony de Padua*, Stasb.org, accessed 09/03/2022: https://stasb.org/documents/2018/7/Rite%20of%20Eucharistic%20Exposition%20and%20Benediction%20at%20St.%20Anthony%20de%20Padua.pdf

then the benediction ritual will supply that need. This rite is very loosely based on the benediction rite used by the Catholic church, although it is deployed for a very different purpose—to magically bless and charge the temple and artifacts.

The ritual of the benediction has four parts: the introit, the litany of the star, the preparation, and the sacramental revelation. The purpose of this rite is to set a magic circle with the eight fragments of the host consecrated in the mass rite, or four if only the four watchtowers are available. This rite is written for a Celebrant and a congregation, where the Celebrant will say a prayer or exhortation and the congregation will respond. The Celebrant and the congregation will have a script that they can read. If there is no congregation, then the Celebrant will fill those parts as well after a suitable pause. There should be three Deities to whom this rite is said. A Father (X), Mother (Y), and their Child (Z). The Child is, of course, the Dying God or Son of the mass rite.

The benediction rite is said after the mass of the Great Goddess is successfully concluded.

Benediction Rite

1. Introit and Revelation

The altar is cleared of the chalice and articles of the mass, leaving the covered dish holding extra consecrated host fragments (eight pieces) sitting in the center of the altar.[27] The Celebrant begins by incensing the altar and temple, and chants while this is performed:

I purify thee, O holy of holies, with the smoke of burnt offerings so that all evil, distorted, and negative influences are cast away and all holiness enters in here.

In the names of X, Y, and Z, whom I summon to guard this holy temple and keep it purified (draws the sign of the ankh), *So Mote it Be.*

---

27 There might also be a need for using consecrated wine, so either a small container or the chalice will have some left over from the mass.

Then the Celebrant takes up the lustral water in a bowl next to the thurible and uses it to asperge (sprinkle) the altar while making the sign of the ankh three times over it, blessing the surface of the altar. The Celebrant then continues asperging the rest of the temple in a deosil circuit. They chant:

I purify thee, O Holy of Holies, with the seed of tears that rends the heart of the Great Mother.

I cast out and banish all iniquitous phantasms of the mind and all unaligned distracting influences; cleansing and purifying this temple with the sacred essence of the Gods: the altar of the spiritual body, the circle of the soul, and the watchtowers of the crossroads of life. In the names of X, Y, and Z, do I bless you!

The Celebrant then bows profoundly before the altar, rises, and chants each of these Psalms to the Planetary Spheres, first naming the planet, and then the chant and the congregation responds.

(Key: C = Celebrant, R = Response of Congregation)

The Sun

C: *Let the light of joy guide our path, for it shall illuminate what is to the eye as darkness.*

R: *Through the joining of hearts and the combining of aspirations is the darkness made light.*

The Moon

C: *Our emotions, let them be guided by a steady heart that cannot be seduced. Let our dreams be free of psychic contagion.*

R: *Through the powers of optimism and the discipline of peace is the light of wisdom reflected through the dreams of artistic creation.*

Mercury

C: *The mind shall not be neglected; for ignorance is the first step toward total dissolution.*

R: *The mind has created all things through the agency of the insightful word, and therefore, we must make our minds a useful container for its inspiration.*

Venus

C: *Human love is a two-sided experience that can be perceived in the light as blissful ecstasy or in the darkness as the pain of rejection.*

R: *Through the blessings of friendship, charity, goodwill, and understanding is the experience of love made both noble and wise.*

Mars

C: *Ever should we guard our anger; for to engage in violence is to be consumed and brought down by those who would persecute us. We must be strong and yet control our passions.*

R: *Never return hate for hate, injury for injury; for therein exists the trap of the passions that cloud our judgment. Through dispassion are we girded to defend our peace with silent resolve.*

Jupiter

C: *Be generous and give to those who are without, lest the world be consumed by its cares. Remember always your own blessings, being filled therefore with thanksgiving for the gift of life and love.*

R: *It is charity which shines like spiritual gold, and the receiving of gifts inspires further giving. Open your hearts, O hidden children, and turn not your face from the plight of humanity.*

Saturn

C: *The oath of ethics binds us so that we have become servants of the Great Mother. We are the agents of spiritual and material change, and through us, the divine plan of the Gods is implemented.*

R: *We follow the immutable guidelines of the secret path of transformative initiation and travel its lonely road for the sake of wisdom, a peaceful death, and a glorious rebirth, which is found at the beginning and end of the eternal cycle.*

Then the Celebrant stands for a moment in silent meditation.

The Celebrant then approaches the altar and carefully removes the veil covering the dish where the eight consecrated host fragments are placed. The Celebrant kisses the altar cloth and bows profoundly. They will then chant the following:

I open the gate between worlds and reveal the Door of Between-ness.

I open the gate between worlds and reveal the Flesh of the Spirit of the Gods.

I open the gate between worlds and reveal the Holy Grail which contains the blood of the mediatrix.

Evohe! Evohe! Evohe!—Here is the Flesh of the Gods, and whatever it touches becomes a partaker of its essence!

The Celebrant carefully recovers the dish and bows when it is accomplished. The Celebrant then takes the thurible and thoroughly incenses the altar. They will then stand a moment in silent meditation before continuing with the Litany of the Star.

2. The Litany of the Star

The Celebrant chants the Litany of the Star while the congregation responds.

C:	*O Lord,*	*R: Grant Us Power!*
C:	*O Lady,*	*R: Grant Us Wisdom!*
C:	*O Lord,*	*R: Reveal Thy Mysteries!*
C:	*O Lady,*	*R: Open Thy Gate!*
C:	*O Light of Life,*	*R: Receive Us into Thy Heart!*
C:	*God, the Father of Heaven and Earth,*	*R: Give Power unto Us!*
C:	*God, the Son, the Light of Gods Manifest,*	*R: Give Power unto Us!*
C:	*Goddess, the Mother of All Creation,*	*R: Give Power unto Us!*
C:	*Holy Quarternary, One Unity,*	*R: Give Power unto Us!*
C:	*Holy Bridget,*	*R: Enlighten Us!*
C:	*Sacrament of Rebirth,*	*R: Enlighten Us!*
C:	*Bringer of Sensual Ecstasy,*	*R: Enlighten Us!*
C:	*All Ye Holy Planetary Intelligences,*	*R: Enlighten Us!*
C:	*Semeliel, the Sphere of Sol,*	*R: Enlighten Us!*
C:	*Levanael, the Sphere of Luna,*	*R: Enlighten Us!*
C:	*Nogahiel, the Sphere of Venus,*	*R: Enlighten Us!*
C:	*Zedekiel, the Sphere of Jupiter,*	*R: Enlighten Us!*
C:	*Madimiel, the Sphere of Mars,*	*R: Enlighten Us!*
C:	*Corabiel, the Sphere of Mercury,*	*R: Enlighten Us!*
C:	*Sabathiel, the Sphere of Saturn,*	*R: Enlighten Us!*
C:	*All Ye Blessed and Holy Anti Apostles,*	*R: Enlighten Us!*
C:	*Magnus Simon Magus,*	*R: Enlighten Us,*
C:	*Magnus Valentinus,*	*R: Enlighten Us!*
C:	*Magnus Seth,*	*R: Enlighten Us!*
C:	*Magnus Hermes Thoth Trismagistus,*	*R: Enlighten Us!*
C:	*Magnus Pythagoras,*	*R: Enlighten Us!*
C:	*Magnus Apollonius of Tyana,*	*R: Enlighten Us!*

C: Magnus Zoistrianos,   *R: Enlighten Us!*
C: Magna Hypathia of Alexandria,   *R: Enlighten Us!*
C: Magna Cleopatra of Alexandria,   *R: Enlighten Us!*
C: Magnus Honorius,   *R: Enlighten Us!*
C: Magnus Agathodaimon,   *R: Enlighten Us!*
C: All Ye Disciples of Magic
     and Mystery,   *R: Enlighten Us!*
C: All Ye Martyrs of Enlightenment,   *R: Enlighten Us!*
C: All Ye Defenders of
     Art and Science,   *R: Enlighten Us!*
C: All Ye Great Goddesses of Magic,   *R: Enlighten Us!*
C: Lady Marah Sophia,   *R: Enlighten Us!*
C: Lady Hokmah,   *R: Enlighten Us!*
C: Lady Shekinah,   *R: Enlighten Us!*
C: Lady Lucianna,   *R: Enlighten Us!*
C: Lady Asherah,   *R: Enlighten Us!*
C: Lady Isis,   *R: Enlighten Us!*
C: Lady Nuit,   *R: Enlighten Us!*
C: Lady Diana,   *R: Enlighten Us!*
C: Lady Lilith,   *R: Enlighten Us!*
C: Lady Medea,   *R: Enlighten Us!*
C: Lady Vivian,   *R: Enlighten Us!*
C: Lady Morgan,   *R: Enlighten Us!*
C: Lady Nimue,   *R: Enlighten Us!*
C: All Ye Masters of the Left
     Hand Path,   *R: Enlighten Us!*
C: All Ye Masters of the Right
     Hand Path,   *R: Enlighten Us!*
C: All Ye Magisters and
     Hierophants,   *R: Enlighten Us!*
C: All Ye Ladies and Priestesses,   *R: Enlighten Us!*
C: All Ye Greater and
     Lesser Adepti,   *R: Enlighten Us!*
C: All Ye Consecrated
     and Initiated,   *R: Enlighten Us!*
C: Aid Us in Our Quest for Truth,
     Eternal Life, Perfect Love, and
     Material Fulfillment.   *R: So Mote it Be!*

C: For it Is Written That:
"Every Man and Every
Woman Is a God!"

C: Give Power unto Us,   R: O Great and Powerful Lord!
C: Grant Us Thy Wisdom,   R: O Great and Wise Lady!
C: From All Harm,   R: Deliver Us!
C: From All Blindness,   R: Deliver Us!
C: From All Errors,   R: Deliver Us!
C: From All Profane and
Foolish People,   R: Deliver Us!
C: From All Threatening
Violence,   R: Deliver Us!
C: From Wars and the
Evils of Nations,   R: Deliver Us!
C: From Disease and
Untimely Death,   R: Deliver Us!
C: Deliver us from all harm,
we beseech you,
O Gods, so that we may live
and fulfill our fate
as it corresponds to thy
immanent design.   R: So Mote it be.

The Celebrant then concludes the Litany by bowing profoundly before the altar in silent meditation for a few moments.

The Celebrant then rises up and says:

We invoke all the potencies that lie within the mystery and magic of the Gods. Give power unto us, O Goddesses and Gods, and we shall return it thrice-fold! Give enlightenment unto us, O Goddesses and Gods, and we shall return it sevenfold! Give deliverance unto us, O Goddesses and Gods, and we shall return it tenfold!
Thus is the vortex of the contagion of all potencies!
Thus is the emanation of the Star, which joins all to it by giving all unto everything!

In the Name of X, Y, Z, and the Spirit of Nature—Gaia, So Mote it Be!

3. Preparation Before the Altar

The Celebrant then takes the magic sword and lays it at the foot of the altar and bows before it, pressing their forehead against the blade.

They will then begin breath control, slowly breathing ever more slowly, and slowing down their heart rate. The Celebrant then rises up on their knees and silently performs the mantle of glory, drawing an equal-arm cross upon their body. They will then kneel and say:

I come to receive the blessings of the Goddesses and the Gods. To partake of their bounty and to dispense this sacred gift to the world, to make it sacred.

The Celebrant rises and makes the sign of the ankh over the sacrament, and then bows. Taking up the vial of consecrated oil, the Celebrant anoints their forehead and then washes the fingers in a bowl of lustral water, drying them with a linen cloth. Then, the Celebrant bows before the altar and says:

In the name of X, Y, and Z, may the life of the manifested Gods shine forth in this temple, properly prepared.

Then the Celebrant incenses the altar for the final preparation.

4. The Revelation of the Manifested Spirit

With great solemnity, the Celebrant removes the veil covering the dish of sacrament and bows before it. They then arise and with arms outstretched in the form of the Tau cross, they say:

Behold the sacrament: the flesh of Gods! For herein is the Mystery of the union between spirit and matter!

The Celebrant takes up the first of the eight host fragments in the folds of their robe and turns to face the magic circle complex. They advance from the altar, cross the center of the circle, and then proceed to the eastern watchtower. Then, the Celebrant halts just before the watchtower and stands momentarily. The Celebrant draws an ankh upon the watchtower using the host fragment which they are holding. The Celebrant then says:

May this Holy Power of the Manifested God charge this place through the blessings of the Flesh of the Spirit. So Mote it Be!

The Celebrant places the host fragment upon the watchtower and bows before it. Then, the Celebrant rises and returns to the altar. They then carefully pick up another host fragment in the above manner after approaching and bowing before the altar. They will then proceed to the next watchtower, repeating the above process.

If there are altars or places set for the four angles, then they are separately set at those points. If there are only watchtowers, then the Celebrant will set two host fragments side by side at each of the four watchtowers.

The watchtowers and angles are set in the following sequence:

1. Eastern watchtower (already shown), southern watchtower, western watchtower, and northern watchtower.
2. Southeastern angle, southwestern angle, northwestern angle, and northeastern angle.

So, with this placement of host fragments, the Octagram of Sacrament is established.

At this point, the Celebrant may seek to bless and charge any artifacts or use the temple so charged for additional workings to be performed within its sacralized environment. This technique is shown in the next chapter.

CHAPTER ELEVEN

SACRAMENTAL TECHNOLOGY— MEDICINES, RELICS, AND AMULETS

> "You're a mystery the way a
> sacrament is a mystery."
> —ANNE RICE, *THE WOLF GIFT*

The art of sacramental technology is where ordinary objects are charged and blessed by the Goddess or God to become imbued with their essence. They are made into magical artifacts that resonate with the spiritual nature of the Deity that caused them to be blessed. Anything, within reason, can be charged and blessed in this manner.

A Witch or Pagan can use the rites of the draw and communion to charge and bless an object, but the best outcome only occurs when the group performing this work adopts the more rigorous methodology of godhead personification, making the communion rite a much more significant operation. Still, this method, while producing the same results, but done symbolically through the artifice of rituals and magic, is greatly simplified, repeatable, and expanded in scope if it's done through the rituals of the magical mass and the benediction.

The key to charging an object is the use of sacraments such as the fragments of the host, lustral water, incense, consecrated oil, and occasionally, consecrated wine. Consecrated sacraments, handled by an authorized priestess or priest (someone who is experienced and knows what they are doing), are the instruments used to pass on the sacralizing influences to target objects, making them, in turn, sacraments.

Other factors to be used in charging and blessing objects are the touching of the hands, making of a sacred sign, the blowing of sacred breath (after having performed the mass rite with a godhead assumption), and the performance of these actions in a highly consecrated temple (after having performed the benediction rite). These actions, along with contact with a sacrament, will powerfully alter the substance of the object through the magical effect of contagion. It is a way of mass-producing artifacts that house the essence of the Deity, making them sacred and holy in themselves. This is the basis of what is called *sacramental magical technology*, and it is an important and integral part of the theurgy of modern Witchcraft and Paganism.

One important consideration is that making an object into a sacred artifact makes it an object that belongs to the Deity. Any item that is chosen to become consecrated to a specific Deity is first made as an offering to that Goddess or God, who may or may not decide to allow it to be used by a priestess or priest in their work. The item must be given back to the recipient, although charged and blessed.

While this might be an issue when dealing with a capricious and fully animated godhead personification, it is automatically assumed in the ritual of consecration that is used with the mass and benediction rites. The object in the consecration rite is offered and then received back again, as a gift, favor, or boon to the one who made the offering. It is assumed that the Celebrant has the proper alignment and associated grace of the godhead to be able to make this a standard part of a ritual. That also means that not everyone can perform this rite in the name of a Goddess or God, but only those who have the proper and developed alignment.

There are also variances with this ritual depending on what is being charged and blessed. A potion, ointment, oil, or medicine will require one kind of consecration rite, while a magical tool, reliquaries (sacramental containers), or an amulet will require another, and vestments, yet another. We saw that appropriate combinations of sacraments are used to perform a threefold consecration for a votive placeholder, and a similar commonsense approach is needed for a specialized consecration rite.

Here are the various combinations of sacraments used to consecrate the classes of sacraments.

1. **Medicines, oils, ointments, potions:** Touched delicately with a host fragment, then a sign is made over it, and a breath blown upon it. (One assumes that the Officiant is free of any problematic pathogens, such as COVID-19.)

2. **Tools, reliquaries, amulets, pre-charged talismans, or any metal or wood objects:** Touched with a host fragment, lustral water, and/or wine or consecrated oil (wiped off afterward), exposed to incense smoke, then a sign is made over it and a breath blown upon it.

3. **Vestments, stole/scarf, hat, cape, phylacteries, bandages, any object made of cloth:** Touched with a host fragment, a light sprinkling of lustral water (wiped off afterward), exposed to incense smoke, then a sign is made over it and a breath is blown upon it.

4. **Sigils for Evocation, or any parchment or paper object:** Touched with a host fragment, exposed to incense smoke, touched briefly with a small metal wand that has been exposed to lustral water or wine, then a sign is made over it, and a breath is blown upon it.

Knowing these different methods for consecrating an object is important so that what is done doesn't damage, stain, or ruin it. These are commonsense methods, and they might vary depending on the material that makes up the object. However, the overall structure of the special rite of sacramental consecration will not change regardless of the material of the target object.

The signs made over the object to be consecrated will follow the logic that it must be the sign recognized by the godhead of the mass rite. Therefore, the Witch or Pagan will have in their repertoire the pentagram, ankh, equal-arm cross, and triangle or hexagram to accompany a Deity that is earthy, watery, airy, fiery, or pure spirit, respectively. The sign that is made with the hand is the most basic of its kind, so any variation will count as a good representative.

We should now discuss the nature of sacred objects, made or discovered. They are also a part of the art of sacramental magic.

Sacred Objects and Relics

There is a special kind of sacramental tool mentioned previously, and it is called a *relic*. Such an artifact will often have a container to hold it, and that is a *reliquary*. A reliquary is a special consecrated container for a relic, allowing it to be displayed to the public, and thus transmitting its powers into magical and liturgical workings. Relics are to be found in many different religions, whether Christian, Pagan, Hindu, or Buddhist. A relic is defined as something that is directly associated with a venerated avatar, saint, teacher, ancestor, or some miraculous manifestation of the Deity in the material world.

Sometimes, a supposed relic is a forgery, like a splinter from the true cross upon which Jesus died, dried blood from his wounds, or any number of bones, skulls, or other belongings of the greater hosts of holy and venerated individuals. At times, the relic is purely a thing of legend, like the Holy Grail. What is important is that the religious adherent believes that the item is authentic, and thereby acting as a kind of shared belief, it can channel the power and holiness of the individual or thing that it represents.

So, the relic doesn't have to be an actual piece of human remains (it can be a possession or something associated with the source of the relic). A relic doesn't even have to be legitimate. It can be a deliberate forgery, a symbolic representation, or an erroneous affiliation. Still, the power of a relic is wholly vested in the faith of those who believe it to be authentic, and that belief alone often has the power to make it a fact. Witches and Pagans tend to create their own relics, but there are cases where venerated objects are kept and displayed by previous teachers or masters.

Since I am not a member of any orthodox religious organization that has a long historical continuity, I don't have access to what would be considered the actual (or assumed) remains of any avatar, holy person, or teacher. I do possess a few practical items from my departed ancestors, but they would not be something that I could make into a relic. For instance, it would be hardly acceptable, nor magically powerful, for me to take one of the silver forks or spoons bequeathed to me from my great aunt and make it into a relic. Whatever virtues my great aunt might have had when alive (and even beyond as a venerable ancestor), anything having to do with magic and Paganism would not have been one of them.

What might be an appropriate relic would be to possess some item from an ancestor who was into the occult or magic, but I don't possess anything like that. It would seem, then, that the whole concept of using relics in magic would be something of a bust for me if I didn't possess anything associated with anyone magical or spiritually significant in my life.

However, there is a third definition of a relic, and that is anything that could represent a miraculous material manifestation or inspired object associated with a Deity. It would therefore be something that was consecrated. Such a thing could also be considered a relic. By means of this definition, I can say that I do indeed possess relics, and I make it a point to manufacture them whenever and wherever needed. Additionally, a picture of an avatar, teacher, or ancestor, whether a photograph or an illustration, can also function as a relic-like representation of the actual person. This allows me, and anyone else who knows how to consecrate an object, to claim any charged and blessed artifact to be a relic of some kind.

One of the most potent (and often used) tropes in my magical work is to enshrine a host fragment from a magical mass performed to a specific godhead. I can take the consecrated host or fragment and place it into a metallic foil wrapper and then use it as a tool for sanctifying and empowering a temple or shrine environment. I have placed such foil-wrapped host fragments at strategic locations, such as the watchtowers and angles, or in front of a statue or upon an icon to empower and sacralize whatever is in their proximity.

If I were a priest in a wealthy Catholic Church, I would use an elaborately decorated monstrance, but metallic foil works quite well because it is a highly conductive material. By placing these kinds of relics at the four watchtowers, angles, and the central altar, each point of the magic circle is profoundly charged and sacralized permanently, even before performing the circle consecration ritual. It's truly marvelous to start with a temple already fully charged to do the work even before the ritual is performed. If ever a magical construct could function as a kind of high-powered battery, then a relic is the logical choice.

Another kind of magical relic is a specially consecrated crystal used to *witness* and thereby absorb the powers and ritual actions associated with a special kind of magical working. Used for this one purpose (and no other), the crystal then contains all of the powers and spiritual intelligences associated with that working. When displayed in a container or placed in a special location, it continues to radiate its power and influences into the magic temple or shrine. I have used such crystals to capture the climax of an important ritual ordeal, and then it becomes an important relic of my magical achievements.

A charged and blessed reliquary is a specialized container or box used to hold sacred objects and protect them. The objects placed into the reliquary do not need to be consecrated themselves, but over time, would become consecrated due to the contagion effect of the consecrated container. Such containers could be used to contain hair, teeth, bone fragments, a token or a picture of a physical or spiritual ancestor, a deck of Tarot cards, cosmetics, medicines, oils and perfumes, incense, jewelry, host fragments, or anything else that would be deemed special and in need of a sacred container. I have a number of such containers, and some of them are quite ornate while others are simple boxes.

Amulets are any kind of medallion or necklace that is charged, blessed, and imbued with the essence and the spirit of the God or Goddess. It is an object that belongs to the Deity, but that is given as a loan to someone who is a worshipper of that godhead. A person who receives an amulet doesn't need to be very religious or even aligned to the Deity ascribed to it. All they need to do is to be open to the Deity and to be part of their outer religious court.

When an amulet is blessed and consecrated, it should also be identified as a gift to a specific person for a specific purpose, one that is allotted to the Deity and the characteristics of the godhead. It has to be something that the Deity can do as part of its manifestation in the material world. After the amulet is blessed and consecrated and the period of incubation is passed (forty-eight hours), then it can be given to the recipient during any special religious gathering by the priestess or priest who crafted it.

Anything that has been consecrated should have a special place for it to be put away or hidden from view, and the reliquary serves that purpose quite well. This is, of course, not true for an amulet, which should be proudly displayed on the person of the owner.

Rite of Sacramental Consecration

This rite is performed once the magical mass and benediction rites have been completed. Whatever is to be consecrated is placed on or near the altar, where the sacraments that will be used are arrayed before the veiled chalice in dishes or vials. The Celebrant is the same who performed the mass and benediction and therefore is filled with the powers and grace of the Deity.

If the object is an oil, ointment, elixir, potion, or medicine, the Celebrant removes the cover from its container, revealing the contents within it. The wand that is used to apply sacrament is short and small, three inches in length. A small spoon or stick could also be used.

The Celebrant stands before the object to be consecrated in front of the altar and raises their arms to the heavens and says the following exhortation:

O God/Goddess, whose name is X, I am here before your shrine to bless this artifact Y in your name. May your holy flesh, blood, tears, breath, and kiss be used to elevate this artifact, so that it will be imbued with your essence; a spark of your spirit will dwell in this holy container so long as it remains in sacred trust.

They then will take a fragment of the host from the dish upon the altar in between their thumb and index finger and make the appropriate sign over the object, and then will touch it three times. (This is for all objects to be consecrated.)

I first bless you with the flesh of the God/Goddess X, so that you are made sacred and holy.

They then will take up the lit and burning thurible from the altar and make the appropriate sign with it over the object, and then circle the thurible around and over it three times. (This is for all objects to be consecrated.)

I twice bless you with the fragrant burnt offerings of the God/Goddess X, so that you are made sacred and holy.

They will then bow before the object on the altar and make the sign over it, then touch it, projecting the power of the Deity into it, and then will blow their breath into and over the object.

I thrice bless you with the holy sign, touch, and breath of the God/Goddess X, so that you are made sacred and holy. Let the essence of God/Goddess X reside within you and be a light in the darkness for all time.

If lustral water is to be used, the Celebrant takes a small wand, dips it into the container of lustral water, and sprinkles a tiny amount on the surface of the object. (If the object requires less water, then touching the wand to the object shall suffice.) They will then say:

I bless you with the holy tears of the God/Goddess X so that you are made sacred and holy.

If consecrated oil is to be used, the Celebrant takes their finger, dips it into the sacred oil, and applies it to the surface of the object. (Then wipes it clean with a cloth after the blessing is completed.) They will then say:

I bless you with the balm of oil from the body of the God/Goddess X so that you are made sacred and holy.

If consecrated wine is to be used, the Celebrant takes the small wand and dips it into the vial of wine and deposits a small drip upon the object. (Depending on whether it is a tool or sigil, it will be wiped clean with a cloth or left to stain the parchment.) They will then say:

I bless you with the blood from the body of the God/Goddess X so that you are made sacred and holy.

Once the sacrament has been used to charge and bless the artifact, the Celebrant holds out their hands over their head and then brings them down to touch the object, perceiving the power of the Deity to pass from the sacralized environment into the object. They will then say:

You are blessed and charged three-fold with the essence of the God/ Goddess X and whose spark of spirit now resides fully within you. I shall ensure that this spark is loved and fed with the magical work that I take upon myself, and gift it to the world at large so that the light of the Spirit shall be ever greater by one in the World. So Mote it Be!

If the artifact is an amulet, then the Celebrant will hold it for a while in their hand and identify the person to whom this godhead jewel is being gifted, along with its function and purpose.

The Celebrant will then put away the dishes and vials of sacrament, and they shall fumigate the altar and the temple one more time. The artifact will be carefully wrapped up and put away so that it might incubate for forty-eight hours before being used or given to its recipient. If the artifact is any kind of vestment, it will be hung up in a dark closet for the incubation period.

Chapter Twelve

Greater Great Rite— Sacramental Sexuality

"In the art of sacred sexuality,
our bodies meet to physically express
what is felt in our hearts and souls."
—Michael Mirdad, *An Introduction to
Tantra and Sacred Sexuality*

O f all the kinds and qualities of sacraments that a Witch or Pagan can generate and experience, sacramental sexuality is the highest and greatest of them all. Witchcraft and Paganism, in the modern Western world, and from my own perspective, are religions that venerate sexuality and seek to experience it in an uninhibited manner. There are also religions where equality is sought between the many genders and sexual orientations, and where differences and diversity are wholly accepted.

Sexuality is something that should never be considered shameful or sinful, nor should consenting women, men, or others be in any way thwarted, penalized, or constrained from expressing their sexual nature however and in whatever form it naturally occurs. This should also be true regarding a woman's right to have control over her body and to determine whether or not she will seek to give birth to another life. To give rights to a fetus or to penalize people for having sex by forcing them to give birth if pregnancy should result is completely absurd and goes against any kind of Pagan morality.

We need to be active and vigilant to protect our freedom of privacy and our right to express ourselves sexually, with some limitations regarding the consent of our partners and the consensus of our close social groups. If that means also being very politically active to prevent a minority fringe of conservative Christian Nationalists from determining laws that govern morality, then so be it.

The sexual revolution occurred back in the 1960s and proceeded to change the social structure regarding gender identification, sexual orientation, and the freedom of some to interact in a less formal and free manner with each other. It began as a struggle that sought equality for all genders and sexual orientations, and rightly so. Yet, this period also had a dark side, as the sexual freedom sought by many was mostly experienced by the upper class, particularly white, cisgender, heterosexual males. That started changing in the 1980s, but we have also experienced backlashes and conservative counter-movements that have shown us that some religious adherents seek to govern all of us with their narrow beliefs and restrictions.

It is sad and disheartening to see over the years that the many victories that have occurred for gender and sexual freedom are threatened by an extreme religious and undemocratic minority. I believe that what is happening now is just the last vestiges of backward thinking and the fear of change, but change will happen anyways, and in fact, has been happening all along. It is already too late to go back to living in the 1950s morality since that time is long gone along with the establishment that made its laws and enforced them.

Still, I believe that Witchcraft and Paganism will continue to move forward, as the younger generations take their place in our community, and the foolishness, exploitation, and coerciveness that has marked the interactions of genders in the past will be overcome and evolved out. Such individuals who have broken the trust of the community regarding their sexual predation have already been excised, and I suspect that this filtering process will continue. We are a very diverse and tolerant community, and that should be seen as a testament to the strength of our religious practices and beliefs.

As I have said, we have discussed all of the various forms of sacraments in this work so far, but we have not covered the most important and powerful sacrament, which is sexuality. I think that I need to define what sacramental sexuality is. Of course, not every sex act is sacred, except perhaps in the most idealized manner. Sacred sexuality occurs when it is done within a consecrated environment, for the purpose of emulating the union of the active (archetypal masculine) and receptive (feminine) polarities and involving two people who have elevated their conscious mind beyond the mundane level of being. In Witchcraft and Paganism, this is where two people assume the personas of two godheads and perform the act of sexual union within a consecrated magic circle, whether symbolic or actual.

Great Rite and Loving Deities

This ritual is called the Great Rite, and it is used to confer upon an initiate the third degree of a consecrated priest or priestess. It represents the highest state that an initiate can achieve in British Traditional Witchcraft (BTW) and its offshoots from a purely liturgical perspective. Those groups and traditions who do not accept a multi-degreed role of initiation would find another perspective to give to the Great Rite, or perhaps it would not be considered an option. I have met Witches and Pagans from many different traditions and lineages and they all seem to support an idea of sacred sexuality. We can, therefore, cautiously adopt this as a primary part of these traditions.

The Great Rite is a thoroughly documented ceremony that can be found on the internet and in books. Representing the highest privilege conferred in the BTW to its initiates, one would think that it would be a well-kept secret. Yet, it is like the rest of the *Book of Shadows,* published in uncountable resources both online and offline. I could spend a few chapters or more going over this ritual in its various forms, but I believe that would be beyond the scope of this book, and it has already been done.

Suffice it to say, the earlier prose version of this ritual borrowed shamelessly from Crowley's Gnostic Mass, but what was borrowed was probably the very core and the best part of that rite. The sacred sexuality incorporated into the Gnostic Mass is definitely a topic that we will want to briefly discuss, but I will assume that you, my readers, already know about the Great Rite. We will pass on this topic of the Great Rite with that idea firmly in mind to talk about other topics.

We have discussed in great detail the godhead assumptions and personifications taken to a higher level of discipline and rigor, where an individual would closely approximate the embodiment of a Goddess or a God to a group or community. The question arises from these considerations as to the appropriateness or facility where this blessed and personified Deity might seek to engage in a sexual manner with one or more of their adherents. Is it appropriate or even something that might or should happen? Do we experience the manifestation of our Goddesses and Gods to have sex with them?

I believe that group consensus and the adopted social morality that a coven or grove adheres to will be better able to answer that question. It is, first and foremost, a group decision. From a purely theoretical perspective, based on Pagan morality, the answer would be affirmative. It is appropriate and even expected that worshipers and their embodied Deities may engage sexually with each other, just as it would be appropriate for a group to engage in group sex magic. These considerations require agreements between the group and individuals, and of course, everyone should be on board with this kind of activity so that it doesn't violate the principles or moral boundaries of any single member. Still, a devotee might approach a person who is personifying a godhead and seek to engage with them sexually, to obtain the ultimate blessing and empowerment that one could obtain from their Goddess or God.

However, the Deity may decline the offer for whatever reason, and it should not be taken as a rejection or that somehow one is unworthy. It is always based on the capricious mood of the Deity, fate, timing, and the unknowable and mysterious threads that bind the Gods and humanity together. Such a blessing need not be conferred by sexual union since it can be done symbolically. Additionally, if such an option should be made available by the group, then a separate area for such activity should also be available. To keep such an encounter private, numinous, and Mysterious, then there should be veils used to obscure entryways and special sequestered locations, comfortably appointed for such activity. It is also possible that the priestess or priest might not be physically capable at that moment of having sex, for various reasons. If and when such an event occurs, then it should be seen as a rare and very blessed moment, but it would more likely not occur since there is so much that must happen within the priestess or priest personifying the Deity to make it a reality.

A sexual encounter with an embodied Deity is a possibility, and, in fact, it might happen without any expectation or preparation. The joy and the rapture of such an encounter is impossible for anyone else to even remotely understand. It is the ultimate fulfillment between a worshiper and their Deity, to be loved and joined at levels beyond the human planes of consciousness. If such a union is fruitful and the person conceives from it, giving birth later to a child, then that child will be the blessed offspring of the Deity, and its life will be forever favored with that remarkable gift. I believe that this is the actual source of all of the myths about children sired from the intercession of Gods and Goddesses and human beings. The Deities in question were likely persons dedicated to personifying a godhead. I have not yet met anyone who either claimed to produce such a child, or any person claiming the parentage of a God. The new Pagan age is still so very young, and such an occurrence may have happened in obscurity or will certainly happen with greater notoriety in the near term.

My thoughts about the practicality of such an occurrence are that it would have to be based on mutual consent, and the request should always come from the worshipper and not the embodied Goddess or God, for otherwise, it might lend itself to being abused. What we don't want is coercion, pressure, and expectation on the part of the priest or priestess who embodies a godhead. It should be a natural occurrence, freely and eagerly requested, and then freely given. I also feel that there are limitations based on the occurrence of pandemic-related diseases and possible STDs that might preclude an actual union and instead, better replaced with a symbolic union as a safer alternative.

Perhaps the best solution to this quandary about the receiving of sexual favors from an embodied Goddess or God is to receive the mark of the Deity on the body of the worshipper. This mark can be a shallow incision with a sharp sacrificial knife or a small burn mark from a branding iron. It should be small and discrete so as to not cause any undue injury or permanent disfigurement. If a shallow cut is made, then it might also be massaged with charcoal to leave a tattoo-like mark. The object is to receive a moment of intimacy with a small token of love, given as a kiss or of pain to mark the sacredness of the occasion. This is, of course, the origin of the Witches Mark, and it represents the physical bond between the godhead and the worshipper. It is also not coincidental that the word for "cutting" in Hebrew is also the word for "covenant" and "circumcise," all of which denote what the mark represents to the Witch who receives it.

Living Altars and Sexual Sacraments

A living and breathing Deity who is manifesting in a human host will make the body of that priestess or priest momentarily an embodiment of all that is sacramental. The oils from the body, tears and sweat, free-flowing blood, semen, and menses would all represent a highly charged sacrament if somehow collected and preserved. These would become powerful relics of the Deity, and could therefore be enshrined and displayed as secret mementos of the materialization of the godhead. I would point out that the sacraments of oil, perfumes, resins, lustral water, wine, and bread are themselves symbolized attributes that would otherwise be the earthly effluvia of the Goddess or God.

The celebration of a magical mass could also place the embodied Deity upon the altar as a place where the symbolic meets the tangible in the guise of the materialized godhead. The Deity may sit upon the altar like a throne, or they might lie upon it like a bed. They might be garbed or nude, or both, depending on the stage or step of the mass rite. Offerings can be given to them, and they would bless the sacraments directly for the Officiant and the congregation. I refer to the mass without the embodied Deity as the *low mass* and one where the embodied Deity is present as the *high solemn mass*. I found that performing this mass rite with an embodied Deity was a truly profound and amazing experience, making the magical mass a truly monumental rite.

In the fictional accounts of Witches performing a Black Mass, there is a naked man or woman on the altar acting as a representative of the Devil and possessed by a demonic spirit. A true host, stolen from a lawful Catholic Mass, is revealed to the congregation, and then defiled, thrown to the ground, and stamped into the earth. The mass rite is a parody of the proper Catholic Mass. It is the celebration of the downfall of the Christ as host and the overturning of the natural order to manifest the rule of chaos and anarchy. Of course, that is all fiction, since a Witch or Pagan would have no interest in degrading Catholic rituals and defiling Christian ethos. We have much to learn from ancient practices and we tend to respect all religions. However, placing an embodied Deity on an altar might make outsiders think of the Black Mass, but they are two very different rituals and approaches to divinity. Only Montague Summers and Dennis Wheatley among modern writers have made this connection between Witchcraft liturgies and the infamous Black Mass.

In thinking about enshrining a Goddess on an altar, I have to consider Crowley's Gnostic Mass briefly, since it would be one of the few rituals that resembles what I have been doing for decades as a Witch and ritual magician. Crowley's Gnostic Mass is worthy of study by anyone who seeks to master the art of sacramental theurgy since it was written as a quasi-magical liturgical rite. Keep in mind that this ritual was written and practiced well before the Witchcraft movement started. And as I have stated, Gardner plagiarized the Gnostic Mass to build up his Great Rite. There would have to be, then, a link between the Gnostic Mass, the Great Rite, and the magical Mass of the Great Goddess.

While there is certainly a link between the Great Rite and the Gnostic Mass, there seems to be not much in common with the Mass of the Great Goddess. The reason for this distinction is the fact that the Gnostic Mass is based on a symbolized and ritualized enactment of sacred sexuality and procreation while the Mass of the Great Goddess is based on the sacrifice of her son, the Dying God, for the empowerment, blessing, and enrichening of her congregation. In fact, the Gnostic Mass is the only mass rite in the Western Mystery tradition that is based on procreation instead of sacrifice. The Mystery of life and death is replaced entirely with the

Mystery of procreation, which actually isn't much of a mystery in our modern age. Death, the potential for rebirth, and the mechanism of the human spirit aligned with that of the God who dies and is reborn, however, is still shrouded in mystery.

Whichever of these is the preferable ritualized Mystery for the practitioners is based on their perspective and spiritual alignment. Witches and Pagans already have the Great Rite, and also the role of the feminine in the Gnostic Mass is not represented by a Deity per se, but by the Scarlet Woman (who is mortal). Therefore, it would seem to me that what is needed to complete the liturgy of modern Witchcraft is the inclusion of the sacrificial Mass of the Great Goddess. We can study the Gnostic Mass, and perhaps even rewrite it to make it a better fit for a Goddess-based religious perspective, but it would likely be redundant to the Great Rite and would have to function as a symbolized version of it.

We have discussed the potential of seeking and achieving the sexual attention or union itself from a priestess or priest who is personifying a fully embodied godhead assumption, representing the kind of union that would occur between a worshipper and their God or Goddess. What would happen if both individuals had assumed their respective godheads and then sought to unite as equals, but within the rigorous discipline of a double Drawing Down rite? Would such an occurrence be considered a Greater Great Rite if both of the participants had assumed their respective godheads first before commencing the Great Rite ritual?

First of all, in order to perform the Great Rite in the altered state of godhead embodiment, it would either require the assistance of helpers (who would then function as witnesses) or it might turn out to be awkward or even fail to happen because one or the other would be somewhat incapacitated. The second consideration is that a full embodiment would overlay the conscious mind of the participants and their intentions, making the outcome suddenly unpredictable. I think that what could be accomplished is for both participants to assume a weaker godhead assumption that would allow for full conscious engagement. My experiences with godhead assumptions and Deity personifications are that the ego and mind of the one who is embodied cease to exist if the embodiment is powerful enough, and then it becomes a matter for the godhead to determine what will occur within their conscious field. It is better for the participants to retain some control and willpower with a weaker godhead embodiment so that their intentions will be realized.

To develop the proper approach to sacred sexuality, an experienced couple should consult some of the many books on the subject and make their sex magic an ordeal of pleasure and intense satisfaction. Learning massage, the art of sensual touching, paying attention to a myriad of details such as lighting, scented oils and lotions, exotic food and drink, and building up a repertoire of rituals of love and lovemaking would be the path to making the Great Rite into a superior experience. I have stated in other books that sex magic requires a couple to know how to effectively engage in a pleasurable interlude of sex as well as having extensive knowledge of ritual magic. The Great Rite requires the highest degree of expressing both sexuality and godhead assumption within the context of an embodiment of loving Deities. That is the ideal, but the means of making it realized are complex and require a lot of study and practice before they can be realized in a consistent manner.

Great Rite and Erotic Mass

In the coven lineage that I was initiated into so many years ago, we developed an erotic mass to be performed after the Great Rite was completed. It incorporated the symbolization of sexual sacraments that were consecrated and consumed as mementos of the real bodily fluids of the Goddess and the God. I was amazed when this Mystery was revealed to me, and I was told that it was an ancient secret practice, given only to members of my lineage.

What I found out later was that this beautiful and supposedly ancient ritual had been completely made up by the leaders of my group and passed off as legitimate lore to the members. Since those times, these same leaders left the Craft in the early 80s and became ardent fundamentalist Christians who targeted Witches and Pagans, telling the public that we were merely dupes of Satan. I, therefore, don't feel that what they gave to me back then as Mysteries were oath-bound rites to my tradition or even my lineage.

I felt that sharing this rite with my readers would be appropriate particularly given the topic that we are presenting in this chapter.

Therefore, let me end this chapter with the ritual mass that was used to consecrate the sexual sacraments of the Great Rite, thereby making it a Greater Great Rite to any who might take this rite and my suggestions and use them.

Erotic Mass of the Fourfold Goddess

This rite is performed immediately after the Great Rite. In the four watchtowers, cups are placed that contain the sacrament of the Goddess, which have been set in their places before the commencement of the Great Rite. Upon the altar is placed a piece of bread that is shaped like a phallus. In the west is placed a cup containing milk; in the north, a cup containing salt water; in the east, a cup containing unfermented grape juice; and in the south, a cup containing honey-dew (honey, oil, and royal jelly). A ceramic chalice and a decorated plate, both consecrated tools, sit on a small altar in the center of the circle.

In many traditions, the Goddess is known as the threefold Goddess; but in our tradition, she is secretly known as the fourfold Goddess. She is seen as representations of the four stages in the life of a mortal woman, who is emulated within the eternal wisdom of the Great Mother. The Goddess has shared in all of these stages of life and even death. It is therefore wise and wondrous to present this Mystery and to reveal the fourfold Goddess to her hidden children.[28]

The priestess stands in the center of the circle and says:

I invoke the sacramental fluids of the Four Stages of the Feminine Potency!

The priestess proceeds to the container in the west and says, making the sign of the ankh:

I bless thee, milk from the Mother in the name of X. ☥ *The Source of All!*

---

28 These, of course, are not the four Goddesses presented in my tradition. I have used Celtic surrogates to help provide an example of this rite.

She breathes her breath into the cup, saying the name of the Mother, *Danu*.

The priestess proceeds to the container in the north and says, making the sign of the ankh:

I bless thee, tears from the Crone in the name of X. ♀ The Source of All!

She breathes her breath into the cup, saying the name of the Lady, *Cerridwen*.

The priestess proceeds to the container in the east and says, making the sign of the ankh:

I bless thee, menses from the Virgin, in the name of X. ♀ The Source of All!

She breathes her breath into the cup, saying the name of the Lady, *Arianrhod*.

The priestess proceeds to the container in the South and says, making the sign of the ankh:

I bless thee, honey-dew from the Lover, in the name of X. ♀ The Source of All!

She breathes her breath into the cup, saying the name of the Lady, *Aine*.

The priestess takes the container in the west and the priest takes the container in the east, and they proceed to the center of the circle where is set a beautiful ceramic chalice, which stands upon a small altar placed there. They both pour the contents of their cups into the chalice.

The priestess takes the container in the south and the priest takes the container in the north, and they proceed to the center of the circle where they both pour the contents of their cups into the chalice.

The priestess then stirs the mixture of the four fluids four times with a consecrated spoon. She says:

From Arianrhod, the Virgin Goddess, comes the first flowing of the Lunar Blood, the first flowing of Life.
From Aine, the Goddess as Lover, comes the honey-dew (the secretions), which flows from the Tunnel of Desire.

From Danu, the Mother Goddess, comes forth the milk from her swollen breasts.
From Cerridwen, the Crone Goddess, comes the pure tears of barrenness, loneliness, and the Wisdom of Knowing.
Into this chalice flow the Rivers of the Goddesses, representing the spectrum of the Feminine Cycle of Life and Death.

From them to us is given the elixir that restores us, regenerates our hearts, and grants us eternal life within their fused spirits. For in drinking of them, they are joined to us, and we to them. So Mote it Be.

Then the priest returns to the central altar, bearing in his hands the great phallus made of bread. He holds it aloft, then brings it down and blows his breath into it, and then says:

I bless this solar phallus of bread of the Great God Y—the Divine Power of creation and pure essence of the God as Man. For the Gods live forever, and we live eternally through them. So Mote it Be.

The priest then slowly dunks the phallus of bread into the chalice of fluids glans first, plunging it into the cup four times. He then removes it and places it on a plate, previously set there. Then, the priest and priestess hold their hands out and say this combined blessing, feeling the power of the five sacraments come alive.

In the Name of X and Y, do we take this elixir and this bread into our bodies. In the sign of the ankh, shall these sacraments be blessed as one with the Gods, and one within us, forever into the timeless worlds of the Mighty Ones! So Mote it Be.

The priest and priestess now partake of the sacraments. The priestess takes up the chalice and takes a drink, and the priest takes a bite of the bread, and they exchange until all of the sacrament is consumed.

164

PART THREE

MAGICAL MYSTERY RITES

CHAPTER THIRTEEN

LUNAR MYSTERY AND MOON MAGIC

"The moon will guide you through the night with her
brightness, but she will always dwell in the darkness,
in order to be seen."
—SHANNON L. ALDER

We turn our attention now to the Mysteries, the ever-changing cycles of light and darkness, life and death, which mark the times and events for working liturgical rites and magic. While it is true that Witches and Pagans can work magic whenever there is something needed or required, performing these same magical rites coinciding with the events in the lunar and solar cycles can make them more meaningful, and therefore, more portentous and significant. I will introduce you to a pattern of Mystery workings for the lunar and solar cycle that allows for a significant combination of magic and liturgy that makes the moment of such a working powerful and significant. Yet, I also need to explain these Mysteries to give them a deeper context.

We will also discuss the Mysteries of working in an outdoor grove, which truly encapsulates the Mysteries of life and death writ large in nature. A grove is unlike any other kind of magical place for Witches to gather and within its domain penetrate the Mysteries of the earth. It is my intention to help Witches and Pagans understand that a grove cannot be used like an indoor temple and that there are some very different rules that apply to its successful use.

Finally, there is the Mystery of the Grand Sabbat, where the Goddess and God come to reside with their devotees for a short time as performed by their dutiful representatives, the priestess and priest, who shall embody them for the benefit of the assembled community. This is an auspicious gathering where the work of a priestess and priest to embody and fully personify a Goddess or God is rigorously tested, and most importantly, objectified by the community.

Witches are typically very focused on the moon and its monthly cycle of changes. We perform our basic liturgical rites based on the cycle of the moon, which are called *esbats*. Every full moon, or at some point convenient to that date, Witches gather together to celebrate the Mysteries of the Lunar Goddess.[29] They will commune with their Deity and also work magic in her name. However, every full moon is a unique occurrence because it happens at a variable time of the month, and it has a specific quality based on the solar season and the month in which it occurs.

Still, I once heard a Witch complain to her coven members that for every full moon, the planned esbat rite was practically the same and that the monthly full moon rites that this person's coven engaged in were boring and repetitious. When I heard this complaint, I was quite surprised. Obviously, this person and her coven didn't know very much about the moon. They also didn't know that each full moon that happens during the monthly calendric year is unique and has a large body of folklore to go along with it.

Many covens have taken the approach to customize their monthly lunar rites, taking into account that each event is unique and different. Some covens, though, probably haven't made that determination yet. Qualifying the full moon is an important step to unleashing the Mysteries of the moon. Otherwise, it would just be another gathering, like all of the rest, and soon lack any kind of meaning or significance.

The moon is probably the most important celestial body in the sky, next to the sun, and it's certainly the most interesting. Yet, hearing this complaint made me realize that the knowledge that

---

29 It is possible that a coven might have a Lunar God and the Solar Goddess, so this perspective of a Lunar Goddess should be taken as based on a traditional approach.

I had acquired about the moon and lunar magic was not equally shared by everyone within the Pagan and Wiccan community. So, for this reason, I decided that it would be prudent to assemble a chapter on the Lunar Mysteries and the art of moon magic for this book. If anyone is seeking to work magic that will affect their material aspirations, then knowing something about the moon is pretty important.

In fact, the most important consideration for any large series of workings involving earth-based magic is to harness the mysterious cycle of the moon and its mythology and folklore. In order to accomplish this task, the Witch is obliged to sift through a lot of moon lore, both scientific and astrological, in order to truly understand the significance and perspective of the moon in the art of celestial magic.

I will perform that task with you in this section and help you to examine all of the various elements required to become proficient at using the moon for both Pagan liturgies and forms of Lunar Mystery magic. There's certainly a lot of material that exists in many different sources, but I decided to pull together a selection of that specific lore that will help you make this mastery a lot easier. I would advise you to acquire some books on the various folklore and myths associated with the moon.[30] Having this knowledge at hand will certainly make your Wiccan full moon rites and practical lunar-based magic much more effective and esthetically pleasing. So, let's take a tour of the practical lunar lore that is available to us.

Folklore, Astrology, and Some Scientific Explanations

We live in an age where everything is seemingly explained away by the prowess of science, where there are no unfathomable Mysteries nor is anything capable of withstanding for long the inquiry of modern empirical minds. Everything is reduced to the objective eye of science, and yet still, the average person stands in awe of the constantly changing cycles of the moon. Science

---

30 I would recommend the book *The Moon in Astrology: The Ultimate Guide to Moon Magic, Lunar Phases, and What Your Zodiac Sign Says About You* by Mari Silva.

has debunked almost all of the myths about the moon, yet they persist in common discussion even amongst educated people. Therefore, it would seem that the moon still casts her spell on the minds of humanity, and the apparent Lunar Mysteries persist despite our scientific explanations and even our most adventurous explorations of her rocky crust.

There are good reasons why all the myths and folklore about the moon persist, and why they will probably continue to exert a powerful influence on the mind and soul of humanity until the end of time. As long as human beings live on this planet and experience the various phenomena of the moon, sun, planets, and stars, they will have a psychological impact on human sentiment. There is no escaping this fact. We are complex psychological beings, and merely the apprehension of facts alone does not rule our life nor dispel superstition or emotional sentiment. We also need to consider that science alone does not have a monopoly on objective truth and that dissenting opinions and the powerful influences of culture are just as compelling as the consensus of science and scientists.

The moon changes its shape throughout the month, seemingly never to appear àt the same place or in the same guise. As the moon transforms itself, the tides of the seas and oceans seem to obey its cyclic passages, and the darkness of night is turned into twilight, illuminating a spectral landscape. The basic nature of the Lunar Mystery is that the moon changes its shape and its brightness, seeming to follow an endless pattern of constant change. The moon appears during both the day and the night, but it's in the darkness of the night when the moon's effect is most dramatic. The moon is a symbol of transformation and seems to represent all that is changeable and ephemeral in our world, including the life cycle of all things living and breathing on this planet. This Mystery is the Mystery of light and darkness, life and death; the changing seasons, which are seen in the apparent movements of the Moon, Sun, and the Earth, and their complex interrelationship.

Science has explained all these phenomena in an undramatic manner, dispelling all of the myths and so-called false assumptions made about the effects of the Moon on the Earth. We should examine these facts because knowing what science has said about this topic does help to shape our opinions and clarify our magical beliefs. These facts will help us in our practice of celestial magic. Science has done a good job of defining the objective and material universe that is both within and all around us, and we would be mistaken to dismiss these cautiously tested and empirically determined facts.

However, science has nothing to say about the nature of the human soul, the nature of Spirit, and the internal perceptions and sentiments associated with the human psyche. In fact, science refuses to even examine a phenomenon unless it can be measured, and that measurement must be verified by repetition. Some might question the methods of measuring these phenomena and the theories that underlie them. These are topics that are outside of the supposed empirical universe, and therefore, are the topical areas most suited to the discourse of religious and magical philosophies.

Therefore, I will not state as a fact that the moon's gravitational effects or the effects of the light of the moon have any dramatic impact on individual human beings, animals, or small inanimate objects. What is affected by the moon is the human mind, its perceptions, sentiments, and inner spiritual reflections, and these, I will address in this chapter. Humanity has been staring into the night sky for untold millennia, and this fact alone has shaped human beliefs and opinions long before science was ever organized as an academic discipline.

We will focus on the folklore and psychological effects of the Moon, Sun, their apparent motion and alignments, and how these may be used to great effect in the practice of theurgy. Therefore, we need to look at a few items as we examine these interesting facts and their use in practical magic. Here is a list of four items for you to consider.

1. **Phases of the moon:** Four quarters, the eight phases of the lunation cycle. How these phases affect human psychology and universal folklore as well as assumed physiological effects. We should examine theurgy as it is associated with the lunar phases.

2. **Seasonal full moon folklore and astrological aspects of the full moon phenomenon:** Each full moon has its own qualities and special characteristics, and these qualify the magic that is performed.

3. **Solar and lunar interrelationships:** Eclipses, both solar and lunar, the cycle of light and darkness, life and death, as projected upon the wheel of the year. Also, we should consider the tidal cycles such as spring, neap, and proxigean spring tides.

4. **Lunar temple:** The key to integrating the lunar and solar cycles into one's magic is learning to incorporate a type of lunar temple. This temple is defined in theurgy as an energy field consisting of a vortex encompassed with a double gateway, where the Mysteries of the seasonal sun and lunar phase are declared and expressed as a kind of symbolic link.

These four items are important to consider when working with moon Mysteries and earth-based magic if our objective is causing material change. They also don't in any way violate the premises currently vogue in the scientific community, since they are concerned with a discipline that science has either nothing to say about or is incapable of making any kind of determination. First, we should examine some of the objective facts about the moon.

If the Moon did not exist, then the Sun would still cause some diminished cyclic tides. Tides are the gravitational effect on large bodies of water—oceans, seas, large lakes, rivers—even the atmosphere and crust of the Earth. (Large things are so affected, but not things that are relatively small.) The gravitational effect of tides is caused by a combination of the Sun, Moon, and Earth. This interrelationship also causes solar and lunar eclipses and the lunar phases of full through new.

The Moon's gravitational force is only one ten-millionth of the Earth's gravitational force, and the Sun's is only 40% of the Moon's force. Therefore, the Moon's gravitation effect has no discernable impact on animals or people. Lunar and planetary light is also insignificant since it is merely reflected light, whose origin is from the Sun. Sunlight, however, does indeed powerfully affect the Earth.

Some of the natural phenomenon associated with the periodic tides affecting large bodies of water has the following qualities:[31]

- The rotation of the Earth and the Moon's orbit causes two tidal peaks and troughs every twenty-five hours.
- Tidal peaks and troughs occur every twelve hours. These events register as only 1.6 feet in the deep ocean but increase at the shores. The effect of tides in bays and estuaries can be dramatic, such as the Bay of Fundy, tidal shifts can achieve 44.6 feet in either direction.
- The Moon's orbit around the rotating Earth produces a variable shift so that the time of high and low tides changes by fifty minutes each day.

Spring tides are exceptionally strong tides that occur when the Sun, Moon, and the Earth are in line, such as when the Moon appears to be full or new to those on the Earth. Neap tides occur when the Sun and Moon are at right angles to the Earth, canceling out their gravitational forces and producing a weaker variation of the high and low tides, such as when the Moon appears to be in either the first or last quarter.

Perigee points are defined as celestial events where the Moon is closest to the Earth, and the Earth is the closest to the Sun. These events occur, of course, during specific times of the year and specific seasons. Lunar perigee occurs twice a year, in late December through January and late June through July, depending on the northern or southern latitude. Solar perigee occurs once a year, also in late December. The lunar perigee is also called a *super moon* when it is closest to Earth and either full or new.

Every eighteen months, an unusually high tide occurs, and this is called a *Proxigean Spring Tide.* It occurs when the Moon is at its closest point to the Earth (called the *closest perigee* or *proxigee*) and during the new moon phase (meaning that the Moon is between the Earth and the Sun).

---

31 Vigdis Hocken, Konstantin Bikos, and Graham Jones, *What Causes Tides?* at TimeandDate, accessed December 31, 2021: https://www.timeanddate.com/astronomy/moon/tides.html

These are significant events in the astrological calendar of the practicing Witch. There are biannual (lunar), annual (solar), and semiannual cycles (lunar and solar) that affect the tides of the oceans on the Earth, and by analogy, the fortunes of individual human beings. This is, of course, a very important point.

Lunar effects on human behavior, also called the *Transylvania effect*, have been pretty conclusively demonstrated to be false.[32] This was done through an effective analysis of whether the full or new moon has any effects on any specific behavior, maladies, or social phenomena, such as alcoholism, mental attacks, menstruation, violence, murder rates, and even stock market variations. All of these correlations have been found to be statistically insignificant. What does seem to be operating are people's beliefs, cultural myths, folklore, and emotional sentiments. Science would judge such causes as not being statistically relevant, but they do seem to impact behavior in an almost predictable fashion.

Phases of the Moon and the Lunation Cycle

Lunar cycles that mark the changing phases of the moon occur over a period of twenty-eight days. There are also lunar cycles that make up the solar year, representing the oscillation of light and darkness, diminishment and increase, which change the apparent shape of the moon and also the times when it is present in the sky. The Moon also changes its shape as it makes its passage across the celestial equator, and this is due to the constantly changing angular relationships between the Sun, the Moon, and the Earth. The Moon travels swiftly through the zodiacal signs, averaging around fourteen degrees in a twenty-four-hour period.

The Moon passes through the entire zodiac in a single month and its synodic period lasts twenty-nine days and twelve hours, which is pretty close to the thirty-day average period for a calendric month. The synodic period is the time that occurs between the apparent conjunction of the Moon and Sun, which is the period of the new moon. It is the period from the new moon to the next new

---

32 Kate Golembiewski, *Why do we still believe in "lunacy" during a Full Moon?* at Astronomy, accessed December 31, 2021: https://astronomy.com/news/2019/08/why-do-we-still-believe-in-lunacy-during-a-full-moon

moon. The sidereal period of the Moon is twenty-seven days, seven hours, and forty-three minutes. What this means is that the Moon makes a complete revolution during that period of time.[33]

When we say that the Moon makes its cycle in twenty-eight days, that is an average approximation of the synodic and sidereal periods. The difference between the sidereal and synodic periods is that the period of the new moon is always progressing slightly when compared to the period of its revolution. Keep in mind that the Moon always shows the same face to the Earth as it rotates and orbits around the Earth.

A full moon occurs when the Moon is at a point opposite of the Sun in relation to the Earth. Therefore, a full moon always occupies the exact point opposite of the Sun within the astrological zodiac. A new moon occurs when the Moon is conjunct with the Sun in relation to the Earth. Therefore, the Moon is in the same zodiacal sign and degree as the Sun when it is in the phase called the *new moon*.

A new moon symbolically represents the time of renewal and reinvigoration, when seeds are planted and ovulation archetypally occurs. The full moon represents when these processes reach their maximum potential, and it is the idealized time for harvesting. The quarter phases are where the Moon is waxing from new to full, or waning from full to new, representing when the Sun and Moon are at right angles to the Earth.

The Moon rises in the middle of the day when it is waxing and in the middle of the night when it's waning. The direction that the horns or tips of the crescent moon are facing indicates whether the Moon is waxing or waning. Horns pointing to the east indicate a waxing moon and horns pointing to the west indicate a waning moon.

The full eight-node cycle of the moon is called the *lunation cycle*. It's symbolized on a personal level as the struggle for conscious evolution, beginning first with awakening into individual self-consciousness and egoic awareness. The Moon also has two qualities that are expressed by the lunation cycle. These two qualities are the zodiacal positions that it occupies as it moves across the celestial equator in a single month and the four lunar phases that it makes as it crosses the path of the Sun and the Earth.

---

33 Vigdis Hocken, *The Lunar Month* at TimeandDate, accessed December 31, 2021: https://www.timeanddate.com/astronomy/moon/lunar-month.html

The elemental quality that the four phases of the moon are:

- **New Moon**—Earth
- **First Quarter**—Air
- **Full Moon**—Fire
- **Last Quarter**—Water

Four phases of the moon are defined in astrology as the specific angular relationships that occur between the Moon and the Sun. These angular relationships are broken into ninety-degree quadrants. The qualities of the phases are symbolized by the aspects of *conjunction, ascending square, opposition, descending square,* and arriving again at *conjunction.*

- **New Moon to First Quarter (0–90 degrees)**—Individualism and impulsiveness
- **First Quarter to Full Moon (91–180 degrees)**—Maturation and fulfillment
- **Full Moon to Last Quarter (181–270 degrees)**—Formulation and objectification
- **Last Quarter to New Moon (271–360 degrees)**—Fruition and dissolution

The lunation cycle uses forty-five-degree angles of the phases of the moon to produce eight divisional segments that track the Moon as it moves from new to full and back to new. Each of these segment periods lasts for three and a half days or eighty-four hours. Each has a use and a focus for working a specific kind of magic or celebrating a Lunar Mystery. What this means is that a Lunar Mystery can be celebrated for any of the eight segments of the lunation cycle and not just at the full moon.

In addition to the basic four phases of the lunar cycle, there are two states of gibbous (swelling) moons and balsamic (healing) moons. There is the gibbous waxing and waning moon that occurs before and after the full moon, and there is a balsamic waning and waxing moon that occurs before and after the new moon, and each has its own meaning and significance.

I have already discussed this process in detail in my other three *For Witches* books, so I don't believe that I need to restate it here, except to succinctly describe it.[34] Yet I feel that reproducing the table of the lunation type would be helpful to identify the quality of these divisional segments.

Here is the table of the eight phases of the lunation cycle.[35]

Lunation Type	Interval Degrees	Key Word	Description
New Moon	0–45	Emergence	Subjective, impulsive, novelty
Crescent	45–90	Expansion	Self-assertion, self-confidence
First Quarter	90–135	Action	Crisis in action, strong-willed
Gibbous Moon	135–180	Overcoming	Clarification, revelation, illumination
Full Moon	180–225	Fulfillment	Objectivity, formulation, manifestation
Dissemi-nating	225–270	Demonstration	Disseminator of ideas, populist, teacher
Last Quarter	270–315	Re-orientation	Crisis in conscious-ness, inflexibility
Balsamic	315–360	Release	Transition, seed-state, germination

---

34 Frater Barrabbas, *Spirit Conjuring for Witches, Talismanic Magic for Witches,* and *Elemental Powers for Witches.*

35 Dane Rudhyar, *The Lunation Cycle: A Key to the Understanding of Personality,* pp. 50–56. I have used the text to distill the entries in this table.

Each of these eight segments has an element of the Lunar Mystery contained within it, and in addition to working magic during these periods, I invite you to engage in these Mysteries to fully realize their qualities through experimenting with a Lunar Mystery rite that would be a part of this work.

Moon in the Twelve Zodiacal Signs and Full Moon Lore

As previously stated, the full moon always occurs in the zodiacal sign opposite the Sun. It has specific astrological qualities since the full moon represents a certain degree of fruition for spiritual and magical activities. The zodiacal sign that the full moon occupies is therefore quite significant since it specifically qualifies it. There is also specific folklore that is associated with the seasonal full moon occurring during a month. This folklore is often used to qualify any full moon working, whether liturgical or magical.

First, we should examine the different qualities of the moon in the twelve signs, so we can examine the qualities of those twelve occurrences in greater detail. The moon signifies emotional energies and internal states of consciousness, and as it passes through the twelve signs, these psychological qualities change according to the attributes of the astrological sign.[36]

1. **Moon in Aries:** Boundless enthusiasm, assertive, emotional outbursts, highly energized, individualistic, impulsive, to live for the moment.
2. **Moon in Taurus:** Easy going, placid, devoted friend and lover, simple and basic needs, emotionally centered and earthy, possessive, love of material things and luxuries, believes happiness can be bought, resistant to change.
3. **Moon in Gemini:** Gregariousness, sociable, good communicator, restless, always seeking new stimulations, important to be unfettered or uncommitted, curious about everything.

---

36 Skye Alexander, *Planets in Signs*, pp. 71–96. I have distilled these definitions to their essential qualities for this list.

4. **Moon in Cancer:** Sensitive feelings, changeableness, emotionally expressive, heart rules head, strong empathy, maternal instincts, nurturing, protective of family and friends.

5. **Moon in Leo:** Self-confident, optimistic, cheerful, natural leader, always seeking attention, self-centered, love of drama, creativity, strong-willed.

6. **Moon in Virgo:** Emotionally subdued, internalized, outwardly aloof, tight self-control, overly critical, self-deprecating, helpful to others, service, selfless, concerned about the welfare of others.

7. **Moon in Libra:** Emotional balance, need for harmonious interactions, displaced emotional expressions, sense of propriety, social tact and social awareness, compromising, indecisive, artistic, musical.

8. **Moon in Scorpio:** Emotionally passionate, secretive, intensely sexual, seeks total union, jealous and possessive, can be vindictive, ruthless.

9. **Moon in Sagittarius:** Happy-go-lucky, optimistic, witty, affable, very sociable, loose emotional ties, importance of friendship, needs to be free, disdainful of smothering and restrictive relationships.

10. **Moon in Capricorn:** Emotionally internalized, unexpressive, deeply serious and sober, depressing, devalues self, fear of rejection, loyal, devoted to friends, family, and lovers, reliable, practical, responsible.

11. **Moon in Aquarius:** Unpredictable, explosive, sudden outbursts, a strong sense of social justice, passionate about causes, rebellious, stubborn, willful, anti-authority, bohemian, radical, visionary.

12. **Moon in Pisces:** Deep and intense emotions, secretive, introverted, psychic, empathic, compassionate, vivid imagination, reclusive, shy, seeks refuge, desires to be alone.

The Moon acquires qualities depending on the sign that it is in as well as the sign that the Sun is occupying. Since the Sun changes its sign around the twentieth of each month, the full moon will occur in the opposite sign. For each monthly full moon and its lore, we have two possible qualities for that full moon, depending on when in the month it occurs. Here is a list of three items to examine and research when planning on any working that would incorporate the moon:

- When seeking to qualify the full moon, combine the astrological qualities with the seasonal full moon folklore.
- Check almanacs and other sources of folklore to qualify the full moon for a given month.
- Build up a booklet of seasonal full moon lore and astrological considerations (Moon in Twelve Signs) to use for liturgical rites and magic.

Here's an example of what you might assemble as information for the full moon in the month of June. I have provided my own definitions for the traditional full moon for the month of June.

June—Strawberry Moon or Mead/Honey Moon

After the abundant flowers of the previous month (May) have bloomed and passed away, then the fruits begin to form, and strawberries are some of the first fruits to be harvested. Flowers also bring the bees which gather the pollen and produce honey, and from that is brewed the beverage called *mead*. June is also the time of the Summer Solstice, the advent of the warm days of summer, and the planting of the rest of the crops in the more northern and less temperate lands. This month is partitioned by Gemini and Cancer.

1. **New Moon in Gemini:** Time for planning gatherings and celebrations
2. **New Moon in Cancer:** Protection against harm, nurturing, and aiding growth
3. **Full Moon in Sagittarius:** Happiness, fulfillment of pleasure, new liaisons
4. **Full Moon in Capricorn:** Material gain through hard work and organization

I assembled most of my full moon lore from, of all places, the *Farmer's Almanac.*[37] You can find that source on an online webpage. There are also lots of other sources for lunar folklore as well since most Pagan publishers will have a book or two on lunar folklore.

Important Solar and Lunar Interrelationships

Solar and lunar eclipses are the most auspicious times for working any kind of magic. If magical workings can be performed during that event, then they will be greatly enhanced and empowered by the Sun and the Moon.

Eclipses of the Sun and Moon occur when the Sun, Moon, and Earth are in a specific and proper alignment. Not only are they auspicious but are typically rare occurrences. This is especially true for solar eclipses, but not as much for lunar eclipses.

Solar eclipses occur when the Moon is new since it is then that the Moon is conjunct with the Sun. If the altitude of the Moon to the ecliptic (celestial equator as seen from the Earth) matches so that the Moon appears to cover the Sun, then an observable eclipse will occur somewhere on the Earth. Solar eclipses, on average, last only around eight minutes if they are total eclipses, less so when they are partial eclipses.

Lunar eclipses always occur when the Moon is full, and the Earth's shadow falls upon the Moon. They are more common than solar eclipses because the Earth's shadow is much larger than the Moon's shadow on the Earth. A partial or nearly complete lunar eclipse is called a *blood moon* because of its red color. Depending on zodiacal signs, the lunar phase, and lunation type, this event could be very auspicious for working magic.

The Moon's altitude is the height at which it appears over the horizon. In the northern latitudes, the Moon is low when it's near the southern part of the horizon, and high up when it's near the center of the sky. (Of course, the reverse would occur when one is located in the southern latitudes.) When the Moon appears to be moving from

---

37 Farmer's Almanac Editors, *Full Moon Calendar* at Farmer's Almanac, accessed December 31, 2021: https://www.farmersalmanac.com/full-moon-dates-and-times.

the Southern to the Northern Hemisphere, it is called the *ascending node,* and when it appears to be moving from the Northern to the Southern Hemisphere, it is called the *descending node.*

Points of intersection between the ecliptic and the Moon's altitude are the points where an eclipse can potentially occur. The inclination of the Moon towards the ecliptic is approximately five degrees and eight minutes, so events when the Moon's shadow would pass over the face of the Earth are rare because they require an exact match between lunar altitude and the ecliptic.

To determine where the Moon will appear in the sky during certain lunar phases and seasons is found in the following table. The higher the northern latitude, the more pronounced the position of the Moon during a lunar phase.

1. **Spring:** The Moon is high in the sky when in the first quarter and down low when in the last quarter.
2. **Summer:** The Moon is high in the sky during the new moon and down low when full.
3. **Autumn:** The Moon is high in the sky when in the last quarter and down low when in the first quarter.
4. **Winter:** The Moon is high in the sky during the full moon and down low when new.

Of course, this is true only when the observer is in the Northern Hemisphere, and it would be the opposite if one were in the Southern Hemisphere.

As far as the northern latitudes are concerned, the most auspicious full moon is during the winter, and the most auspicious new moon and waxing moon phase is during the summer. During the spring, the full moon is part of the ascending node, and during autumn, the full moon is part of the descending node. These two facts also have an impact on the magic, giving a greater impetus or slightly detracting from the magic that is worked during these two seasons respectively. An ascending moon is auspicious and a descending moon is somewhat inauspicious.

Additionally, in the northern latitudes, a solar eclipse is most likely to occur during the summer when the new moon is in alignment with the ecliptic, and a lunar eclipse is more likely to occur in the winter. This is important to consider when seeking to incorporate either a solar or lunar eclipse into one's magical working.

The Moon plays a very important part in determining whether a magical working is auspicious and also when a working should be performed. Because the Moon moves so quickly in the sky, passing through the entire zodiac in a month, it also produces the largest share of transit aspects with the other planets.

These are all of the relevant facts about the Moon that you would need to consider when seeking to build a Lunar Mystery rite that can encapsulate all of the phenomena of the Moon and use it to harness some very specific kind of magical operations. What we need to consider next is assembling this information and presenting a ritual working that would combine both the liturgical and magical workings into a single rite.

CHAPTER FOURTEEN

LUNAR MYSTERY RITE REVEALED

"There are nights when the wolves are silent
and only the moon howls."
—GEORGE CARLIN

This Lunar Mystery rite uses ritual components covered in the *For Witches* books *Spirit Conjuring* and *Elemental Powers*. However, we will be repeating them here so that the explanation for this rite is complete. This rite can be performed by a group or an individual. If a group performs this rite, then there should be an Officiant of the Lunar Mysteries chosen for this work. Additionally, there should be someone who is going to perform a godhead assumption and light trance state (level two) to channel the Lunar Goddess or God. If a single individual performs this rite, then that person must assume all of the roles in this working, including the godhead assumption and a mild trance state. Widdershins is the cyclic direction of this working, to symbolize the qualities of the moon.

This Mystery rite uses a combination of the rose-ankh vortex (set to the four watchtowers), a simple pyramid energy vortex (set to the four angles), and a western gateway portal rite to establish the energized field for the Mystery.[38] Within the western gateway underworld, a sacred circular perimeter is established and the Mystery concept is presented to establish the foundation of the Mystery. The Mystery itself consists of the lunar phase and the lunation cycle

---

38 Frater Barrabbas, *Spirit Conjuring for Witches*, pp. 62–66—Reference this title for a complete analysis of the rose-ankh vortex, how it is performed, and what it does.

stage. The zodiacal sign in which the moon occurs during the performance of this Mystery rite is also important and would qualify all of the meditations and considerations about the moon. All of these qualities are meditated upon while the Officiant circumambulates the circle, traveling widdershins for a period of time, making many revolutions of the inner perimeter, and reciting from memory the basic elements of the Mystery rite.

Setting the rose-ankh vortex is a simple affair without any qualifications or verbiage. The Officiant may decide to verbalize a concept to each point of the circle, or they may be silent and focused on the work. The rose-ankh rite should be a basic staple in the coven's or individual's repertoire of rituals.

The pyramid vortex is set with invoking pentagrams of the element associated with the moon phase to the four angles. Invoking pentagrams are drawn at the four angles, starting with the northwest angle and proceeding widdershins around the circle. An invoking pentagram of spirit receptive is set to the center zenith point of the circle, then the four angle devices and drawn to the center apex and then to each other (to form a square on the circle base). At each angle, the Officiant should invoke one of the four Goddesses representing the Maiden, Lover, Mother, and Crone as discussed in Part Two, Chapter Seven. These four Goddesses should represent the aspects of Deity as associated with the pantheon of the group or individual.[39] The center apex should represent the Great Goddess in whatever form the coven or individual recognizes her.

A western gateway is set using some simple representations of the guide, guardian, and the ordeal associated with the Mystery. I will present an example of how they might be qualified, but they will be determined and qualified based on the pantheon associated with the group or the individual. These entities are the same for all of the Lunar Mysteries, but they are no less important to the overall process of the rite.

The climax of this rite is the godhead assumption of a lunar Deity (of any gender), the blessing of lunar sacraments such as milk or cream, cheese, rice cakes, plain yogurt, and communion with the Moon Deity. No moon pies, please, though that might

---

39 I am using some stock Celtic Goddesses in my example. They are not the actual Goddesses that I use in my own personal version of this rite.

have humorously passed through your mind. Then, the Officiant expresses a magical wish or desire (this could be a custom sigil on a consecrated parchment) and projects it into the element energy pyramid. This is followed by the exteriorization of that energy, the thanksgiving and departure of the Moon Deity, and then ascent through the eastern gateway portal and the sealing of the vortex.

As you can see, this is not a complex ritual, but it is quite effective in presenting and engaging with the Mystery of the Moon, communing with a Moon Deity, and setting a charged pyramid vortex into the mundane sphere imprinted with a desire. The element chosen for the element pyramid vortex is based on the phase in which the moon is appearing, and these have been covered in the previous chapter.

The nature of the desire, determined by the group or an individual, should be a single and simplified thing, expressed in the graphic representation of a custom sigil drawn on parchment and consecrated beforehand. The parchment sigil is then left on the altar until the next phase of the moon occurs when it will be burned in a Cauldron to release it.

The Lunar Mystery rite has the following sections, as above:

1. Rose-ankh vortex is set
2. Pyramid Energy vortex is constructed
3. Western gateway portal is opened
4. Inner circle perimeter is set
5. Mystery presentation and meditation
6. Lunar Deity godhead assumption
7. Sacramental Communion
8. Imprinting the pyramid energy field
9. Exteriorization of the pyramid energy field
10. Thanksgiving and departure
11. Ascension and eastern gateway portal is opened
12. Vortex sealing

I can now proceed to present to you the actual Mystery rite as outlined above. This ritual is performed within a regularly consecrated magic circle. The Officiant and attendees are properly prepared, and the temple is ready for the working. A consecrated sigil is placed on the altar to be used in the working.

Lunar Mystery Rite

1. Setting the Rose-Ankh Vortex

The Officiant takes up the wand from the altar and proceeds to the northern watchtower, where they draw above the watchtower light a rose-ankh device and visualize it being filled with violet-colored energy, and then draw an invoking spiral around it.

They then proceed to the western watchtower and perform the same actions, drawing a violet-colored rose-ankh device and activating it with an invoking spiral.

They proceed to the southern watchtower and perform the same actions as previously.

They proceed to the eastern watchtower and perform the same actions as previously.

They proceed to the center of the circle and draw a rose-ankh device in the nadir, projecting a violet energy down into it and activating it with an invoking spiral.

The Officiant deposits the wand on the altar and takes up the sword. They then proceed to the northern watchtower and take the sword and draw a line of force from the rose-ankh device drawn there to the rose-ankh device in the central nadir of the circle.

They then proceed to the western watchtower and perform the same action.

They proceed to the southern watchtower and perform the same action.

They proceed to the eastern watchtower and perform the same action.

They then return the sword to the altar and proceed to the northern watchtower. They will face the west with their hand projecting the forces before them and will walk around the circle three times, proceeding in a spiral transit until they reach the center of the circle. They will then project the energy into the nadir below the floor of the temple. The vortex is now completed.

2. Pyramid Energy Vortex—Mystery of Women's Lifecycle

The Officiant then takes up the wand from the altar and proceeds to the northwest angle of the magic circle and stands before it. They will draw an invoking pentagram of the lunar phase element with the wand and seal it with an invoking spiral to the angle. The Officiant then holds the wand and points to the pentagram device and says:

"I invoke you, O Cerridwen, Mistress of Magic and great wise woman, to come and appear in this sacred angle."

Then the Officiant proceeds to the southwest angle and draws the invoking pentagram with the wand. They will then summon the Goddess, saying:

"I invoke you, Danu, Great Mother and nurturer of all living things, to come and appear in this sacred angle."

They proceed to the southeast angle and perform the same action as previously. They say:

"I invoke you, Aine, alluring divine seductress and sovereign mistress, to come and appear in this sacred angle."

They proceed to the northeastern angle and perform the same actions as previously. They say:

"I invoke you, Arianrhod, strong and unyielding, virginal maiden, to come and appear in this sacred angle."

They proceed to the center of the circle to the zenith and perform the same actions except drawing an invoking pentagram of receptive spirit. They hold the wand, pointing to the zenith, and say:

"I invoke you, Cliodna, Triple Goddess, divine singer of the universal creation song, queen of the sidheog (faerie), and great healer, to come and appear in this temple apex."

The Officiant bows then proceeds to the northwest angle and draws a line of force with the wand from the empowered pentagram and godhead to the central zenith of the circle. They proceed to the southwest angle and perform the same action. They proceed to the southeast, perform the same action, and the northeast where they perform the same action. Then they proceed again to the northwest angle and with the wand, draw a line of power from that point to the southwest, then to the southeast, then to the northeast, and completing the line of force in the northwest.

The Officiant proceeds to the northwest angle and then begins to walk in a deosil spiral from that point in the outer circle to the center of the circle, making three rounds of the northwest angle before completing the circuit. They use the wand to project the energy before them, facing forward until they reach the center of the circle where they project the power into the zenith. The pyramid vortex is now complete.

3. Opening the Western Gateway of the Mysteries

The Officiant returns the wand to the altar and proceeds to stand in the eastern watchtower facing the west.

They draw an invoking spiral to the southeastern angle and say:

"Behind me is the guide who assists me to open the Mysteries of the Moon, and to reveal the secret powers of light and darkness."

They draw an invoking spiral to the northeastern angle and say:

"In front of me stands the guardian, who will test and judge my insights and wisdom to witness the Mysteries of the Moon and will allow me to pass only if I prove myself worthy."

They draw an invoking spiral to the western watchtower and say:

"Before is the ordeal, where I am reduced, transformed, and reborn by the secret knowledge of the Mysteries of the Moon. I must be willing to surrender myself to the greater power and wisdom of the Lunar God/Goddess."

Then the Officiant slowly advances from the eastern watchtower to the western watchtower, stands before it, and makes the sign of the opening threshold portal (like parting a curtain). Next, they will advance a step into the imaginary veil, turn, and raise their arms to receive the light of the west, pouring down upon their head and body. They then advance forward to the center of the circle, imagining themself descending into an underworld grotto. The gateway passage is completed.

4. Lunar Mystery Presentation

The Officiant goes to the altar and takes their sword. They will then proceed to the northwestern angle and trace a circle proceeding in a widdershins circuit, making a full circle and returning to the northwestern angle. They then proceed to the altar, return the sword, and pick up the staff. They will then proceed to the center of the circle to begin the Mystery presentation.

They will stand in the center of the circle and say the following invocation to the Moon Goddess. If there are others in attendance, they stand around the periphery of the inner magic circle of the Mysteries to listen to the Officiant calling the Goddess of the Moon. Of course, the name of the Moon Goddess or God would depend on the pantheon of the group or individual.

"I summon forth the brilliant nocturnal light of Rhiannon, O Great Goddess of the Moon, to listen to your Mysteries in awe and wonder, and deeply plumb the depths of your spectral magic. Lady of the Sidhe, who rides the mare of the moon through the fields and is never caught, whose love, wealth, and bounty make her the Queen of the Fey, and whose magic spans the wide reaches of earth and sky, come to me who seeks your wisdom and magic. I am your hands and feet, and I am your eyes and heart. Come forth into me!"

Then the Officiant proceeds to walk around the middle part of the inner circle slowly while reciting the Moon Mystery for the particular phase of the moon, over and over again until they come to the end, as sensed by them at the moment. (These recitations are examples of what might be written.)

The Officiant starts this action by saying:

"I begin this rite in the lunar phase of [new/first quarter/full/last quarter] in the lunation stage of [name of lunation stage] in the sign of [zodiacal sign], and I sing my song of the Mystery of the Moon, so listen, learn, and master the hidden knowledge."

The Officiant begins their circumambulation while reciting their poetic Mystery as many times over as deemed sufficient while walking the circuit. The Officiant and the attendees should also internally focus on the quality of the moon as determined by the phase, lunation stage, and zodiacal sign.

New Moon:

"We summon the White Lady of regeneration and preparation.
For the dark moon is a time of planning and divining,
of planting new seeds, of learning, and seeking reparation."

First Quarter:

"We summon the Scarlet Lady of passion and flight.
For the waxing moon is a time of action, the enacted designs
that will grow to fruition with the waxing lunar light."

Full Moon:

"We summon the Blue Lady of exaltation and reflection.
For the full moon is the time of completion and fruition—
the matter has come to its ultimate manifestation."

Last Quarter:

"We summon the Black Lady of Death and Dissolution.
For the waning moon is the time of release; the work in completion
Shall bear witness to the ultimate unknowable decision."

When the Officiant has completed their circumambulations, they have returned once again to the center of the circle where they will stand with their staff in the silence of the moment, meditating on the Mystery of the Moon. Then, when this moment has passed, they will stamp their staff four times and say:

"The Mystery is revealed, and now comes the God/Goddess of the Moon."

The Officiant proceeds to the altar and returns the staff.

5. Lunar Godhead Assumption and Communion

If the Officiant is the only attendee, then they will be the one to perform the godhead assumption of the chosen lunar Deity as the Medium, otherwise, a selected Medium from the group will take the part. If a group is performing this rite, then the Officiant will stand slightly off to the north of the Medium in the center of the circle. The group will array themselves around the periphery of the circle.

A chair is placed in the center of the circle for the Medium, facing west, and a small, foldable table is also situated nearby, with the sacraments, a cup, bowl, spoon, and plate placed on it. The consecrated sigil is also placed on the table for later use. The Medium stands in front of the chair, facing the west, and performs the following actions to assume the godhead of the chosen lunar Goddess or God. The Medium is anointed and specially garbed to perform this godhead assumption. The prayers and invocation have been previously written and memorized, allowing for a degree of spontaneity.

1. The Medium bows deeply and then holds their arms up in the pose of offering and says a prayer to the target Deity.
2. The Medium performs the ascending wave, visualizing energy traveling up their body from their feet to their head and beyond.
3. They intone the invocation to the target Deity and then stand in silence for a short time.

4. The Medium performs the descending wave, visualizing the energy traveling from above their head down through their body to their feet.

5. They make the sign of the equal-arm cross on their body with their hand, touching the right shoulder, left shoulder, forehead, and groin, then folding their hands before their heart while imagining a cross of glowing energy on their body. They pause a short time to absorb the effect and feel the energy coursing along their body.

6. The medium then draws a triangle gateway centered on their heart, touching the points of the right shoulder, left shoulder, groin, and heart. They raise their arms in supplication, drawing the target Deity into their heart, and feel it enter into them. They embrace their body and bow their head, linking their consciousness with the godhead.

7. They perform the ascending wave, visualizing energy traveling up their body from their feet to their head and beyond. They then carefully seat themself on the chair and allow the trance state to deepen, to achieve a level two embodiment.

After a short time, the Medium will regain a level of functional consciousness and through the power of the godhead in their mind and body, they will address the group and acknowledge their godhead assumption, or if working alone, will affirm to themself the acknowledgment of the Goddess or God. Then, the Medium will stand and go to the table with the sacraments and make the sign of the ankh upon them, touch them with their hands where appropriate, and bow down to blow their breath upon them. They then will say:

"I bless, charge, and empower these sacraments of the Moon, in the name of X, whose guise I have assumed."

The Medium will also take up the consecrated sigil in their hands, make the sign of the ankh upon it, and then blow their breath upon it. They will then set it back down on the folding table. They will look to the zenith of the circle and make the sign of the ankh, saying:

"I bless this pyramid of power in the name of X so that it might manifest the secret desire of this gathering in the light and darkness of the Moon."

The sacraments, sigil, and energy pyramid are now consecrated, and the sacraments may be shared with the group, or left for the Medium to partake in later if they are working alone.

6. Exteriorization of the Charge and Departure

The Medium stands, facing the west, while the Officiant performs the exteriorization. If there is only one attendee, then the Medium assumes the role of Officiant while still lightly embodied.

The Officiant proceeds to the altar to take up the staff with their left hand, walks to the folding table in the center of the circle, and takes up the blessed and consecrated parchment sigil with their right hand. Standing in the center of the circle, they then say the following:

"In the name of the God/Goddess X, I take this desire that we have designed and walk the pathway of manifestation so that the divine powers blessed and charged herein may work to make this desire truly realized!"

The Officiant then turns to face the northwestern angle and then begins to walk a widdershins spiral around the circle with ever-widening arcs until they have made three circuits of the northwestern angle and arrive at the outer perimeter of the circle. They will imagine pushing the energy of the circle as they walk the spiral, and that the forces arrayed there become ever more resistant as the Officiant proceeds.

Once the Officiant has arrived at the northwestern angle for the third and final time, they will take the staff in their left hand, place the right with the sigil on it so that the sigil is pressed onto the staff, and extend it out towards the angle. The Officiant will exhale loudly as they imagine all of the energy being projected out of the vortex circle and rippling in waves of force into the material world beyond. They will then return the staff next to their body, still holding the sigil against it, and make three taps with the base of the staff.

The Officiant then proceeds to the altar where they placed the sigil on the altar and return the staff to its proper place. They then proceed to the center of the circle. If they are the only attendee, they will sit in the chair as the Medium and briefly meditate, otherwise, they will return and stand before the Medium who will sit again on the chair and meditate for a short time.

The Medium will then release the conscious connection with the target Deity and say the following departing words and thanksgiving.

"O God/Goddess X, we thank you for your appearance, your gifts, and your assistance in our magical work. We bid you farewell, love, and deep respect, and hope to call on you again to commune with us, your secret children."

They will then make the sign of the ankh before the west three times and the assumption is completed. Then they make the sign of the closing threshold portal (like closing a curtain) before the west and bow.

The Officiant and the group (if there are attendees), remove the chair from the center of the circle and take the folding table and place it next to the altar. If the Officiant has performed this rite alone, then they will partake of the sacrament to help them ground and fortify them for the next stage of the rite.

7. Opening the Eastern Gateway of the Mysteries

The Officiant proceeds to stand in the western watchtower facing the east.

They draw an invoking spiral to the northwestern angle and say:

"Behind me is the guide who assists me to close the Mysteries of the Moon and to reveal the secret pathway of light and ascension."

They draw an invoking spiral to the southwestern angle and say:

"In front of me stands the guardian, who will bar my passage into the light and seek to keep the secret knowledge in the realm of the Mysteries

of the Moon and will allow me to pass only if I am steadfast and clear in my intentions."

They draw an invoking spiral to the eastern watchtower and say:

"Before is the ordeal, where I am reborn, invested with knowledge, and able to transmit the secret knowledge of the Mysteries of the Moon. I must be willing to act as the mediator for the greater power and wisdom of the Lunar God/Goddess."

Then, the Officiant slowly advances from the western watch-tower to the eastern watchtower, stands before it, and makes the sign of the opening threshold portal (like parting a curtain). They then advance a step into the imaginary veil, turn, and raise their arms to receive the brilliant light of the east pouring down upon their head and body. They then advance to the center of the circle, imagining themself ascending into the world garden. The gateway passage is completed, and the rite is ended.

CHAPTER FIFTEEN

SOLAR MYSTERY RITES
AND SUN MAGIC

"She turned to the sunlight
And shook her yellow head,
And whispered to her neighbor:
'Winter is dead.'"
—A.A. MILNE

The Sun is one of the more important celestial bodies since the Earth's orbit and its rotation around the Sun define the period of light that we call the day and the changing of the seasons that occur in the course of the year. The apparent motion of the Sun is steady and consistent, and it is only the weather that can diminish or occlude its illumination. This is unlike the Moon, which moves quickly across the sky and appears in different forms and at different times of the day and night. The Sun was an obvious object of worship from the earliest times, and people venerated it because it appeared to give life and light to the world. The Sun opposed the darkness of the night and gave visual clarity to the world of daytime.

Witches who are practicing an earth-based religion will celebrate the Sun and its daily and yearly passage, including associating it with a God named Lugh, Helios, Apollo, Shamash, Ra, or even Lucifer. It can also be personified by a Goddess, such as Hathor, Bast, Sekhmet, Brigid, Olwen, Sunna, or Alectrona. The Sun and Moon are objectified place markers for the Deities of the Witchcraft religion, as is the Horned God of Life and Death. Since Wicca has formed a kind of consensus that there is a Goddess and a God, then it would seem that the Sun and the Horned Hunter take turns acting in that role, unless polytheism is adopted to allow all variations.

A simpler approach would be to admit that there is a real polytheism operating in Wicca and that Witches can deify all the elements of terrestrial existence and worship them in a pluralistic manner. That is the path that I have forged over the years, and I think that it works best with a more nuanced understanding of the nature of Deity. That makes the Sun and Moon into Deities, but it also deifies the rest of the planets, stars, and constellations, as well as the various geographic features of the locale of the covenstead.

The Mysteries of the Sun have already been covered previously, being presented within the diurnal cycle of day and night and the four basic seasons that occur throughout the year. The combination of weather, monsoons, floods, and inundations along with the waxing and waning heat and light of the Sun produce the ever-changing seasons.

Those of us who inhabit the northern latitudes of the Earth experience four seasons, but different cultures in different locations see a different kind of seasonal pattern. Those who live either at the equator or in the southern latitudes experience a particularly different seasonal pattern—from no differences except wet and dry periods or the reverse seasonal occurrences during the same monthly period. In the southern latitudes, the Winter Solstice occurs in June, and the Summer Solstice occurs in December.

I have simplified this discussion by taking the perspective of the northern latitudes with its four basic seasons. Other students who live in other locations can still apply this perspective with some differences and come up with a similar pattern that would somewhat resemble the four seasons.

Still, the cycle of day and night and the passage of the annual seasonal cycle of the year represent the basic elements of the magic of the Sun. How this affects theurgy is that the time of day or night, the month, and the season of the year, including the local weather, represent the characteristics that will determine the quality of the sacramental magic.

Eight Solar Celebrations and the Wheel of the Year

Modern earth-based religions celebrate seasonal changes with gatherings, feasts, music and dancing, and ceremonies and rites that depict the mythological characteristics of the season. These celebrations are the age-old and venerable solstices and equinoxes that have been part of the liturgical calendars of many people since before recorded history. Certainly, our Neolithic ancestors celebrated the Winter and Summer Solstice since they built megalithic monuments to measure and exactly determine those events. The celebrations of the Vernal and Autumnal Equinoxes were added to the astral-religious festivities later in the Bronze Age, and these seasonal celebrations varied depending on the regional seasonal cycle.

The Celts had their own calendar of four seasons, but the Greek city-state of Athens had a more complex calendar. Agriculture was key to these calendars, but so were the temperate climate and the local conditions. Egypt celebrated the annual flood of the Nile River sometime between June and September when Sirius rose above the horizon. For ancient Athens, the time of spring planting coincided with the rising of the Pleiades star group, where the spring and autumn seasons were short, and the summer and winter seasons were much longer.

Somewhere along the relentless passage of time, many other festivals, feast days, and celebrations were accumulated. Christianity had a habit of accumulating Pagan feasts and turning them into ones dedicated to Christian Saints—or so we were told. It was probably in this manner that four more calendric events were added to eventually become the eight sabbats of Witchcraft. There is some argument about whether or not the cross-quarter celebrations were holdovers from our distant Celtic past or muddied Christian feasts with later Pagan overtones. The celebrations of Imbolc, Beltane, Lughnasa, and Samhain became as important as the solstices and equinoxes.

Ronald Hutton, in his excellent book, *Stations of the Sun* has essentially demonstrated that our present-day seasonal calendar was not the result of stollen or abrogated Pagan festivals, and in fact, very little, if any, of the Pagan past has had much impact on our present calendar.[40] All of the so-called Pagan sabbats are lifted

---

40 Ronald Hutton, *Stations of the Sun*, p. xi.

out of a matrix of deep folk tradition and Catholic liturgy and combined with our imagination to produce the lore of the modern calendric liturgy of Witchcraft and Paganism.

Some may find this judgment to be unpleasant, but I believe that modern scholarship has shown that both Witchcraft and Pagan religious practices are quite modern and newly, imaginatively revised from antique folkloric sources, all of which were fully indoctrinated by Christianity. This fact neither negates these important seasonal celebrations nor makes their practice questionable. The reason why these dates are very important has to do with magical and astrological reasons. Let us investigate them together.

We start our seasonal Wheel at the beginning of the year, which is the Vernal Equinox, also known as the first day of spring. The Vernal Equinox begins when the Sun enters the sign of Aries. It represents the beginning of all things, the quickening and the rebirth from the death of winter. This is a time for potential and the planting of seeds, of change, and starting new chapters in the book of our lives. The kind of magic best worked during the spring is represented by new business, starting a new career, looking for new opportunities, or getting some needed training and education, and also repairing and replacing things that are worn out or no longer functioning optimally. Change is a good thing in the season of spring. Aries is the cardinal sign of fire, representing new beginnings and the fires of ambition.

As the season of spring begins and starts to develop, the energies of growth and renewal are firmly set, and the path forward is determined. When the growing power of spring reaches its zenith of power, then the first cross-quarter sabbat occurs. All cross-quarter sabbats happen at around the same time, which is around the mid-point between the solstices and equinoxes. The mid-point between March 21 and June 20 is around May 1. The Sun is in the fixed earth sign of Taurus, representing the fullness of the season of life and renewal. There is desire and a passion for all of the good things in life, and this is a magical time for material fulfillment since the seeds planted in the Vernal Equinox are beginning to manifest and grow in Beltane.

The light and life reach a crescendo during the advent of Summer Solstice. This is the longest day of the year and symbolizes the power and majesty of the Sun as a living Deity, which is life and light. If we are seeking wisdom and knowledge, enlightenment, and perfect peace, the Sun can gift us that need. This is also a time for truth and acknowledgment, the making of family bonds (weddings and handfasting), and the opening of the tribe or group to new members. The Summer Solstice occurs when the Sun enters into the sign of Cancer, which is the cardinal sign of water. It symbolizes the union of all living things into the family of life on Earth, our forever home.

As the season of summer commences and the crops begin to wax and grow to fulfillment, the Sun is beginning its descent from the apex of ascendency that occurred at the solstice. As the Summer reaches its zenith of power, the cross-quarter of the sabbat Lammas or Lughnasa occurs on August 1, around a month and a half after the solstice. At this event, the Sun is in the sign of Leo, which is fixed fire, representing the golden light and heat of the coming harvest of grains and vegetables. It is a time to celebrate what has been accomplished and what is near-term in regard to growth and work. It is a time for play, celebrating children, travel, and parties. The magic of this seasonal event is to briefly let loose, blow off steam, and celebrate the wondrous Mysteries of life, love, and liberty.

The power of Lughnasa is such that I always shut down my temple, dismiss my fellow initiates, and depart for traveling vacations, feasting and celebrating until September. I figure that with the heat of the summer month and its drowsy effects on the mind and soul, this time is better served with a much-needed break from magical and liturgical work. To this day, I have never executed a celestial magical working during this particular season. Still, the qualities of the season could be used for many magical projects—if the heat of the day doesn't impair one's concentration. It would be better served if such magical workings were performed in the nude at night outdoors.

Summer ends sometime between the end of August and the Autumnal Equinox, but in the last few decades, it seems that summer continues well into October. However, the Autumnal Equinox begins when the Sun enters the zodiacal sign of Libra, the cardinal sign of air. This is the proper harvest feast that is both a celebration and a giving of thanks for all that has been accomplished in the year. Light and dark are now equal in the length of day and night, but the darkness is growing. As the Vernal Equinox was a time for new material beginnings, so the Autumnal Equinox is a time of new spiritual and psychic beginnings. The energies of life are beginning to decline, but internal gateways are opening, and the darkness is ready to enfold us with its Mysteries. This is the time for beginning internal quests, soul searching, talking, and holding long conversations with spirits and ancestors. It is time for the start of great internal workings.

Autumn matures through October, and the light continues to diminish. Vegetative life has passed away and appears in the dark browns and bronzes of its funeral clothes. It is a month and a half between the equinox and the Winter Solstice. The harvest has reached its end with the fruits and tubers, and the life energy of the land is turning ever inward and away from the material world. At the end of October and the very first day of November, the gateways of the dead and the ghost roads of the ancestors open. It is the time of Samhain, also known as Halloween, and it is the folksiest of all the cross-quarter celebrations. It is ironically under the auspices of the sign of Scorpio, fixed water. This is a time when the magic of darkness ascends and opens the doors to the underworld. It is a time of great undertakings, transformative initiations, spiritual metamorphosizes, and conversations with dead ancestors. Inner psychic Mysteries are opened and revealed, and then close again in the coldness of darkness and death.

The end of autumn is the beginning of winter, and the light diminishes until it is thoroughly dominated by the darkness. The days become shorter and the nights longer, and the weather turns cold, wet, and icy. Through November and into December, the days shorten until that day when the Sun enters into the sign of Capricorn, which is cardinal earth, ushering in the shortest day and the longest night.

The Winter Solstice is a time of endings and beginnings. It is a time of nightly vigils, prayers, and thanksgiving. Death and rebirth happen on the day and night, and once passed, the days will become longer, and light will be in the ascendancy once again. The Winter Solstice is a time of precarious balancing between anticipating the future rebirth of life and acknowledging the passing of the old ways and business. It is a moment of respite, hope, rest, and deep thoughtfulness before the resumption of activities to restore the life previously lost in the turning of the season. As for magic, the Winter Solstice is a time for recollections, closing the gateways and pathways of darkness and the dead. It is a time for celebrating the rebirth of light, realization, the reaffirmation of life, and an intuitive understanding of the necessary cycle of darkness and light.

As winter progresses and the cold winds and icy storms dominate the landscape, the light is slowly in ascension, where each day becomes longer and each night of shorter duration. A month and a half from the Winter Solstice, when the Sun has entered into the sign of Aquarius, which has the quality of fixed air, the event of Candlemas Eve (Imbolc), on February 1, occurs. The rebirth of the Sun and the ascension of light gives humanity the promise of the coming spring, even though it is the middle of winter.

It is a time for planning, preparations, and beginning new enterprises. It is a time of purification, fasting—a celebration of light, and the promise of life renewed. During this time, we bless and light many candles, perform divination, make reed crosses, and open the house for the Goddess of Life (disguised as St. Bridget) to bless the young and old. As a magical event, Candlemas Eve is a time for deep divination, the stirring and beginning of major projects (to be fully revealed in the spring), and the summoning of light to quell the darkness of injustice and inequity.

The Wheel of the Year steadily turns, and the eight spokes represent the forces of change and fixation of each of the four seasons. Each has its own particular magical qualities, and each qualifies the seasonal period that it spans. An individual or group working theurgy during any of these periods must take into account the quality of the season and even the weather that happens on that chosen day. Everything that occurs on a sacred day during a sacramental working can be significant, even mundane occurrences. The Witch must examine and weigh all of the auspices when considering the outcome of a particular working. Some events, whether natural or astrological, will be significant, while others will just be part of the overall process. Deciding what is important is an art form by itself, and we will be visiting these methodologies in Chapter Fourteen of this book.

The four seasons have two celebratory events each. One is the advent or beginning of the season, and the other represents the midpoint of that season. Each of these events is qualified by one of the four elements, a zodiacal sign, and whether it is cardinal or fixed. The qualities of cardinal and fixed represent the initial and creative qualities of the season and the static and unchanging qualities of the season. It makes sense that the four cardinal signs represent the beginning of a season, and the four fixed signs represent the middle of the season.

Table of the Eight Sabbats

Event	Element	Sign	Quadruplicity	Quality
Spring Equinox	Fire	Aries	Cardinal	Rebirth of life, beginnings executed
Beltane	Earth	Taurus	Fixed	Fertility, growth, material happiness
Summer Solstice	Water	Cancer	Cardinal	Zenith of light, blessings of life
Lammas	Fire	Leo	Fixed	Celebrations, first harvests, travel
Autumn Equinox	Air	Libra	Cardinal	Full harvest, thanksgiving, preparations
Samhain	Water	Scorpio	Fixed	Opening spirit gates, night of the dead
Winter Solstice	Earth	Capricorn	Cardinal	Longest night, rebirth of light
Candlemas Eve	Air	Aquarius	Fixed	Purification, fasting, celebration of light

The table above displays the elements and qualities associated with each of the eight seasonal events, and this can aid us when we want to determine the best time to execute a theurgic Mystery working. We can also see that aside from the folklore and modern Pagan considerations for these dates, they are also imbued with a potent magical energy mixed with archetypal symbols and astrological portends. As Witches engaged in a nature-based theology, mythology, and a calendric liturgy, we are already very much aware of these eight sabbats. Yet, we now know that these events mark the kind of magic that is best worked at these times, which might have seemed obvious or perhaps intuitively imagined by those so attuned.

Sabbat Rites and the Book of Shadows

The ritual ceremonies for the eight seasonal sabbats are written up in the traditional *Book of Shadows* and they are sparse and extremely rudimentary. I can say for a fact that when I got my own copy, I was quite disappointed in how little there was for each sabbat celebration. What I discovered is that our coven had greatly embellished the practices, rituals, and folklore with what was available in books and various modern traditions. The *Book of Shadows* was pathetically sparse and brief in its liturgical rites, but the coven practices and rites were more complex and seemed to meld modern and ancient sources into a system of belief that was easily assimilated by nearly everyone. The eight sabbats were, then, manufactured and differed, sometimes considerably, between groups and traditions.

Where did all of this additional lore come from? How did coven lore differ so much from what was in the Gardnerian *Book of Shadows*? What was produced for the sabbats was a mixture of modern themes and tropes mixed liberally with folklore traditions from the British and Gaelic cultures to produce something both recognizable and seemingly mysterious. However, these rituals and practices seemed far removed from the life and death struggles of an agricultural and Pagan-based ancestral past from which we all have descended. In our modern world of abundance, we have forgotten the privations and sacrifices of our ancestors who lived by the results of their farming abilities and the cooperation of nature. A year of bad crops would be an acute problem, a few years of bad crops would mean the starvation and death of the tribe or clan.

From the perspective of our Pagan ancestors, the powers of light and darkness and the passing of the seasons and their outcome were more dire and immediate to them. Nature was to be not only respected but revered, placated, and even coerced to produce a bountiful harvest and a healthy population of livestock. While in a normal year, the period of autumn and winter were times of plenty, spring was a time of belt-tightening, hope, and magic to help make the coming agricultural year bountiful. The first fruits of June were a deliverance, and the progress of the growing season was watched and tended with great care to ensure that the harvest would be blessed with abundance. To the mind of the community, the magic of the Goddesses and Gods of the earth and sky, and even the underworld, were an important and significant part of their liturgy and folk beliefs. This is no longer the case because as a people, we no longer face the annual jeopardy of feast or famine.

If the old perspective of seasonal light and darkness, life and death, are no longer a part of our concerns in our modern world, then what is important in the eight sabbats is the recognition of the Mysteries of life and death as represented by the seasons and the fact that all living things are born and must, therefore, die. It would seem that the magic of the seasons represents, in a microcosm, the greater cycles of our individual lives and the lives of our society and our culture. What these seasonal changes can provide us are the symbolic tools to cause positive outcomes and material manifestations in our annual recognition of the waxing and waning of life and light.

The Lesser Mystery, in my opinion, is life itself, although it is still a profound and amazing occurrence despite the fact that science has explained it quite well. The Greater Mystery, then, is death and what happens beyond the cessation of life, such as the mysterious rebirth into a new life. In response to this Mystery, science is silent, but religion has much to say. Still, underlying the Mystery of death is the Mystery of Spirit, the variations of the manifestation of Deity, and the ultimate resolution of the many into the One. These are the Mysteries that are still relevant today, and they represent what should be developed as a Solar-based Mystery rite where a special magic can be unleashed.

The magic of the solstices and the equinoxes is symbolized by the never-ending cycle of light and darkness, particularly the transition from one state to another. It is the magic of transformation and transmutation, which is the ability to apply the power of change to emphasize the darkness or the light for the material gain of the individual or the group.

However, the magic of the cross-quarter seasonal sabbats is quite different. Since there is no transition in these times, then the full Mysteries of life and death are presented. While Beltane symbolizes the rebirth and awakening of the living, Samhain symbolizes the rebirth and reawakening of the dead. The gateway of Beltane and Samhain is the gateway of the underworld, where life and death are the powers and potentials that reside within that place. Beltane is where the gateway opens to admit new life into the material world and Samhain is where the gateway opens to admit the dead who can enter that place as newly deceased to seek regeneration, or who can emerge in their ghostly guise as the heroes, heroines, and ancestors of the clan. The gateways of the Mysteries of life and death are represented by these two seasonal events.

The Lesser Mysteries, although no less significant, involve the sabbats of Lughnasa and Imbolc, which symbolize the time of labor rewarded, feasting, and the time of deprivation and fasting for the vigil of inception. The feast of Lughnasa is when the materialization of one's efforts can be celebrated; it is not so much a time for sending out magic as it is receiving it. The fast of Imbolc is when the empty bareness and darkness of winter is illuminated with hope and strengthened with the overnight vigil of the inception or inauguration of a determined life path. The magic of this sabbat will determine if the treasures of life will be obtained or whether another completely different path must be sought. There is time before the transitional equinox to make this judgment.

Light and darkness are the dance steps through which we all must participate, and the interplay of the Sun, Moon, and the Earth, and their divine representatives symbolizes this process of eternal change. Yet it is the cross-quarter seasonal events that partake of the Greater Mystery of life and death, and so they are the greater focus of the magical sabbat. This is not to say that the equinoxes and solstices are unimportant or unnecessary. To harness the powers of transformation and transmutation, they are quite pivotal and significant. Yet to explore the Mystery of death and rebirth, the cross-quarter sabbats are used, especially Beltane, Samhain, and Imbolc.

Therefore, to represent a magical Mystery presentation of the eight sabbats, we must segregate them into quarterly and cross-quarterly events in order to better represent their Mysteries and the magic that can be generated through their performance. I will distinguish these Mysteries as those of light and darkness and those that represent the Mystery of death and rebirth, the first will be the Lesser Mysteries, and the second, the Greater Mysteries.

Similar to the Lunar Mystery rite, the Solar Mystery rite uses Deities to personify the season. However, the Lesser Mysteries of light and darkness would focus on a Solar Deity based on the pantheon of the group or individual, and the Greater Mysteries of death and rebirth would focus on a Dying God or the Horned God. These two Mystery cycles represent the overall Mysteries of the Sun, symbolizing the interplay of light and darkness and the occurrences of death and rebirth. Why these Mysteries are separate can be easily determined by the growing season in the northern latitudes. The transition between seasons, as represented by the solstices and equinoxes, does not immediately alter the flora and fauna of the earth, but the cross-quarter sabbats do represent a change in the quality and occurrence of life. The changing of the quality and occurrence of life lags behind the changing quality of light, and so these two Mysteries are presented as two distinct but intertwined Mystery cycles.

What I have explained in this chapter is the background needed to perform a magical Mystery rite for the Sun, so now that we have covered all of the pertinent information, we can proceed with examining the actual ritual.

Chapter Sixteen

Solar Mystery Rite Revealed

"The glorious lamp of heaven,
the radiant sun, Is Nature's eye."
—John Dryden

This Solar Mystery rite uses rituals that are found in *Elemental Powers* and *Spirit Conjuring* of the *For Witches* series of books. I will also include them in this working so my reader doesn't have to refer to those books to find them. Like the Lunar Mystery rite, this ritual can be performed by a group or an individual. The pattern for this working is very close to the pattern for the Lunar Mystery rite with some notable exceptions. If a group performs this rite, then there should be an Officiant of the Solar Mysteries chosen for this work. Additionally, there should be someone who is going to perform a godhead assumption and light trance state (level two) to channel the Solar or earth-based Deity. If a single individual performs this rite, then that person must assume all of the roles in this working, including the godhead assumption and a mild trance state. Deosil is the cyclic direction of this working, to symbolize the cyclic qualities of the Sun and the Earth.

As explained previously, the Solar Mystery rite has two tracks, and so there are two possible target godheads for this working. The first should be a solar godhead and the second, a godhead of the earth and underworld representing the Dying God. The Mystery path of the solar godhead is the one that is focused on the transition of light and darkness that represents the changing of the season and the passage of time through the year. The Mystery path of the dying godhead is the one that is focused on the cyclic Mystery of death and rebirth that is symbolized by the vegetative growth and dying cycle, and also by the life, death, and rebirth of animals and humans. I have structured this Mystery rite so that a person or group performing it can easily follow either path, and the verbiage for either path is written into the ritual lines.

I believe that the easiest way to represent these two pathways in the Mysteries of the season is to present them separately as they appeared in the table of eight sabbats in the previous chapter. If we examine them distinctly, then I believe that the two separate Mystery paths will be identified.

Mystery of the Light and Darkness—Mystery of the Sun Deity

- **Spring Equinox**—Aries—Element: Fire
- **Summer Solstice**— Cancer—Element: Water
- **Autumn Equinox**—Libra—Element: Air
- **Winter Solstice**—Capricorn—Element: Earth

The associated element for each of the solar-based seasons of light and darkness is used in the Mystery rite to set the four angles with an invoking pentagram. These will vary whether the Mystery is solar or earth-based.

Mystery of Death and Rebirth—Mystery of the Dying Deity

- **Imbolc** (Candlemas Eve)—Aquarius—Element: Air
- **Beltane**—Taurus—Element: Earth
- **Lughnasa** (Lammas)—Leo—Element: Fire
- **Samhain**—Scorpio—Element: Water

This Mystery rite of the Sun uses a combination of the rose-cross vortex (set to the four watchtowers), a simple pyramid energy vortex (set to the four angles), and a western gateway portal rite to establish the energized field for the Mystery. Within the western gateway underworld, a sacred circular perimeter is established, and the Mystery concept is presented to establish the foundation of the Mystery. The Mystery itself consists of the two-part seasonal paths of the quarter sabbats and the cross-quarter sabbats, and this qualification makes the Mysteries distinct from each other. These qualities are meditated upon while the Officiant circumambulates the circle traveling deosil for a period of time, making many revolutions of the inner perimeter, and who recites from memory the basic topic of the Mystery rite.

Setting the rose-cross vortex is a simple affair without any qualifications or verbiage. The Officiant may decide to verbalize a concept to each point of the circle, or they may be silent and focused on the work. The rose-cross rite is a slightly more advanced ritual working that is used to project a solar vortex energy field that is based on the qualities of the device of the rose-cross. I would recommend that you study this ritual as presented here and also in the book *Elemental Powers* in order to fully grasp the context of this rite.[41]

The pyramid vortex is set with invoking pentagrams of the element associated with the solar or earth-based Mystery cycle to the four angles. Invoking pentagrams are drawn at the four angles, starting with the northwest angle and proceeding deosil around the circle. An invoking pentagram of spirit active is set to the center zenith point of the circle, then the four angle devices and drawn to the center apex and then to each other (to form a square on the circle base).

At each angle, the Officiant should invoke one of the four Gods representing the warrior, storm God, chieftain, and underworld lord to qualify the four-fold elements of the archetypal masculine Deity. These four Gods should represent the specific godhead Deities as associated with the pantheon of the group or individual.[42] The center apex should represent the Solar Deity or the Dying Deity in whatever form the coven or individual recognizes that entity. Solar Gods need not be exclusively masculine, nor should the Dying God be an exclusive male representative. In fact, there are representatives of these Deities of any gender. Like humanity in real life, the Deities are not tied to specific genders

---

41 Frater Barrabbas, *Elemental Powers for Witches*, pp. 165–167.

42 As with the Lunar Mystery rite, the selected Deities are taken from stock Celtic Deities and do not represent what I use in my own version of the Solar Mystery rite.

or sexual archetypes—they are even more dynamic and protean than humans, as suits their nature.

A western gateway is set using some simple representations of the guide, guardian, and the ordeal associated with the Mystery. I will present an example of how they might be qualified, but they will be determined and qualified based on the pantheon associated with the group or the individual. These entities are the same for all of the solar and earth-based Mysteries, but they are no less important to the overall process of the rite.

The climax of this rite is the godhead assumption of a Solar Deity or an earth-based Dying Deity (of any gender), the blessing of solar or earth-based sacraments, such as white wine and honey cakes, or dark beer and crusty dark bread, and communion with the Solar or Dying God. Then, the Officiant expresses a magical wish or desire (this could be a custom sigil on a consecrated parchment) and projects it into the element energy pyramid. This is followed by the exteriorization of that energy, the thanksgiving and departure of the Solar or Dying God, and then the ascent through the eastern gateway portal and the sealing of the vortex.

Similar to the Lunar Mystery, this is not a complex ritual, but it is quite effective in presenting and engaging with the Mystery of the Sun or Earth, communing with an associated godhead and setting a charged pyramid vortex into the mundane sphere imprinted with a desire. The element chosen for the element pyramid vortex is based on the Mystery type and the stage of the season that the Sun is appearing, and these have been explained both above and in the previous chapter.

The nature of the desire, determined by the group or an individual, should be a single and simplified thing, expressed in the graphic representation of a custom sigil drawn on parchment and consecrated beforehand. The parchment sigil is then left on the altar until ten days have passed when it will be burned in a Cauldron to release it.

The Solar or Earth-based Mystery rite has the following sections, as discussed above:

1. Rose-cross vortex is set
2. Pyramid energy vortex is constructed

3. Western gateway portal opened
4. Inner circle perimeter is set
5. Mystery presentation and meditation
6. Solar or dying godhead assumption
7. Sacramental communion
8. Imprinting the pyramid energy field
9. Exteriorization of the pyramid energy field
10. Thanksgiving and departure
11. Ascension and eastern gateway portal opened
12. Vortex sealing

I can now proceed to present to you the actual Mystery rite as outlined above. This ritual is performed within a regularly consecrated magic circle. The Officiant and attendees are properly prepared, and the temple is ready for the working. A consecrated sigil is placed on the altar to be used in the working.

Solar Mystery Rite

1. Setting the Rose-Cross Vortex

The Officiant takes up the wand from the altar and proceeds to the eastern watchtower, where they draw above the watchtower light a rose-cross device, visualize it being filled with golden-colored energy, and then draw an invoking spiral around it.

They then proceed to the southern watchtower and perform the same actions, drawing a golden-colored rose-cross device and activating it with an invoking spiral.

The Officiant proceeds to the western watchtower and performs the same actions as previously.

They proceed to the northern watchtower and perform the same actions as previously.

They proceed to the center of the circle and draw a rose-cross device in the zenith, projecting a golden energy up into it and activating it with an invoking spiral. Then they will draw a rose-cross device in the nadir, projecting a golden energy down into it.

The Officiant deposits the wand on the altar and takes up the sword. They then proceed to the eastern watchtower, take the sword, and draw a line of force from the rose-cross device drawn there to the rose-cross device in the central nadir of the circle.

They proceed to the southern watchtower and perform the same action.

The Officiant proceeds to the western watchtower and performs the same action.

They proceed to the northern watchtower and perform the same action.

The Officiant then returns the sword to the altar and proceeds to the eastern watchtower. They will face the north with hands projecting the forces before them and will walk around the circle widdershins three times, proceeding in a spiral transit until they reach the center of the circle. They will then project the energy into the nadir below the floor of the temple, stand in the center, and draw the energy up in an ascending wave from the nadir through their body to the zenith. The vortex is now completed.

2. Pyramid Energy Vortex—Mystery of Masculine Lifecycle

The Officiant then takes up the wand from the altar and proceeds to the northwest angle of the magic circle and stands before it. They will draw an invoking pentagram of the solar or earth-based Mystery element with the wand and seal it with an invoking spiral to the angle. They then hold the wand and point to the pentagram device and summon the God, saying:

"I invoke you, O Arawn, lord of the domain of dead and the powers of rebirth, to come and appear in this sacred angle."

Then, the Officiant proceeds to the southwest angle and draws the invoking pentagram with the wand. The Officiant then summons the God, saying:

"I invoke you, Dagda, Father, Chieftain of the Gods, just ruler, to come and appear in this sacred angle."

They then proceed to the southeast angle and perform the same action as previously. They say:

"I invoke you, Taranis, Storm God and great sky phallus, to come and appear in this sacred angle."

They proceed to the northeastern angle and perform the same actions as previously. They say:

"I invoke you, Gwydion, trickster and wise youth, to come and appear in this sacred angle."

They proceed towards the center of the circle to the zenith and perform the same actions except drawing an invoking pentagram of active spirit. They hold the wand, pointing to the zenith, and say:

"I invoke you, Manawydan, wise man and knower of secrets, teacher of the Mysteries and magic, to come and appear in this temple apex."

The Officiant bows then proceeds to the northwest angle and draws a line of force with the wand from the empowered pentagram and godhead to the central zenith of the circle. They proceed to the southwest angle and perform the same action. They then proceed to the southeast, perform the same action, and then move to the northeast where they perform the same action. Then, they proceed again to the northwest angle and with the wand, draw a line of power from that point to the southwest, then to the southeast, then to the northeast, and complete the line of force in the northwest.

The Officiant proceeds to the northwest angle and then begins to walk in a deosil spiral from that point in the outer circle to the center of the circle, making three rounds of the northwest angle before completing the circuit. They will use the wand to project the energy before them, facing forward until they reach the center of the circle where they will project the power into the zenith. The pyramid vortex is now complete.

3. Opening the Western Gateway of the Mysteries

The Officiant returns the wand to the altar and proceeds to stand in the eastern watchtower facing the west. They will choose either Sun or Death depending on the Mystery to be presented.

They will draw an invoking spiral to the southeastern angle and say:

"Behind me is the guide who assists me to open the Mysteries of [the Sun/Death], and to reveal the secret powers of light and darkness."

They then draw an invoking spiral to the northeastern angle and say:

"In front of me stands the guardian, who will test and judge my insights and wisdom to witness the Mysteries of [the Sun/Death] and allow me to pass only if I prove myself worthy."

They draw an invoking spiral to the western watchtower and say:

"Before is the ordeal, where I am reduced, transformed, and reborn by the secret knowledge of the Mysteries of [the Sun/Death]. I must be willing to surrender myself to the greater power and wisdom of [the Sun/Death]."

Then, the Officiant slowly advances from the eastern watchtower to the western watchtower, stands before it, makes the sign of the opening threshold portal (like parting a curtain), and advances a step into the imaginary veil, turns, and raises their arms to receive the light of the west pouring down upon their head and body. They will then advance forward to the center of the circle, imagining themself descending into an underworld grotto. The gateway passage is completed.

4. Solar and Earth-based Mystery Presentation

The Officiant goes to the altar and takes their sword. They then proceed to the northwestern angle and trace a circle, proceeding in a widdershins circuit, making a full circle, and returning to the northwestern angle. They then proceed to the altar, return the sword, and pick up the staff. They proceed to the center of the circle to begin the Mystery presentation.

They will stand in the center of the circle and say the following invocation to the Son God for that Seasonal Mystery of equinoxes and solstices. If there are others in attendance, they stand around the periphery of the inner magic circle of the Mysteries to listen to the Officiant calling the God of the Sun. Of course, the name of the Sun God or Goddess would depend on the pantheon of the group or individual. (I am presenting here only an example.)

"O Lugh, Lord of Light and Darkness, the Sun traveling through the seasons, where light ascends and descends in its eternal dance with darkness. You are the exemplar of the life force that emanates from the Sun, the great repository of knowledge and wisdom, and the revealer of deceit and truth-teller. Let your light illuminate our minds, let us be facile and flexible, and above all, appreciate irony and the humor of the Gods of fate. Come down to me who seeks your clarity and insight. I am your hands and feet, and I am your eyes and heart. Come forth into me!"

For the cross-quarter seasons, the Officiant would say the following invocation of the Dying God. They say:

"O Cernunnos, Horned One, Lord of the Trees and Master of the Hunt, the powers of light and darkness revealed as death and rebirth. You stand at the crossroads of life, witnessing birth, death, and rebirth, and yet you know this great Mystery in your spirit, for you have died with us and been reborn to us every year into eternity. The cycle of birth, growth, maturity, decline, and death that happens in a single cycle of the seasons is imprinted on the material bodies of all living things. Yet this fate of death has within it the Mystery of rebirth, although not the rebirth of the individual. We share in the spirit of life so that when we die, we shall come to the eternal source, and there, know you, and realize rebirth in that great collective of life. Come up from the underworld to me who seeks your elixir of rebirth. I am your hands and feet, and I am your eyes and heart. Come forth into me!"

Then, the Officiant proceeds to walk around the middle part of the inner circle slowly while they recite the solar or earth-based

Mystery for the particular seasonal sabbat, over and over again until they come to the end, as sensed by them at the moment. (These recitations are examples of what might be written.)

The Officiant starts this action by saying:

"I begin this rite of the Mystery of [the Sun/Death] of the sabbat season of [sabbat name], and I sing my song of the Mystery of eternal change, so listen, learn, and master the hidden knowledge."

The Officiant begins their circumambulation while reciting their poetic Mystery as many times over as deemed sufficient while walking the circuit. The Officiant and the attendees should also internally focus on the quality of the Moon as determined by the phase, lunation stage, and zodiacal sign.

Spring Equinox:

"Spring melts winter's ice and snow, bringing renewed life to the barren land. Light is waxing and there is balance between darkness and light to keep. Seeds of potential are sown, and plans are made that can be later reaped."

Beltane:

"Beltane is the gateway of life and death, where life in abundance shall come to us.
We dance to the tune of the piper of life and wend our way through the misty paths.
To love, to join, in pleasure and pain, to give life and make life our fated thane."

Summer Solstice:

"Summer comes to the land to bring its zephyr winds and soft sighing rain. Light is in ascension and the darkness in is retreat, hidden in the earth. While the fruits of love's labor begin to grow, and the urge to rejoice comes again."

Lughnasa:

"Lughnasa is fullness, exultation, feasting, and forgetting pain and sorrows.
Guilt and remembrance overturned, the joy and exuberance of life cannot be denied.
Festivals of light and laughter hide the darkness, the fear, that death nearby lurks."

Autumn Equinox:

"Autumn cools the summer's heat and brings to the table many things to eat.
Still more labor for every living thing, to bring in the harvest against the chill.
Yet darkness grows and nature is soon to die, to become dormant in light's defeat."

Samhain:

"Samhain, the gateway of life and death, where white-shrouded death comes to us.
Our fate is the same as living things, our departed ancestors demand good cheer.
To die is to be reborn, to be reborn is to be held, the eternal round of death and life."

Winter Solstice:

"Winter comes in and autumn bows its head, and the light grows dim; cold and ice.
Labor is done, the storing is set, to brave the icy storms of winter's freezing breath.
Darkness is ascendant as the sunlight dims, yet the Earth's return of light is seen."

Imbolc:

"Imbolc, time of emptiness, stillness, fasting, and remembering life in death. Joy and love have passed, we are like the dead who seek life but are ever forbidden.
Our way is to design, name, and devise, to bring back light who still have life."

When the Officiant has completed their circumambulations, they will return once again to the center of the circle where they stand with their staff in the silence of the moment, meditating on the Mystery of the Sun or Death. Then, when this moment has passed, they will stamp their staff four times and say:

"The Mystery is revealed, and now comes the God/Goddess of [the Sun/Death]."

The Officiant proceeds to the altar and returns the staff.

5. Solar or Life-based Godhead Assumption and Communion

If the Officiant is the only attendee, then they will be the one to perform the godhead assumption of the chosen solar or earth-based Deity as the Medium, otherwise, a selected Medium from the group will take the part. If a group is performing this rite, then the Officiant will stand slightly off to the north of the Medium in the center of the circle. The group will array themselves around the periphery of the circle.

A chair is placed in the center of the circle for the Medium, facing west, a small foldable table is also situated nearby with the sacraments, a cup, bowl, spoon, and plate placed on it. The consecrated sigil is also placed on the table for later use. The Medium stands in front of the chair, facing the west, and performs the following actions to assume the godhead of the chosen solar or life-based Goddess or God. The Medium is anointed and specially garbed to perform this godhead assumption. The prayers and invocation have been previously written and memorized, allowing for a degree of spontaneity.

1. The Medium bows deeply then hold their arms up in the pose of offering and says a prayer to the target Deity.
2. The Medium performs the ascending wave, visualizing energy traveling up their body from their feet to their head and beyond.
3. They will intone the invocation to the target Deity and then stand in silence for a short time.
4. The Medium performs the descending wave, visualizing the energy traveling from above their head down through their body to their feet.
5. They then make the sign of the equal-arm cross on their body with their hand, touching the right shoulder, left shoulder, forehead, and groin, then folding their hands before their heart while imagining a cross of glowing energy on their body. They pause a short time to absorb the effect and feel the energy coursing along their body.
6. The Medium then draws a triangle gateway centered on their heart, touching the points of the right shoulder, left shoulder, groin, and heart. They raise their arms in supplication, drawing the target Deity into their heart, and feel it enter into them. They embrace their body and bow their head, linking their consciousness with the godhead.
7. They perform the ascending wave, visualizing energy traveling up their body from their feet to their head and beyond. They then carefully seat themself on the chair and allow the trance state to deepen to achieve a level two embodiment.

After a short time, the Medium will regain a level of functional consciousness, and through the power of the godhead in their mind and body, they will address the group and acknowledge their godhead assumption. If working alone, they will affirm to themself the acknowledgment of the Goddess or God. Then, the Medium will stand and go to the table with the sacraments and make the sign of the cross upon them, touch them with their hands where appropriate, and bow down to blow their breath upon them. They then say:

"I bless, charge, and empower these sacraments of [the Sun/Death], in the name of X, whose guise I have assumed."

The Medium will also take up the consecrated sigil in their hands, make the sign of the cross upon it, and then blow their breath upon it. They will then set it back down on the folding table. They look to the zenith of the circle and make the sign of the cross, saying:

"I bless this pyramid of power in the name of X so that it might manifest the secret desire of this gathering in the light and darkness of [the Sun/Death]."

The sacraments, sigil, and energy pyramid are now consecrated, and the sacraments may be shared with the group or left for the Medium to partake in later if they are working alone.

6. Exteriorization of the Charge and Departure

The Medium stands facing the west while the Officiant performs the exteriorization. If there is only one attendee, then the Medium assumes the role of Officiant while still lightly embodied.

The Officiant proceeds to the altar to take up the staff with their left hand, walks to the folding table in the center of the circle, and takes up the blessed and consecrated parchment sigil with their right hand. Standing in the center of the circle, they will say the following:

"In the name of the God/Goddess X, I take this desire that we have designed and walk the pathway of manifestation so that the divine powers blessed and charged herein may work to make this desire truly realized!"

The Officiant then turns to face the northwestern angle and then begins to walk a widdershins spiral around the circle with ever-widening arcs until they have made three circuits of the northwestern angle and arrive at the outer perimeter of the circle. They will imagine pushing the energy of the circle as they walk the spiral and that the forces arrayed there, becoming ever more resistant as they proceed.

Once they have arrived at the northwestern angle for the third and final time, they will take the staff in their left hand, place the right with the sigil on it so that the sigil is pressed onto the staff, and extend it out towards the angle. They will exhale loudly as they imagine all of the energy being projected out of the vortex circle and rippling in waves of force into the material world beyond. They then return the staff next to their body, still holding the sigil against it, and make three taps with the base of the staff.

The Officiant then proceeds to the altar where they place the sigil on the altar and return the staff to its proper place. They then proceed to the center of the circle. If they are the only attendee, they will sit in the chair as the Medium and briefly meditate, otherwise, they will return and stand before the Medium who will sit again on the chair and meditate for a short time.

The Medium will then release the conscious connection with the target Deity and say the following departing words and thanksgiving.

"O God/Goddess X, we thank you for your appearance, your gifts, and your assistance in our magical work. We bid you farewell, love, and deep respect, and hope to call on you again to commune with us, your secret children."

They will then make the sign of the cross before the west three times and the assumption is completed. They will make the sign of the closing threshold portal (like closing a curtain) before the west and bow.

The Officiant and the group (if there are attendees) remove the chair from the center of the circle and take the folding table and place it next to the altar. If the Officiant has performed this rite alone, then they will partake of the sacrament to help ground and fortify themself for the next stage of the rite.

7. Opening the Eastern Gateway of the Mysteries

The Officiant proceeds to stand in the western watchtower facing the east.

They will draw an invoking spiral to the northwestern angle and says:

"Behind me is the guide who assists me to close the Mysteries of [the Sun/ Death], and to reveal the secret pathway of light and ascension."

They draw an invoking spiral to the southwestern angle and say:

"In front of me stands the guardian, who will bar my passage into the light and seek to keep the secret knowledge in the realm of the Mysteries of [the Sun/Death], and will allow me to pass only if I am steadfast and clear in my intentions."

They draw an invoking spiral to the eastern watchtower and say:

"Before is the ordeal, where I am reborn, invested with knowledge, and able to transmit the secret knowledge of the Mysteries of [the Sun/ Death]. I must be willing to act as the mediator for the greater power and wisdom of the [Solar/Life-based] God/Goddess."

Then, the Officiant slowly advances from the western watchtower to the eastern watchtower, stands before it, makes the sign of the opening threshold portal (like parting a curtain), and advances a step into the imaginary veil. They will then turn and raise their arms to receive the brilliant light of the east pouring down upon their head and body. They then advance forward to the center of the circle, imagining themself ascending into an above-world garden. The gateway passage is completed, and the rite is ended.

CHAPTER SEVENTEEN

SACRED GROVE—MYSTERY
AND MAGIC OF NATURE

"I have seen dawn and sunset
on moors and windy hills
Coming in solemn beauty
like slow old tunes of Spain:
I have seen the lady April
bringing in the daffodils,
Bringing the springing grass
and the soft warm April rain.

I have heard the song of the blossoms
and the old chant of the sea,
And seen strange lands from under
the arched white sails of ships;
But the loveliest things of beauty
God ever has showed to me
Are her voice, and her hair, and eyes,
and the dear red curve of her lips."
—JOHN MASEFIELD, *BEAUTY*

There is nothing more beautiful, intense, real, and meaningful than having an outdoor place to worship and work magic, particularly if it is a special private place, maintained over a period of time. I call such a semi-permanent place to worship and practice

Witchcraft outdoors a *sacred grove* and I have been lucky enough to have once owned a three-acre section of wooded land that had such a place within it. A grove demands a basic perspective that you cannot find in an indoor temple. Witches who work in a sacred grove are expected to be able to be flexible with the variables of nature. Since nature is capricious and changeable, those who seek to work within it must adapt and accept whatever occurs as part of the sacred unveiling of blessed events.

A basic premise that Witches and Pagans should follow is that nature is, by itself, sacred when approached as a place of mystery and magic. Whether that land is cordoned off and meticulously maintained or it is wild and unkempt as nature left by itself can occur, it is a sacred place. Everything that occurs within its locale is part of the sacred interplay of spirit and matter, and everything that resides within it, both animate and inanimate, is also sacred. The strange jutting mossy rocks, the great gnarled oak, hills and valleys, creeks and lakes, the deer that secretly wander through its wetlands, from the humblest insects to the falcons flying overhead are all sacred.

What, you might ask, makes this distinction? How does a humble glade, den, or even a suburban backyard suddenly become a holy of holies? The answer is quite simple. Nature doesn't change, only our perception of it changes. To enter into sacred space is to modify the way that we apprehend that place. When we see it as sacred, then it is sacred, but truly, it was sacred all along, we just were not paying attention. Therefore, a grove is never consecrated like a temple or a temporary room with a magic circle. It doesn't need a ritual to signify its exalted state, and it doesn't need to be charged with the distribution of sacraments (incense and lustral water); it is naturally consecrated at all times. Instead of performing a consecration rite at the start of a working, when one operates in a grove, only the mind and the senses of the attendees need to be altered.

Another important concept about outdoor rites and workings in a sacred grove is that there are no real definitions, rules, scripts, prejudices, demarcations, or expectations in nature. We bring those things into nature as our own personal baggage, but they are steadfastly artificial and have no part in the real occurrence of a sacred grove. Thus, the rituals that we successfully use in a temple are practically meaningless when applied in a grove. We can force them to be meaningful, but then we do so while ignoring what is really there, and in some fashion, insulting the Deities of locale and ignoring the mysterious emanations of nature itself. As Witches and Pagans, we are not people of the book. We have no sacred writings. All we have is the ever-present material reality of nature and the impressions of Spirit that wholly and completely pervade it. Nature is our holy writing, and the experience of the Mysteries of nature is our true teacher. The best approach to engaging with the Mysteries and magic of an outdoor grove is to be completely open, flexible, and without prejudice. We need to listen, be aware of all that is happening, and see and experience it as manifestations of the divinity of nature.

In my many decades of practicing Witchcraft and attending outdoor gatherings, Pagan festivals, or even grand conclaves of various traditions, what I see happening typically seems to completely miss the point of gathering outdoors in nature. Everything that is done, from lectures, teachings, discussion groups, rituals, and ceremonies are conducted in the same exact manner that they would be if the event were held at someone's home or a hotel. Seldom have I seen nature walks, discussions of the flora and fauna of the present location, or its geographic topology. The site chosen for this event is more or less forgotten in the hustle and bustle to meet, greet, teach, and perform rituals and ceremonies within the allotted time for the gathering. While all of this is going on, nature itself quietly presents the most important lessons and Mysteries, yet the attendees seem to be insensitive and oblivious to this amazing occurrence happening around them.

What seems to me to be even more redundant is when a ritual is enacted at such a gathering, lustral water is made and sprinkled around, incense burned, and the four quarters are called. The four elements are identified, even though they are already abundantly defined in the natural environment itself. The four quarters are already there and have been since the beginning of life on this planet—we hardly need to call them. What is really there are the many directions of what has been called the *compass round*, and the winds can blow across the land from any of the sixteen directions. What features are there in the land where this gathering occurs are ignored by the attendees, who presume to overlay it all with their symbols, models, names, and expectations.

All of these practices have a great element of error built into them because many folks have not actually tried to fathom what it is they are trying to do and where they are trying to do it. They have not altered their perceptions and opened their minds to see and experience what is really there. I have found this approach to be perplexing, and I am not alone, since elders that I have talked to have agreed wholly that this way of working with nature is just wrong.

What is needed to fix this problem is a whole new approach, or at least, it will be new to some. Nature is self-contained. Most of what we need is already there. The four elements are in abundance in some manner, so they don't need to be identified in a ritual. The same is true regarding the four quarters, and, in fact, there are 360 degrees to that circle, so there are many points of reference in a grove setting and all of them are valid. Air is the wind that blows the leaves in the trees; water is the rain, creeks, rivulets, lakes, and ponds; and earth is the ground with or without the vegetative covering of mosses, grasses, trees, weeds, thickets, and bushes. Fire could be seen as the brilliant light and warmth of the sun, but it is also the one element that folks might bring into a sacred grove and set up in a controlled fire pit. The various insects, birds, and creatures are the residents that partake of the glory of the grove, and the herbs, mushrooms, and untended fruit are the sacraments that are used, or not, in a guarded and guided manner. The weather is a manifestation of the interactions of the sky and earth, and it, too, is sacred. If a storm comes and disrupts a working, then it is a representation of the regard or communication of the Deities of nature to their human recipients. All of this must be absorbed, engaged, and venerated in order for the Mystery of the grove working to be truly realized. Anything less will distort or even occlude the experience of the sacredness of nature.

Building a Sacred Grove

We enter a grove without personal expectations. We set aside our scripts and schedules so that we can apprehend nature with as little bias as possible. We seek, first and foremost, to observe and to be taught by our observations. We make ourselves openly sensitive to natural occurrences, and we still our thoughts and temporarily drop all of the worrying concerns of the mundane world. Entering a grove requires us to perform a kind of decompression exercise, a type of mindfulness that draws us away from our ego-centric life into a state of awe, wonder, and appreciation of something outside of ourselves, but also right in front of us.

Nature has the qualities of directness, immediacy, wonder, and also subtlety. To apprehend it, we must first undergo an internal mental change that a period of deep meditation can achieve, to be supported with a state of mindfulness that can obverse all things without an internal dialogue interpreting what we see and experience. I would recommend spending time meditating in nature in order to arrive at this state of openness and sharpened acuity. That is the first step needed before contemplating working in a sacred grove.

Once this state is achieved, then the second step can be taken, which is to enter into the sacred grove and ask it what needs to be done and how it should be done. This may sound kind of absurd, but when you consider that I have been advocating talking to spirits, then making this offering to a sacred grove is similar to conjuring unknown nameless spirits. You approach the sacred grove and ask it with reverence to open itself up to you, so that you may perceive and interact with it as it truly exists. You have discarded all expectations, so it is up to the sacred grove to draw you in, teach you its name, and guide you through your experience. You will hear the grove spirit speak if such are your talents, or you can use dice or knucklebones to determine the nature and the personality of the grove spirit.

Does this approach mean that there are no rituals or actions to be learned and mastered when engaging with a sacred grove? Of course not, there are rituals and ceremonies, and even some basic ground rules that are common to all types of sacred groves. We will discuss them in this chapter, but the first step must be engaging with the sacred grove on its terms. You should open yourself to its spiritual wisdom and power in order to be certain that what is done in that space is in accordance with the naturally occurring elements and features that are a part of its foundation. The rituals that are developed for a specific sacred grove will have variances unique to that environment, even though the basic structures will be essentially the same. Over time, those differences can also grow and expand to produce a unique set of practical lore used only in that particular grove.

Treating a sacred grove as a deified entity that has a special name and character is an important starting place for grove workings. Even if that place is a temporary or rented campground, one should still take the same approach of engaging with the spiritual entity residing within the collective of that grove. Adopting this approach then requires that you engage in a dialogue with this grove spirit, identify it, and then give it votive offerings as if it were a Deity, since by doing so, you have made it into a Deity. Ironically, these offerings are always organic, human-made things consisting of food, drink, (vegetable) oil, tobacco, and other things that have been taken from nature to nurture and feed us humans.

We give these things back to the earth to show that we aren't selfish and that we want to feed the earth as well as ourselves. Of course, these offerings should be organic and not polluted with unnatural chemicals and preservatives, so that what is given will quickly meld back into the earth. Once you have obtained this kind of relationship with the grove spirit, then you can commence building the sacred topology of the grove so you can tap and engage with the powers and Mysteries inherent in the sacred grove.

Once you have determined the location for a grove—or at least its designated boundaries—then you will need to map out the topology of the grove as it exists in its natural state. Boundaries are determined limits based on human-measured land boundaries, and these can be the boundaries of a permanent grove on private land or a temporary one that is carved out of a semi-public campground. Wherever the grove exists, it will have some kind of legal-based boundaries that will encapsulate the area. What can also occur is that the grove area is exceeded by the sacredness of the land formation and may actually include many miles of additional territory. However, every grove has an area of focus, and that is where the grove workers will focus their efforts.

There are three basic human-built attributes introduced to the sacred grove for establishing a sacred topology where human beings and the powers and Mysteries inherent in the grove will interface. These three attributes are the flat space used for the compass round, a fire pit, and a natural entry point that acts as the gateway threshold of the grove. You could ignore these attributes and work with the space completely unaltered but adding at least these three will greatly assist the workings of the grove environment.

The compass round is a circular area of around twelve to twenty-five feet or more of flat land that can be walked by the group who will perform rites and workings in this space. The size is determined by the number of individuals who would be working in this place. If the weeds can be trimmed and the area of the compass round cleared of debris so that walking is easily done without accident, then that effort should suffice for typical grove workings. The preparations of the compass round should also include noting or even marking the cardinal and in-between points outside of it. It is an important consideration that those who are to work in a grove will know the points of the compass orientation for their chosen working environment.

A fire pit can be placed at a point either around the periphery of the compass round or it can be set in the center. I have found that a fire pit, which can be used to brew potions and cook sacramental food, is better served at the edge or just outside the compass round than in the center where activity could interfere with the main workings. A fire pit is a hole dug in the earth around two feet deep and three to five feet wide. A wood pile should be placed close by as well as the Cauldron and its iron stand. Other items may also be employed, such as a cup, bowl, plate, spoon, and knife. A mortar, pestle, and a flat stone for cutting and preparing herbs or meat could also be used, depending on the elaboration of the drink and food that would be shared in the rites. There can also be more than one Cauldron as well, and each can be fully consecrated.

An entry point to the compass round should also be determined, based on the features of the grove as one approaches it. While the preferred entry point is the north or northwest, this entry will be determined by clearings and natural paths that lead to the place in the grove. The entry point is the natural boundary for the grove, with the intrinsic idea that passing this point in a procession will require the all-important change in consciousness so that the sacred nature of the grove will be readily perceived. My grove had its entry point to the east because there was a natural opening to the woods in that direction.

There are some optional attributes that can be added to the grove to further develop it, and there are some attributes that can be added if the site is a permanent one. These optional attributes are torch lights and the use of chalk to mark the boundary of the compass round. Adding torchlights and a chalk circle are esthetic additions that can be used to make the compass round more visible to the human eye, and the torch lights can also illuminate the compass points that are to be used in grove workings during the evening. I chose to use eight torch lights and set them up just outside the compass round to mark the eight points of the compass at night.

Some of the more advanced attributes that could only be added to a permanent site involve some more intensive terraforming of the grove area. The entry point can be enhanced with an actual archway that people must pass under as they process into the grove. This can be made of metal (such as an arbor gate) or stone blocks with a decorated keystone at the top. Whether metal or stone, the archway should be decorated to represent the boundary and perimeter of the grove and symbolize the single traditional entryway into that sacred place.

If it can be done, a hill should be constructed and planted with grass or natural cover that will overlook the compass round but be outside of it. Another feature would be the construction of a well since such an edifice would be the perfect representative of the earth godhead as the provider of water. Drinkable water is preferable, and if it smells and tastes of iron, then that would be optimal.

A permanent grove site can house both the red Stang of life and the black Stang of death. I chose to place my two Stang poles in the west and northwest respectively, outside of the compass round. You would have to determine the best location based on your topological map of the grove area. These two Stangs are treated as permanent shrines and are given periodic votive offerings to keep them active and empowered. There should also be a shrine placed somewhere in the grove area but well outside of all activity for the grove spirit itself. This shrine will also receive votive offerings from time to time. For a temporary site, these two Stangs could be set up if they can be readily taken down, otherwise, the priestly Stang will suffice for such a working.

The formidable tools that are used in the grove are the portal priestly Stang, the Besom, the dagger, and the wand. These are wielded by individuals and brought into the grove for the working, then transported out when the working is completed. These are not permanent fixtures, unlike the Cauldron and its associated regalia, which remain with the fire pit. For a temporary grove, the more permanent features are left in the grove until it is time to clear the site and remove all of the human-introduced attributes. Except for the grove shrine, which should be obscure and not easily located, the rest of the site should be cleaned up thoroughly and left as natural as possible to allow the grove area to become wild once again.

A sacred grove is ready to be used when the following items have been established to facilitate the human and nature interface.

1. Establish a spiritual rapport with the grove spirit of the land so that the spirit has a name and an identifiable personality.
2. Ask the grove spirit what kind of magic can be worked in this domain and how it should proceed. You will have rituals, but they might need to be adjusted to build a harmonious relationship with the grove spirit.
3. Build a map of the designated boundary of the grove area—this can be done mentally by exploring the grove area or by drawing a physical map.
4. Locate and build an obscure shrine for the grove spirit—make offerings to it before continuing.
5. Establish the compass round and perform simple tasks to make it useable—this will be the area where the group will circumambulate the inner grove area. Mark the eight directions on the outside of the compass round area.
6. Build a fire pit and stock it with firewood, set up the Cauldron, stand, and outdoor kitchen station.
7. Add torch lights and a chalk circle—you can also groove the ground to make a circle, but these are optional tasks.

Once these seven steps are completed, then the grove is ready to be used for the first of many times.

Sacred Gove Magic

A sacred grove is active at all times, so it can be engaged at any time, day or night. Grove magic in the day can focus on the sun and the elements of the day while grove magic performed during the night can focus on the moon, celestial occurrences, and the nocturnal state of nature that presents the greatest Mystery in darkness. The passage of the day and night, the variations of weather, the occurrences of storms, high winds, and perfect quiet are parts of the sacred theater of the grove.

Anything that occurs is to be perceived through the mindset of the fully engaged grove, where all is perceived as the expressions of the Deities and the manifestation of Spirit within matter. Being in the grove should make anyone aware of this kind of Mystery and magic as it dynamically occurs if they have made the proper alignment to the grove spirit and the glory of nature, unnamed and undetermined by the mind of humankind.

Grove magic done in the day is more transparent, accessible, and observable, and therefore, it is represented by the healing arts; the way of nurturing, making food and potions, and preparations for the evening events. It is a time of building, the giving of offerings, and maintaining the readiness of the grove. I have witnessed some wonderful rites of healing done during the day, and also witnessed, and even engaged in, handfastings in a grove. The compass round is easily seen and the markings of the compass points are readily determined. All of this, of course, completely changes when the night comes.

Nighttime in the sacred grove is a whole different kind of experience. If there is no lit fire nor any torches present, then the grove will be dark and indiscernible, depending on any ambient light from the moon. A dark and stormy night would be quite a spectacular scene and would likely require some steel nerves to withstand the onslaught. Weather, of course, will affect the quality, or even the ability to perform a working. Any possibility should be accorded a respectful and patient sentiment if the scheduled event for a working is interrupted by inclement weather—this occurrence is always a possibility when working in a grove.

Additional lights, like fire and torches, help to make it less dark and more navigable. At night, the full glory of the grove Mysteries can be experienced, and the magic can have a variety of focuses. Still, the Greater Mysteries are those that cycle around life, death, rebirth, and the seemingly endless cycle of nature in its seasons. Lunar Mysteries can be explored in the magical grove-based esbat, and the Solar Mysteries explored in magical grove-based sabbats. A temporary gathering will typically occur around some seasonal or celestial event, so that will determine the theme and the kind of magic available to the group.

What I have presented in the previous chapters for the Lunar and Solar Mystery rites could be the starting model for the grove-based version of this rite. It should be a scaled-down version in keeping with the simplicity and immediacy of grove workings. The basic pattern can be kept, but most of the verbiage should be eliminated and replaced with simplified ritual actions.

An important consideration for grove workings is that they should be simple and easy to perform in an outdoor environment. There is also no need to set magical devices to the compass round, but simply pointing them out with the appropriate intent should suffice. Verbalizations, as they would occur, are replaced with simple single-word utterances or spontaneous verbal expressions as the ideas in the stages of a working are performed. The key to working complex rituals in a grove is to make them simple and easy to perform by memory. Sometimes the most powerful ritual activities in a grove are completely unscripted actions and suddenly inspired discoveries.

Perhaps the most important part of the Lunar and Solar Mysteries in a grove is the personification of a godhead at its climax. All that is really needed in those rituals are the godhead assumption of the chosen Deity within the grove environment, the communion to be followed with the compass round, and a circle dance to churn and exteriorize the power to do the will of the assembled folk in the simple and old-established traditional manner. The grove will add a considerable volume of power to this working since the magic will be drawn from the resources of the grove itself.

As it is known in basic shamanic examples (and discussed in my book *Spirit Conjuring*), there are three levels of being in the sacred grove. The sky, earth, and underworld. These can be made as accessible to grove magical workings as they are in a temple working.

The main difference is that there is no gateway to cross since one is already in a sacred domain. All that is required to focus on is the sky, the earth, or below it to realize the mystery and power of those three domains. A tree could be climbed, or a gully traversed (or a temporary grave or pit previously dug in the earth) to facilitate access to these three worlds.

I will let you figure out how to build Lunar and Solar Mystery rites for use in a grove using the points that I have set out here. It has to be something that is simple, immediate, and conforms to the harmonious interaction of the grove spirit and the magic that is to be enacted within that domain.

Finally, there is a basic ritual format or pattern that is worked in a sacred grove. It is a simple rite because it should be easily memorized, and it may need to be able to be spontaneously altered as needed in the moment. Grove magic must be adaptable and dynamic, and this is what should be used to tap into that Mystery and perform its associated magical spells.

Passage to the grove is a procession where the group forms a single line and proceeds to walk solemnly along a predetermined route to the entry point for the grove. The grove is dark yet prepared for the working, and the leader or leaders of the group will hold a torch to light the way. There may have been others already at the grove to help begin the work, or the grove may be deserted. Regardless, the leader or leaders will then proceed into the grove to light the fire and the compass round torches (if there are any) and return to allow the rest of the group to enter and take their position.

The Besom is placed just after the entry point, and everyone walks across it signifying that they have entered the sacred gathering place (having traveled by broomstick). The Besom is then used to sweep the area of the compass round as a last stage to prepare it for the walking circuits. The portal Stangs are taken into the grove and placed in their previously determined places, where the iron-shod poles are stuck into the earth. The sacraments are prepared for use and covered with cloths, and when all of the initial tasks are completed, then the group will take their places around the compass round.

The basic ritual movement is to travel around the compass round either deosil or widdershins, depending on the kind of energy that needs to be generated. Ritual actions in the compass round of the grove produce harmonic resonating energies from the earth itself, thus amplifying any magic that is done in the grove area. When beginning a grove working, the first walk around the compass round is done sunwise or deosil, in emulation of the sun's travel through the sky of the grove. This movement of the group will generate a stronger than assumed energy in the grove, making it ready to be used for other purposes.

Principle rituals in the grove consist of the adoration of the Stang, the night travel of the Besom, then the personification of Deity in a more potent variation of the Drawing Down rite for either a chosen celestial Deity (Moon Goddess), an earth-based Deity (Horned God) or some other variation. At any grove working, invocation of the grove spirit, and offerings to it are performed by the whole group.

Godhead personifications of the higher sort would be followed with a special communion, charging, and blessing, and also the setting of an energy field and its exteriorization to manifest a simple request or desire. There can be a special feast or dinner as provided by the Cauldron, a sumptuous potion, or a special heated drink. At the least, there should be dark beer and dark, crusty bread with some cheese to fortify the group with a consecrated meal as blessed by the attending Deities and the grove spirit.

At the end of the grove working, everyone gathers around the compass round and performs one final series of circuits while the group gives thanksgiving to the grove spirit and all of the Deities summoned to participate and then gives them a fond farewell and peaceful release to them all. Then the lights are extinguished, the fire thoroughly put out, and the group assembles in a line as once before. They may file out of the grove, or they may make a few serpentine circuits of the compass round as they wend their way ultimately through the entryway and back to their assembly point.

What is left for me to do here is to present to you an example of the grove magical workings with associated suggestions for you to design and construct your own grove Mystery working. Like all of the rest of the rituals in this book, the grove Mystery rite is an example, but it is not exactly what I have used in these kinds of working—nor do I reveal the Deities that are a part of my private practice, of course.

CHAPTER EIGHTEEN

GROVE MYSTERY RITE REVEALED

"The Valley Spirit never dies;
It is the woman, primal mother.
Her gateway is the root of heaven and earth.
It is like a veil barely seen.
Use it; it will never fail."
– LAO TZU, *TAO TE CHING*

T he grove Mystery rite is a Mystery involving the immanent materialization of Spirit through nature. It can involve the Mysteries of the moon and the sun since it is irrevocably exposed to the elements. It is a place where all of the manifestations of nature are deemed to be sacred and profound, from the humblest insects to the exalted exhibitions of the sky and weather. From the moment that an individual or group enters through the entry point or the gateway arch and crosses over the Besom so placed there, then they are in sacred domain where the Goddesses and Gods can freely engage with their devotees. The key to performing ritual actions in a grove is that they are deliberate and often spontaneous. Script and written actions are not used, but practiced patterns accommodated over a period of time through use and experimentation are very much the methodology employed in grove workings.

To write a grove Mystery rite is to actually propose patterns and ideas, and then with practice and use, a formulation will become adopted by a group. I will not, therefore, write an example ritual with ritual actions and scripted dialog, I will instead assemble practices that I myself have adopted and adapted, and present these to you for your consideration. There is a theme and a plot to a grove Mystery rite, but the dialog, interactions, and exact sequence of events will be what you will discover when you seek to perform this kind of working, whether alone or with a group. Since there are many tasks that should be performed, both before and during the grove working, I would recommend that you perform this kind of rite with the aid of fellow practitioners, since many hands will make the preparations and the performance function smoothly and be less taxing.

I will focus on a grove working that would happen during the night since I have found that nighttime workings are more dramatic and meaningful. The play of light, darkness, and shadow is more pronounced, therefore making the rite more exciting and significant. That is my opinion, of course, so you will have to experiment and determine whether workings at night or during the day have a greater precedence for you. In fact, I can say without any doubt that grove Mystery workings require a fair amount of experimentation and practice before they can become a natural and harmonious enterprise. It is my experience that getting the bugs out of cooperative work and finding the best tools to develop and maintain the grove, as well as to quickly ready it for a working and then to quickly take it down, requires some planning and practice. I have experienced grove workings where the torches failed to light, the fire went out, or some other kind of human-caused delay made it less than optimal.

Achieving perfection, or something close to that goal, requires effective planning, teamwork, and also keeping things simple and succinct. Elaboration or trying something that hasn't been attempted before (or worked out and practiced) will likely produce a less-than-desirable outcome. Additionally, sometimes the Deities will intervene or interrupt a working with rain and storms, high winds, or some other calamity, and the grove workers must be prepared to deal with that kind of occurrence. Sometimes, a working will have to be delayed as if the Powers-That-Be have decided that it won't happen that night. We must be flexible and accept what happens with the same wonder and gratefulness that we might have for a very successful working. This is a difficult thing for anyone to accept, but to faithfully work with a grove is to take on the responsibility of carrying the right attitude toward nature at all times.

The basic pattern for a grove Mystery rite is that the workers walk to the grove in a procession and that they leave in a similar manner. There are two sets of grove workers, however, and the larger group engages in the procession to and from the grove, and a smaller group of attendants arrives early, before nightfall, and works to prepare everything for the working. These individuals will build up the fire pit and prepare it for being quickly lit and will care for the torches to ensure that they have a proper quantity of fuel and that their wicks are ready for lighting. If there is to be a potion or sacramental food and drink at a feast, then someone will have to prep and cook it prior to the start of the grove working. When the working is to start, any lights that were used to illuminate this work are extinguished and the grove becomes dark.

An assembly point is selected for the start of the procession, and it should be at least a ten-minute solemn walk to and from the grove. The procession is headed by the leader of the group and those who will carry torches. Others will carry the portable Stangs and the Besom. If the sacrament is to be a simple meal of dark ale and dark bread (the red meal), then it can be carried in baskets by the member of the procession.

The leader of this gathering is a single person who will direct the group and function as a kind of master of ceremonies. They will guide and direct the proceedings of the grove Mystery. It is the leader's responsibility to know what is being performed that evening, and they will also be the voice of the group, invoking the grove spirit and the associated Deity. They will also give the signals for the movement of the group, calling out what is to be done beforehand so that the group can focus on their directions and not have to memorize anything. As I have said, speech should be brief, to the point, and be as spontaneous as possible. The way to do this is to realize the whole point and topic of the moment when speech is required and then to say what is in one's heart. The leader should be a good speaker and be experienced and know how to direct the group to a successful grove rite enactment.

Once the group has entered the grove and all of the preparations are completed, then all of the members will form a ring in the

245

cleared compass round and perform a deosil circumambulation around the circle many times until a certain level of energy can be sensed by the group. This walking around the circle will be a brisk walk, but not running or going too slow. A deosil circle will automatically churn up the energy latent in the grove and make it available for use. A widdershins circumambulation will either exteriorize the energy raised, or it will produce a vortex wave. You can experiment with either movement and see what it does for you and your group. A fair amount of time is spent walking around the circle, and at times, the pace can become a near trot if a pulse of energy is required. A grove working also allows cross-walking, such as walking from the cardinal points to the center of the circle, then through it to arrive at the cardinal point on the other side. Individuals or groups can engage in this kind of cross-walking. A widdershins circumambulation with a cross-walk will produce the required kind of vortex energy to produce a Mystery domain since the gateway at the entry point has already been crossed.

There are no quarters to be called since the compass round distinctly represents all terrestrial directions, and that should suffice to set the directions of the grove. Sightings of the moon and stars can be done, and noted to the group, to add to the dimension of meaningfulness that the natural elements of the grove offer to the workers. The primary focus of the grove Mystery is to connect and engage with the spirit of the grove, making offerings to it, and seeking for the spirit to show its will (either through spontaneous mediation or through the use of a divination tool, runes stones, or sticks). A place and a portable board to throw knuckle bones, dice, or some other kind of divination tool is a necessary tool for grove work. The group seeks a message from the grove spirit; an affirmation, a sign, or even a manifestation as part of its grove work. Whatever is received in this manner would represent the core work of the group, since it is the grove itself that teaches, guides, and directs the grove workings. This would include the adoration of the Stangs, the Cauldron, and the Besom, the principal tools in the grove.

Secondary Mystery rites can also be included, such as a Lunar or Solar Mystery rites. These rites would require a godhead personification, which should be part of the grove Mystery rite as well, so a person or persons who would take upon themselves that responsibility could assume the role and be sequestered and then brought into the grove after it had already been set up and fully activated. A Lunar Mystery rite requires a widdershins-based energy field, and a Solar Mystery rite would require a deosil-based energy field. The grove workers would perform the requisite circle walk to generate the needed energy for that Mystery.

Godhead assumption, communion, blessings, prophecy, and words of wisdom are all enacted as they would in a temple. A chair or temporary throne can be set up when the Medium ceremoniously enters the grove (with or without helpers). Platters, baskets, and chalices of sacrament are presented to the Medium for consecration, and then amulets can be charged, and individuals or small groups blessed, questions asked and prophetically answered.

At the end of this work, the purpose or teaching of the grove spirit is brought up, and the group will perform a circumambulation many times around the circle to exteriorize the energies and to manifest what the grove spirit has given to the group as a request or a boon. Once released after a pulse, the boon will become manifest.

The final actions of the grove working are to give a loving farewell to the attendant Deity after a brief thanksgiving. Then, the assembled group will gather in the compass round and begin to walk in a widdershins circuit, and the leader will break hands with their partner and lead the group in a snake dance that will circulate the compass round in a sinuous path of spirals and turns, imitating the movements of a giant snake. The members will circle around and back and forth, both widdershins and deosil, until the serpent wends its way to the entry point. The group that performed the preparation will break off before the exit while their surrounding members will fill the gap and hold hands so the missing members will not interrupt the snake dance. The members will head in this manner to the assembly point.

Those left behind will pick up all of the items left behind, including the portable Stangs and the Besom, douse the torch lights, and carefully put out the fire. Then, they will walk slowly through the entry point and proceed back to the assembly point and to their final destination.

Grove Mystery Rite

The grove attendants who are to prepare the grove will meet at the assembly point and depart to the grove. There will be sufficient supplies already placed there, including the development and maintenance of the grove area. This will be done at or just before sunset. The workers will be at the grove site for a duration of time until the other members lead a procession to the grove site. The place where the grove spirit resides has been given offerings and a votive long-burning candle is lit at that site, making it ready to be accessed and making its position known. This small altar set off from the central grove will be the heart of the Mysteries to be performed. The grove workers will perform their work with as little noise or talking as possible.

A throne (a folding chair covered with cloth) is placed in the east or west for either a solar or lunar Deity. This chair will be brought to the center of the circle when it is needed.

1. Assembly and Procession

At the appointed time, the grove members will gather at the assembly point with their instruments and tools for the work. Once all are there, they will receive any additional instructions for the evening from their leader. A question or request will have been decided by the group to seek from the grove spirit—this will be mentioned to the group by the leader as a reminder. Then they will form a line with the leader at the front, with the torchbearers standing close by them, and the rest forming behind them all. At the signal from the leader, they will begin a slow-stepped procession in silence, as if to listen to the sounds of nature and to disturb the peace as little as possible.

2. Entry Point Passage and Fire Prayer

When the procession comes to the entry point archway, everyone will stop. The torchbearers will pass the entryway and stand on either side, and the person carrying the Besom will walk through and place the Besom on the ground perpendicular to the archway. This person will stand aside as the leader and the members pass through the archway and into the grove. After everyone has passed, they will retrieve the Besom and proceed to the compass round, where they will then sweep the circle before anyone takes their place. Then, the Besom will be placed before the throne in the west or the east.

One torchbearer will go to the emplaced grove torches and light them one by one. When this occurs, those attending the firepit will light it as the leader approaches the firepit. Everyone will gather around the firepit as the leader says a prayer to the Deity of the fire and welcomes its presence in the grove, adding the element of fire to the working. Everyone will stand before the firepit and focus silently on the fire for a short while. Then, everyone will proceed to the compass round and form a circle.

3. Compass Round and Energy Generation

The group stands in a ring in the compass round and they each turn to the right and begin to walk briskly around the circle. They can chant together as they proceed, neither too slow nor too fast, making several circuits around the circle. They will not hold hands while walking around the circle. Then, finally, at a signal, they will step more quickly (to form a pulse) and then stop where they are and face the center of the circle. A leader will step forward and stand in the center, assuming a place of honor and responsibility. The leader will use their hands to draw the energy above their head. Then, the leader will stand in silence while everyone else meditates.

4. Summoning and Appearance of the Grove Spirit

The leader in the center of the circle then turns and points to the illuminated space where the votive candle is lit at the small altar shrine of the grove spirit. While everyone else quietly intones or recites a summoning chant, the leader calls out the name of the grove spirit and asks it to become known to the group. If possible, they will assume a light trance while standing and seek to commune with the grove spirit. If there is a question or desire that the group seeks, the leader will ask the grove spirit to aid the group in their quest. Otherwise, the leader can ask for a board with knuckle bones or dice to be brought to them and they will divine right there in the center of the circle as the group continues their quiet, whispery chant.

Once contact has been made with the grove spirit, the group, assisted by the leader, will say prayers and thanksgiving to the grove spirit for its gift. Then, all become silent again and the leader will ask for a sign to be delivered to the group as the night's events progress. Everyone will be attuned to this possibility for the rest of the night, and a special honor will be given to the one who recognizes it.

5. Mystery of the Moon or Sun—Cross Walk

As the leader rejoins the group, they will face the right and begin to walk deosil or turn left to walk widdershins, depending on whether the Mystery is for the Sun or the Moon. They proceed with their circuit of the circle and pass the first full circuit. When the leader passes the north, then they will turn to the center and proceed to walk across the center of the circle to the south while the rest follow them. They will then turn right or left to resume a deosil or widdershins arc, being careful not to overtake or step on any members of the group they might meet. The leader will continue on their course followed by the group until they reach the west, and then they will walk across the center of the circle to the east and turn either right or left with the group following them. They will perform a few more circuits around the circle, then everyone will step forward quickly and then stop. The vortex for the Mystery is now set.

6. Godhead Drawing Down, Communion, and Dance Round

Someone in the group will fetch the temporary throne and set it up in the center of the circle. At this time, the Medium is brought into the grove and they will be seated upon the throne. The group, standing in the compass round, will sit with heads bowed and hands in supplication to the Medium while the leader invokes and summons the elected Deity to descend down into the Medium. The Medium will make the signs of the cross upon their body and then the triangle on their torso and hold their hands in prayer before their heart. They will assume a deep trance and then channel the Deity. After a short period, once they regain a certain degree of consciousness, they will speak to the group. The leader will ask them the three questions of identity, character, and purpose so the group can weigh the level of the godhead possession.

Once the godhead assumption is confirmed, then the sacraments will be brought before the Medium and they will bless them by drawing the appropriate sign over them, touching them where appropriate, and blowing their breath over them. They will also bless any amulets that have been placed before them, and when that is completed, individuals may come before them to receive their blessing, ask questions, and receive prophecy. If there is to be a feast, it will happen at this point in the grove working. Once communion is completed, then the leader will stand with the seated Medium, and the rest of the group will assemble in the compass round to begin the next stage of the working.

At this point in the working, the leader can direct the grove members in the compass round to dance around the area while drums beat out a dance rhythm to celebrate the appearance of the Deity and the communion they have received. They should move in a deosil direction to wind up the power, but their movements and dance steps are individualized. They can overlap each other, or even dance in small groups, as long as they don't attempt to cross over the center of the circle where the leader and enthroned Medium reside. This activity can go on for a while, reaching a kind of crescendo at the signal of the leader. Then all is still and silent for a moment. Afterward, the group will resume their positions on the compass round.

7. Exteriorization, Thanksgiving, and Deity Departure

Grove members in the compass round will turn to their left and proceed widdershins around the circle at a brisk rate, while the leader will direct the power to their hands that are held up over their head. They will proceed in this manner, making a few circuits of the compass round until a signal from the leader will cause them to quickly move forward and then stop. This pulse will send the energy in the compass round out of the grove and into the material world. The leader will direct this energy and speak about the purpose and eventual result of this energy release. When this action is completed, the grove workers in the compass round will turn to the center of the circle and bow their heads while the leader gives the final thanksgiving to the Deity and bids them a fond farewell to depart.

8. Snake Dance and Exit

Workers will come to help the Medium stand and they will take both the Medium and the throne to the side of the compass round and out of the way. Two will stay with the Medium to ensure that they are stable and they may be given some of the remaining sacrament. The leader will join the members in the compass round, they will hold hands, and when ready, begin to move in a widdershins direction. After making a circuit, the leader will let go of the person to their right and start to move off of the compass round to begin the snake dance. The leader will move in circular and spiral directions, both deosil and widdershins, to emulate the movement of the snake. However, the pace will be slow so that the members on the end can keep up with the movements. The grove attendants will join the end of this snake dance, and if possible, the Medium and their assistants will join as well. The grove attendants are at the end because, as the serpent dance heads towards the entryway arch, they will drop off and remain in the grove.

The leader and the grove members will wend their circuitous serpent dance out of the grove and will continue in this manner until they reach the assembly point. The grove attendants will extinguish the torches, put out the fire, and gather together any remaining items in the grove that should be moved. They will proceed solemnly to the assembly point and then disperse.

This is the grove Mystery rite as presented in its most basic and rudimentary form. Based on this ritual pattern, the group that performs it may also embellish it, and certainly, the grove spirit may also teach or present new lore to be incorporated into the working if it is a permanent grove. Embellishment is most successful when it is approached with practice and practicality. Keeping the working simple and straightforward is the key to success for an outdoor working such as a grove Mystery rite.

CHAPTER NINETEEN

RITE OF THE GRAND SABBAT

"During these frenzied debaucheries witches
perform the carnal act with incubus devils"
—MONTAGUE SUMMERS, *WITCHCRAFT
AND BLACK MAGIC* P. 204

The Witches' Sabbat has quite the reputation from a historical perspective, and medieval clerics thought that it was a perversion of the High Solemn Mass held outdoors at sites notorious for their malefic reputation. Witches were thought to fly on their broomsticks to gather together with their master, Satan, and engage in a dark, cruel, and evil pageant of whippings, beatings, and sexual debaucheries. Of course, the fever dreams of self-denying clerics, and later, with Montague Summers' paranoid delusions, could not be further from the truth.

What happened long ago, perhaps in the time of antiquity is, to this day, unknown. This mysterious vacancy led many to imaginative heights of forbidden pleasures and torturous pain, but in today's modern world, such things are just products of the imagination. However, the Great Sabbat, better known today as the Grand Sabbat, holds a very special place within the Witchcraft and Pagan communities. Like the Black Sabbat of ill repute, it involves Witches and Pagans commuting from around the region to a specific place and appointed time to perform their rites as a community. Unlike the Black Sabbat, the means of transportation are not broomsticks and hallucinogenic anointments, and the rites themselves are quite tame and wholly respectable.

A Grand Sabbat is very similar to a grove Mystery working except that it draws in people from many traditions, liturgical practices, and techniques of magical working. These many diverse groups and individuals give up their traditions to follow a specific general kind of working with which everyone can assist and partake. The most important feature of this gathering is that it takes more than one day to assemble and perform the Sabbat rite, so those assembled are expected to form a kind of temporary community. The shortest period for this kind of gathering would be three days, and the longest is a week or even two. Because many have jobs and careers, the longer period would not be practical, so typically, the gathering would be for three to five days.

There are two reasons why a Grand Sabbat needs more than one single night to be successful. First, there should be time allotted for the diverse crowd to meld together into a community, and this can only happen when the attendees camp together and interact over a period of time. The second reason is that inclement weather may force the Grand Sabbat rite to be postponed from one evening to the next. This degree of flexibility will ensure an optimal time when the evening event can be successfully enacted.

A Grand Sabbat requires at least one person to be the experienced and practiced priest or priestess who will completely assume and personify a chosen Deity. Traditionally, a Grand Sabbat is a time for the Old Craft Deities to make an appearance, those being the Horned God Herne, or the Goddess Hecate, Lady of Witches. If one or the other is to be personified, then the single night for the Grand Sabbat can be planned, yet, if there are two people with the gift of emulating both the Horned God and Hecate, then they would occur on separate nights. It could be argued that having one prime event with a godhead personification is more than enough to occupy this kind of gathering, but it could be also stated that having both a traditionally masculine and feminine Deity personification would be more equitable. I leave that decision-making to those who would plan such an event.

During this gathering, the priest and/or priestess who is to personify the God and/or Goddess will meet the group of attendees during the inauguration rite, the night of the Grand Sabbat, and the final parting. They can be seen together, if there are two of them, at both the inauguration rite and the final parting rite. Otherwise, they each will have a separate night in which to engage with the attendees. When they are not performing as the Deities, they can mingle with the other attendees, or they can exclude themselves if that is their wish.

There should also be two leaders, one for each Mystery of the Goddess and the God if there are both, and a single leader if there is only one Deity to be celebrated. The leader acts as a master of ceremonies and conducts the ritual activities for the three planned ritual events. The leader should not be either the priest or priestess who is to assume the godhead for the rituals, of course. The leader will also conduct brief meetings and be responsible for all liturgical activities.

The Grand Sabbat gathering, therefore, has three major ritual enactments that will occur. The first is the rite that officially begins the gathering followed by the main event for the Grand Sabbat, and then the final parting rite that happens before the camp is struck and people pack up and leave. The inauguration should happen at least a day after the folks have gathered for a short event, or as much as two days for a longer one. The main event should be planned for the last couple of days before the event closes. During the interlude between events, people can gather in groups to talk and exchange ideas, and there can be live music, dancing, and merriment. A Grand Sabbat is a joyful occurrence because it doesn't happen every year, but only at interludes, as determined by the Goddess and the God. It can include adults, teenagers, and even young children. Special care should be exercised to ensure that children are not engaged in adult activities.

There must be time for the attendees to make their camp, meet and greet, exchange lore, and make or renew friendships. Feasting and drinking for the whole camp is something that happens, although it is not required, and the same goes for live music, whether planned or spontaneous. Everything that happens should be kept to a level of cordial respect for the gathering and for the other people who are attending. Uncontrolled drunkenness, wanton exhibitions, sexual coercion, and even sexual assault are not permitted. It is the responsibility of the various tradition leaders to control their members or for the leader of the event to select a security force to ensure that the interactions and celebrations of the attendees are positive and non-aggressive. People who break these rules should be ejected from the event and forced to leave if they cannot behave themselves. I have seldom seen such things happen, but they can and do happen whenever people get together in large groups. When they sadly occur, they must be quickly remedied to head off any crisis.

Grand Sabbat Rituals—Inauguration and Parting

While I will only loosely describe how a Grand Sabbat is to be enacted, I feel that those who wish to organize such an event should have the freedom and the knowledge to assemble and perform these rites. There is a requirement for a few individuals with informal roles to help with the assembling and performance of these rites, including the leader(s), but for the most part, the larger population of the attendees will gather and engage with these rites and not have to be responsible for their setup and enactment. Volunteers are always a blessing in such matters because they make the labor for assembling the grove site and warding the rituals more pleasant and easier to complete.

Those who are going to help construct and develop the temporary grove can arrive a day or even two days earlier than the rest of the attendees. They will then construct the grove of the Grand Sabbat, and this is what it might look like:

The Sabbat grove is a lot like the sacred grove of the previous chapter, except that there is a raised central altar erected that is large enough to accommodate the priest or priestess who is assuming the godhead, and any equipment that they might need. The priest and/ or priestess can stand before the gathered crowd or they can be initially enthroned, depending on the time and materials available to the group building the grove. Everything else is set up, including two Stangs, placed in the appropriate quarter (north for the Death Stang, south for the Life Stang, or whatever is decided), and a broom is put upon the altar stage at the edge. There should also be twin torches placed on either side of the altar stage to illuminate the animated godhead. Other regalia can be placed before the ritual begins. The rest of the Sabbat grove is set up just like the sacred grove as already discussed.

The inauguration rite can be presented at the Sabbat grove, or it can be presented at the temporary village camp. In either case, the attendees will ultimately end up in the Sabbat grove to walk the compass round and establish the first generation of the grove energies.

If this rite is performed at the Pagan village, then the garbed priest and priestess will appear as the God and Goddess and be accompanied by torchbearers. When they appear at the outskirts of the village, people will stop what they are doing and make way for the procession of Deities into their camp. When they pass, people will take off their caps (if they have them), bow their heads, and hold their hands out in supplication. The Deities will proceed to the center-most point in the camp and the leader will welcome them. They may impart a word or two in response or be completely silent, making the appropriate sign to the people, and then turn and depart from the village camp. Once that happens, the people will assemble and proceed to the Sabbat grove to celebrate and perform a simple rite to encourage the magical and divine energies to manifest. The Deities will not be in the grove at that time to celebrate with the people since their time will come when the full Sabbat is to be enacted.

Another way this rite can be conducted is for the leader to call the people to assemble just outside of the camp and then for the Deities to make an appearance nearby and make their sign to the assembled mass. Either the intrusion or the pass-by can be used to kickstart the Grand Sabbat, and each has its own particular esthetics.

The parting rite is performed in the same manner as the inauguration, and it can be enacted with a visit to the village camp or with a pass-by. This time, the Deities will speak, giving a message to their people about the conduct of the Grand Sabbat and its success, as well as a message about the next gathering and when it might occur. The timing for the next gathering is always determined through the throwing of knucklebones or dice to divine the will of the Deities. Then the God and Goddess (or just one of them, if it is a single event) will bless the people and send them home charged with hope and peace.

Grand Sabbat Rite—Main Event

The Grand Sabbat occurs in the evening, but not too late nor too early. The people in the village camp have been preparing for this event and are garbed in their best outfits suitable for the auspiciousness of the gathering, their role and position in the community, sumptuously made up, glittery and beautiful. They meet at the place of assembly and form a procession line with the leader in front. Once everyone is together, they begin their solemn and silent walk to the Sabbat grove.

When they arrive, they find that the fires are lit, the torches are illuminated, and everything is in preparation. The altar stage is empty, and the northern corner is kept clear of people as a passageway for the Deity. At the entry point, they are stopped by folk dressed in black and armed with daggers who demand to know who is the Mother of everyone. Any answer will do, or one might be told before the rite, but everyone passes the warden after being stopped to enter the grove.

Once everyone has entered, then the Deity makes their appearance through the northern corner of the compass round and proceeds to the center of the stage and mounts it, to be enthroned there and given the regalia of their power and authority. Then, the drums begin to beat and the people march and dance widdershins around the circle for a time while the Deity bestows blessings, making the sign and saying appropriate words of encouragement. Then, after a time, the Deity signals the leader, and the group will stop what they are doing and face the Deity. Incense braziers add a smoky aroma to the atmosphere, and some may leap and dance before the altar stage at the instigation of the Deity.

The Deity gestures for the people to come forward from the compass round to meet at the stage altar. Helpers at the edge offer trinkets and flying ointment to those who wish them. The Deity then stands before their people. The drums resume, beating to a crescendo while the people chant the name of the Deity (*Horned God!* or *Hecate!*), and then at another sign, the drums are silent.

Then, the Deity may bless an appropriate food and drink to be handed down to the celebrants or whoever wishes them. There are cut pieces of bread blessed together in large baskets and many cups of drink are also blessed. The Deity makes the sign over them and they are so blessed. The Deity will say something like "Eat of this bread, for it is my body," and "Drink of this wine/beer, for it is my blood." All who wish to have sacraments are given time to receive and consume them.

When this activity is completed, everyone will become silent, and the Deity will give a speech, somewhat memorized and more often spontaneous. The basic structure for this speech is something like the following:

1. The Deity greets their people and tells them that they have suffered, and they know this.
2. The Deity tells the people that they are special and that they have an agreement to help and abide by them.
3. The Deity seeks loyalty to their cause, saying that the blood and flesh of the people are their own blood and flesh, and the cause is for freedom, love, and peace.
4. The Deity warns of difficult times ahead, about their detractors and enemies, and that steadfastness will overturn the evil in the world.
5. The Deity asks the people to remember and to never forget their ancestors and loved ones; to know and celebrate their unique heritage.

At this point in the rite, the Deity will ask the people if there are any who are new to the faith or who are newborn or very young. These children and newly-initiated adults are brought before the Deity who blesses them by anointing them on the forehead with consecrated oil. Either holding them up or turning to them to face the crowd, the Diety asks the attendees to name the child or newly initiated adult and therefore confirms that given name. The Deity may also bless the parents in a similar manner, wishing full lives for them and their child. If both Deities will be present during the two-night Grand Sabbat, then either the God or Goddess will perform this rite.

Then, the Deity asks if anyone would choose to receive the favor of their blessing in the form of a mark. Those who come forward will receive a mark from a sharp knife on their back or another part of their body, as they choose. This will be a very shallow cut that will bleed slightly. An attendant nearby will hand a small piece of tissue to help staunch the blood.[434]

Once these actions are completed, the Deity is handed an ornate book and asks the crowd if there is anyone who seeks to be initiated into the Craft. If there is someone, they are presented to the Deity, and if not, then the Deity will renew the vows of the assembled Witches and Pagans, and these are general and specific enough to include all faiths. The Deity will read this vow, line by line, and the assembled folk will repeat and respond to each one. The new initiate will also repeat and respond with their hand over their heart and head bowed. When the vow is completed, the new initiate will receive the consecrated oil upon their brow, touched by the hand of the Deity, and the Deity will kiss the hand offered to them. Then if they are willing, they may receive the mark of an initiate upon their body with a shallow cut of the knife. They will later sign their name in the book, and the Deity will remind everyone of the significance of this book.

The Deity will then direct everyone to crouch down, put their hand upon the earth and the other on their head, and bless themselves, making themselves an instrument of the Witchcraft and Pagan faith and to the sacred earth of the Sabbat grove.

If the Deity is the Horned God, then an enactment of ritual sacrifice is done where the Deity is killed and dismembered by a priestess, and the heart is extracted and shown bleeding to the crowd, who cheer and scream. This is, of course, all staged and made to appear as if the God has been killed. Then, after a moment, the Horn God rises up, with fake gore on his body, laughing, and saying:

"I die but I am reborn!"

If the Deity is the Goddess Hecate, then she will present a youth as her son to the crowd on the altar stage, and the son will be killed before them in the same manner as the Horned God. After a short

---

43 It is a good idea in all instances of large gatherings to have first aid supplies readily available, especially when skin may be intentionally broken.

while, Hecate will speak barbarous words of evocation and then reach down and raise up the youth, saying:

"My mortal lovers shall die, but through my powers, I shall make them reborn!"

Once this Mystery is completed, the Deity will bring forth the priestess or the youth, and they will be honored, crowned with a flower wreath, and presented to the community as exemplars of their tradition.

Finally, the drummers will begin a powerful drum beat and the Deity will urge the people to dance and cavort around the circle in honor of them. This revelry will go on for a while as the Deity, from their perch, will urge them to do more and more. The drums will continue to beat harder and faster until reaching a crescendo, and then the Deity will shout for them to stop. Everyone will stop and the drums will be silent.

The Deity will then make a final speech, exhorting the crowd to remember this moment, and to celebrate their uniqueness by feasting and enjoying themselves without any guilt. At that moment, the Deity will turn, and with their attendants, will exit off of the altar stage and proceed to leave the grove. The attendants will watch over the priest or priestess and help with the grounding, disrobing, and cleaning that is always required after a full-garbed godhead personification. Food and drink are very helpful, but so is putting the hands into the earth to drain away all of the energy absorbed by the assumption process.

After the Deity has departed, then the people will slowly exit the Sabbat grove individually or in groups. At the village camp, the revelry may continue until folks finally fall asleep due to exhaustion. Folks should note their dreams that occur through the night, write them down in the morning, and share them with their clan.

The rite of the Grand Sabbat is completed.

THE FOUR PATHWAYS AND WITCHCRAFT MASTERY

We began this journey, in the series *For Witches*, with the missing three paths of lore that I believed was a necessary addition to the basic modern Witchcraft repertoire. These three paths are spirit conjuring through a familiar spirit, advanced energy magic, and talismanic magic. A Witch who has mastered these three paths would become a magus or a fully empowered Witch with all of the knowledge that was bequeathed to us from the philosophers, goetic sorcerers, and Witches of antiquity. All of the lore of the past has now been brought together and given a modern interpretation and deployment. This presentation of three additional paths is a veritable treasure of magical lore now within the provenance of modern Witchcraft, making it as complete and as powerful as any system of Ceremonial Magic.

This book, *Sacramental Theurgy*, offers the practicing Witch a new dimension in their liturgical and magical practices. Like the book on *Elemental Powers*, the rites in this work are an extension of existing praxis, but that extension is quite profound. It pushes the knowledge and practice of Witchcraft beyond what is normally accepted as Witchcraft practices.

Since many of my sisters and brothers were orphaned from the Catholic religion or some other form of high church practices such as Orthodox, Lutheranism, Episcopalians, and the Church of England, and because they turned their backs on these practices, I believed that it would be difficult to get such people to look at certain practices and beliefs with new eyes. The mere words of *sacrament, mass, benediction,* or *transubstantiation* are fraught with difficult associations with a religion that seeks to enforce its morality and religious beliefs on even those who are not a part of that faith.

This is also true of Protestant Evangelicals who believe in the supremacy and exclusive truth of their faith over any other. Such an attitude toward other authentic and legitimate faiths represents a major social problem for anyone who does not share these religious beliefs. Therefore, appearing to appropriate rituals and beliefs from those faiths, as I have been accused, would be considered very wrong-headed and even contemptible. One might think that a true Witch would make certain that their practices are as far away and different from anything that might be practiced by people who they see with suspicion or even outrage.

However, having read through this work, you will have seen that how I promote my rituals, practices, and beliefs adheres more firmly to a Pagan perspective than a Christian one and that I am indeed much more immersed in a Pagan perspective than others might think, based on my writings on other subjects. How I have approached my liturgical workings is to view them in a practical manner, and that anything that is touched by a Deity must be considered sacralized and sacramental.

Since we have the honor and privilege to assume and channel our Deities and to impersonate them under controlled conditions, then the work that they engage in and promote must be considered sacramental. The magic that drives the transformation of substances into sacraments is something that has been practiced for untold ages, although our version of this practice is modern and newly established. Catholics called it *transubstantiation,* but it is really a form of magic. They also used sacraments to bless and consecrate their devotees, materializing the spiritual power of their godhead into their churches and even mundane material objects and living creatures. These are purely magical actions, which is why the Catholic Church has moved away from them as articles of their faith.

Still, for Pagans and Witches such as myself, these beliefs and practices are a goldmine for repurposing our liturgical and magical practices. Since we have an exclusive source for the sacralizing of substances and objects, which is some form of god-head assumption, then we use these sacraments and the Deities that we embody to perform a greater magic to impact and affect the world around us in a positive and constructive manner. We are not alone, since we can impersonate our Deities. It is then that they are with us and can help us to achieve our objectives, both individually and as a community.

Working magic through the Deities is the basic definition of theurgy as a magical practice, so as modern adherents, we can use these techniques to greatly empower our work. After all, if we can get the Deity to aspire to achieve something for us, then it will naturally occur without obstacles or personal issues to stop it.

This is what I have proposed in this book: that Witches and Pagans can repurpose the tools and beliefs that were once an important part of the Catholic faith from a completely modern Pagan magical perspective. We might use the words *mass, benediction, transubstantiation, consecration,* and *sacraments,* but they have a whole different meaning within the context of Pagan rites and magic.

If we can understand that point, then we can take back ideas, beliefs, and practices that are far older and have a deeper history than what we might have if we simply avoided them. Catholics were only a half-step towards Christianity from Paganism, and they kept a lot of Pagan magical beliefs and practices as a means of satisfying their Pagan congregants. They used theology to make these Pagan magical practices seem canonical, but they were able to divest themselves of these kinds of practices when it was more embarrassing to keep them than exclude them. What they left behind were Pagan magical vestiges of a faith long removed from our modern era, but they are perfect for a modern Pagan mindset.

I was born a mainstream Protestant Christian, so even though my faith taught me to see Catholicism as some kind of erroneous Pagan practice more in league with the Devil than being an actual Christian faith, I was, overall, immune to the anger and pain associated with attempting to leave that faith. I was not really embraced by the church authorities in my Protestant Christian faith because I asked too many questions that were seen as annoying and irrel-evant. I was never confirmed, nor did I become a member of the church. I opted out before any of that could occur and then stewed for a few years as a seeker until I discovered Witchcraft.

Because I was not raised a Catholic, I saw the rites and rituals of Catholicism, especially the pre-Vatican II variety, as particularly magical and useful to reverse engineer into Pagan-based magical rituals. I found this quite successful, even though some of my Witch friends who had been Catholic found them averse to their practices and beliefs. I hope to change that opinion by starting with a godhead assumption, sacralizing objects, and then going from there.

What I found in my experimentation and the reverse engineering of old Catholic liturgy was a whole new class of magical rites and ceremonies. It opened a whole new world to me and added considerable spiritual power and meaning to the rituals that I now utilized. Some people found my ideas to be intriguing, and others found them to be terrible, but no one could deny that what I was doing was impactful and seemingly within the Pagan perspective. When I would explain it, some rejected the terminology, and others just couldn't abide by the supposed source of my rituals. Still, others found what I was doing to be quite amazing and so very useful. While some dismissed what I was doing with a social stink-eye, others adopted the very rituals and workings that I had assembled. They were open-minded and saw a great deal of potential in the rituals that I had proposed. I then applied this perspective to nearly every level of my liturgical and magical workings and discovered yet another pathway within Witchcraft lore.

I also saw the need to reform practices that were already being performed, most notably the Drawing Down rite for the specifically named Goddess or God. I saw what was going on in the greater Witchcraft and Pagan communities and I saw that this rite was being abused by a few leaders. I also saw that it was a phenomenon that was unjudged and unable to be scrutinized. If a rite can't be objectively judged and examined in a critical manner, then it becomes dogma, and such an object of faith cannot be questioned. I believe to this day that any form of dogma represents a closed door in Witchcraft and that we should avoid any and every closed door, since otherwise, we will cease to grow and evolve.

Everything that we do, whether in magic or liturgical rites, should be examined and questioned. The only thing that should be sacred to us is the experience of the Divine and the manifestation or revelation of Spirit in nature. Our rites are just the means to achieve that sacred vista, and we should work on changing and perfecting them. Our religion is young, so we must continue to revise and develop our practices so that we might achieve a greater level of perfection at some future date.

So, because I sought to reform our practices, I also sought to develop a greater regimen of achieving godhead personification. I found that Aleister Crowley and his short work *Liber Astarte vel Berylli* had gone down this path, but I had already worked out my own methodology that remarkably coincided with his. It was good to see that another mind had approached this problem from a different perspective and came up with a similar methodology. It also helped me to see my technique from another view and to refine what I had originally put down. I felt that this technique of godhead personification represented the highest level that we mere mortals could achieve, but even so, it allowed us to channel the power and authority of the Deity directly into the material world and that it could be the source of all kinds of potent and meaningful magic.

I also learned about the power and potential for magic using placeholders for the Deities, and the Stang was probably the most amazing tool of them all. When I first encountered a Stang, I found it a freaky and kind of idolatrous thing, but it seemed to hold a great degree of power for me. Once I got over my awkward feelings toward it, I learned to love what it was and what it represented.

That was a time when I had been losing my Witchcraft religion, having been impugned with some mild derision from high-level occultists and Ceremonial Magicians who thought that I should have outgrown my juvenile attachment to that religion. My meeting with the Stang at a Pagan gathering in 2001, and also meeting the Baphomet Bunch (or Bapho-bunch, as they called themselves), along with my friend Steve, helped me to revitalize my faith and to be proud of my Witchcraft achievements, both religiously and magically. From that moment on, I embraced what I learned of Old Craft Witchcraft tools and techniques and brought them into my practice without qualms or hesitation.

Still, it was some years later when I had qualified all of the practices that I had developed or adopted over the years as a single lore pathway in Witchcraft that I realized the common thread that pulled them together. They were techniques and rituals that used sacraments and they depended on the presence in some manner of the godhead in order for them to be fully realized and successful. This pathway that I had discovered incrementally and in piecemeal was a path of sacramental theurgy.

I had already determined to publish three books in the *For Witchcraft* series that covered the explicit magical techniques that I had developed over the decades, and these nicely fit into empty niches of the Witchcraft tradition. I knew that I had a whole other segment of lore that I wanted to share with you, my readers, but I didn't immediately realize how that could be done. I was deeply involved in writing the other three books, not understanding that there was one more to be written. I was proposing not three, but four additional lore pathways for Witchcraft.

The fourth pathway was an important and powerful extension of existing lore, but proposed as I had developed it years ago, it was also quite different. Now, in this book, where all of the pieces are assembled together under the rubric of cultic practices and the Mysteries that embody them, it represents the highest level of philosophic magic in the Neoplatonic tradition, which is Theurgy. I have modernized it, indeed, but what is produced through this methodology is practically the same.

What do we have when the three lore pathways of spirit conjuring, elemental powers, and talismanic magic are joined together? We have a complete magical tradition that is equal to, or even greater than, what Ceremonial Magicians use. These three pathways are grounded in the Witchcraft tradition, although talismanic magic extends the magical paradigm to include methods and techniques that are part of a Pagan-based ritual magic. Yet, all three of these pathways represent the full spectrum of magical possibilities set into the hands of the practiced and experienced Witch. These are the lore pathways that can lead to a mastery of life for the individual and the clan, and they can also push the practitioner to methods and techniques that are beyond what even I have written. All of that potential is here in these books, waiting for Witches to achieve the level of experience and ability to make use of them.

The final question that should be asked is: *What happens to these three pathways when this fourth one is mastered? What happens to the seasoned adept who seeks and achieves to master this new pathway that I have fully revealed in this book?* Where the other pathways helped the practitioner to bend material reality so that it conformed with their desires and needs, this pathway integrates the Deity with the magic and fully embodies and empowers it with divine force, making it nearly infallible. This is because such magic as this takes on a macrocosmic dimension and focuses it directly on the microcosm, all with that tremendous force.

Where working the three pathways makes us similar to the Deities in our ability to change the material world, adding the element of the godhead persona and sacramentation to our magic brings us to the equal level to the Gods for a single instance. That single instance makes our magic irresistible. The fourth pathway, integrated with the other three, makes us a Deity for just a moment, but in that moment, all things are possible. We not only can manifest our will in the material world, but we may also experience ecstatic union and Oneness, enlightenment, and total clairvoyance. Just for a moment, we *are* the Gods, and that is the greatest Mystery of this magical path, which I bequeath to you, my steadfast readers.

May the Gods and Goddesses of all Wiccan and Pagan faiths bless and make fruitful all of your endeavors.

Frater Barrabbas

BIBLIOGRAPHY

Alexander, Skye. *Planets in Signs*. Atglen, PA: Whitford Press, 1988.

Bailey, Michael D. *Origins of the Witches' Sabbath*. University Park, PE: Pennsylvania State University Press, 2021.

Crowley, Aleister. *Magick in Theory and Practice*. Secaucus, NJ: Castle Books, 1991.

(This book is no longer print—alternative online text: Sacred Texts Thelema. Accessed Sep 3, 2022: https://www.sacred-texts.com/oto/lib175.htm)

——. "Liber Astarte Vel Berylli Sub Figura CLXXV," *The Equinox*. Simpkin, Marshall, Hamilton, Kent & Co., 1912.

Farrar, Stewart and Janet. *A Witches' Bible: The Complete Witches' Handbook*. Paranormal eBook series, fwMedia (no published date).

Frater Barrabbas. *Talismanic Magic for Witches*. St. Paul, MN: Llewellyn Publications, 2023.

——. *Elemental Power for Witches*. St. Paul, MN: Llewellyn Publications, 2021.

——. *Spirit Conjuring for Witches*. St. Paul, MN: Llewellyn Publications, 2017.

——. *Mastering the Art of Ritual Magic – Omnibus Edition*. Stafford, UK: Megalithica Books – Immanion Press, 2013.

"Full Moon Calendar." *Farmers' Almanac*, https://www.farmersalmanac.com/full-moon-dates-and-times.

Golembiewski, Kate. "Why Do We Still Believe in 'lunacy' during a Full Moon?" Astronomy Magazine, 21 Aug. 2019, https://astronomy.com/news/2019/08/why-do-we-still-believe-in-lunacy-during-a-full-moon.

Hocken, Vigdis, et al. "The Moon Causes Tides on Earth." *Timeanddate.com*, https://www.timeanddate.com/astronomy/moon/tides.html.

——. "What Is a Lunar Month?" *Timeanddate.com*, https://www.timeanddate.com/astronomy/moon/lunar-month.html.

Hutton, Ronald. *The Stations of the Sun—A History of the Ritual Year in Britain.* Oxford, UK: Oxford University Press, 2001.

Jones, Evan John and Valiente, Doreen. *Witchcraft – A Tradition Renewed.* Custer, WA: Phoenix Publishing, 1990.

Leland, Charles Godfrey. *Aradia.* David Nutt, 1899.

Paprocki, D.Min., Joe. "What Are the Spiritual Exercises of Saint Ignatius? Loyola Press." *Loyola Press*, 23 May 2019, https://www.loyolapress.com/catholic-resources/ignatian-spirituality/examen-and-ignatian-prayer/what-are-the-spiritual-exercises-of-saint-ignatius/.

Peterson, Joseph. *The Sworn Book of Honorius – Liber Iuratus Honorii.* Lake Worth, FL: Ibis Press, 2016.

Robin of Sherwood, created by Richard Carpenter, HTV and Goldcrest Films, 1984–1986.

Ritual of Evil, directed by Robert Day, performances by Louis Jourdon, Belinda Montgomery, and Diana Hyland, Universal Television, 1970.

Rudhyar, Dane. *The Lunation Cycle: A Key to Understanding of Personality.* New York, NY: Aurora Press, 1986.

Silva, Mari. *Moon Signs: The Ultimate Guide to Understanding Your Sign, Different Sun-Moon Astrology Combinations, and Compatibility.* Franelty Publications, 2021.

Smith, Jonathan Z. "Dying and Rising Gods," in *The Encyclopedia of Religion* Vol. III & IV, edited by Mircea Eliade – New York, NY: Macmillan, 1995.

Index